Practical Front-End Testing

Strategies and Best Practices for Developers

Hsin-Hao Tang

Apress®

Practical Front-End Testing: Strategies and Best Practices for Developers

Hsin-Hao Tang
Taipei, Taiwan

ISBN-13 (pbk): 979-8-8688-1450-1   ISBN-13 (electronic): 979-8-8688-1451-8
https://doi.org/10.1007/979-8-8688-1451-8

Copyright © 2025 by Hsin-Hao Tang

This work is subject to copyright. All rights are reserved by the Publisher, whether the whole or part of the material is concerned, specifically the rights of translation, reprinting, reuse of illustrations, recitation, broadcasting, reproduction on microfilms or in any other physical way, and transmission or information storage and retrieval, electronic adaptation, computer software, or by similar or dissimilar methodology now known or hereafter developed.

Trademarked names, logos, and images may appear in this book. Rather than use a trademark symbol with every occurrence of a trademarked name, logo, or image we use the names, logos, and images only in an editorial fashion and to the benefit of the trademark owner, with no intention of infringement of the trademark.

The use in this publication of trade names, trademarks, service marks, and similar terms, even if they are not identified as such, is not to be taken as an expression of opinion as to whether or not they are subject to proprietary rights.

While the advice and information in this book are believed to be true and accurate at the date of publication, neither the authors nor the editors nor the publisher can accept any legal responsibility for any errors or omissions that may be made. The publisher makes no warranty, express or implied, with respect to the material contained herein.

    Managing Director, Apress Media LLC: Welmoed Spahr
    Acquisitions Editor: Anandadeep Roy
    Development Editor: James Markham
    Editorial Assistant: Jessica Vakili

Cover designed by eStudioCalamar

Distributed to the book trade worldwide by Springer Science+Business Media New York, 1 New York Plaza, New York, NY 10004. Phone 1-800-SPRINGER, fax (201) 348-4505, e-mail orders-ny@springer-sbm.com, or visit www.springeronline.com. Apress Media, LLC is a Delaware LLC and the sole member (owner) is Springer Science + Business Media Finance Inc (SSBM Finance Inc). SSBM Finance Inc is a **Delaware** corporation.

For information on translations, please e-mail booktranslations@springernature.com; for reprint, paperback, or audio rights, please e-mail bookpermissions@springernature.com.

Apress titles may be purchased in bulk for academic, corporate, or promotional use. eBook versions and licenses are also available for most titles. For more information, reference our Print and eBook Bulk Sales web page at http://www.apress.com/bulk-sales.

Any source code or other supplementary material referenced by the author in this book is available to readers on GitHub. For more detailed information, please visit https://www.apress.com/gp/services/source-code.

If disposing of this product, please recycle the paper

To all developers committed to building robust, reliable, and high-quality web applications. May this book be a valuable guide in mastering front-end testing strategies and best practices, empowering you to write code with confidence and create exceptional user experiences.

Table of Contents

About the Author xiii

About the Technical Reviewer xv

Acknowledgments xvii

Introduction xix

Forewords xxiii

Chapter 1: Getting Started with Testing 1
    What Is Front-End Web Testing? 2
    Why Write Tests? 2
    How to Start Writing Tests? 3
    Types of Front-End Testing 4
        Unit Testing 5
        Integration Testing 8
        End-to-End Testing 10
        Visual Testing 11
        I Only Have One Hour, Which Tests Should I Write? 12
        Summary 13
        Notes 15
    Testing Techniques 16
        What Are the Testing Techniques? 16
        How Are These Testing Techniques Applied in Development? 17

TABLE OF CONTENTS

- Are These Testing Techniques Suitable for UI Development? 18
  - Notes 20
- Naming Conventions 22
  - Given-When-Then 23
  - it should 24
  - 3A Pattern 25
  - Conclusion 26
  - Notes 27
- Mock, Spy, and Double 27
  - Mock 27
  - Spy 28
  - Double 30
  - Notes 31
- Chapter Review and Summary 32

Chapter 2: Unit Testing 35

- Unit Testing 36
- Environment Setup, Installation, and Tool Comparison 39
  - Jest 39
  - Cypress 48
  - Notes 53
- Minimal Scope Validation Logic 54
  - Breaking Down Overly Complex Code 56
  - Isolating Dependencies 58
  - Conclusion 60
  - Notes 60
- How to Write Tests for Components? A React Example 60
  - Testing Implementation vs. Testing Behavior 61
  - Splitting Logic and Presentation 69

TABLE OF CONTENTS

    Summary 80

    Notes 81

Shallow Rendering and Full Rendering 82

    Shallow Rendering 83

    Full Rendering 89

    Summary 94

    Notes 95

Chapter Review and Summary 96

Chapter 3: Integration Testing 99

Integration Testing 99

    Notes 108

Testing Features from the User's Perspective and
Maximizing Realism 108

    Testing Features from the User's Perspective 108

    Maximizing Realism 110

    Notes 112

Mocking Components, API Responses, and Third-Party Libraries 113

    How to Mock Components? 114

    How to Mock API Responses? 116

    How to Mock Third-Party Libraries? 122

    Why Aim for Realism? Is Mocking Not Good Enough? 125

    Can Testing Be Done Without Using Mock Data? 129

    Notes 129

Snapshots 130

    Notes 140

How to Write Tests for State Management? A Redux Example 141

    Notes 148

Chapter Review and Summary 148

TABLE OF CONTENTS

Chapter 4: End-to-End Testing 151
End-to-End Testing 151
Notes 154
Environment Setup and Installation 154
Notes 156
Verifying User Flow 159
Memori 160
Conclusion 167
Notes 169
Chapter Review and Summary 169

Chapter 5: Visual Testing 171
Visual Testing 171
Mixtini 172
How Snapshot Comparison Works 174
Notes 176
Verifying Visual Accuracy 177
Component-Level Testing 178
Page-Level Testing 189
Workflow 192
Summary 192
Notes 193
Tool Comparison 194
Snapshot File Types and Structure 195
Reviewing Snapshots Based on Pull Requests or Branches 197
Merge Checks 197
Component-Level Testing 198

Page-Level Testing 198

Browser Support..199

Summary..199

Notes 201

Chapter Review and Summary 201

Chapter 6: What to Do After Writing Tests: When and How to Run Them 205

Pre-commands and Manual Test Invocation 206

Pre-commands 206

Manual Test Invocation 207

Summary..209

Notes 209

Run Tests Before Merging Code 210

pre-commit...210

pre-push 211

Running Tests During PR Submission..213

Summary..214

Notes 214

Running Tests Regularly in CI..215

Should Code Be Merged into the Main Branch When Tests Fail? 216

How to Reduce the Likelihood of Test Failures After Code Merges? 217

Notes 217

Inferring Use Case Coverage from Code Coverage 218

Conclusion 223

Chapter Review and Summary 223

TABLE OF CONTENTS

Chapter 7: Frequently Asked Questions 225

What to Do When UI Updates Cause Test Failures? 225

The Element Selection Method Is Too Loose, Strict, or Lacks Clear Meaning 226

Tests with Too Many Implementation Details 234

Summary 248

Notes 249

How to Handle Duplicate Tests? 249

Notes 253

How to Test the Timer? 254

Notes 258

How to Mock Only Part of a Module? 258

How to Debug? What If an Element Can't Be Found? How Do You Trace the Data Flow? 260

What If the Element Can't Be Found? 263

How Do You Trace the Data Flow? 265

Notes 267

How to Test Localization? 267

Notes 271

How to Use Setup and Teardown? What Are beforeEach, afterEach, beforeAll, and afterAll? 272

Repeated Setup 272

One-Time Setup 275

Summary 276

Notes 276

Should Tests Include Type Checking? 277

Option 1: Implement Type Checking Inside the addNumbers Function 277

Option 2: Use Tools for Type Checking 278

Notes 279

Why Do Some Test Cases Succeed Sometimes and
Fail Other Times? 280
    Resource Dependencies 280
    Test Dependencies 283
    Conclusion 286
    Notes 286

How to Run Specific Tests? An Example Using Jest 287
    Skipping Specific Test Blocks 287
    Skipping Specific Test Cases 288
    Notes 292

Chapter 8: Leveraging AI for Writing Tests 293

How to Effectively Use GitHub Copilot for Writing Tests 293
    Simple Example 294
    Implementing Unit Tests 296
    Implementing Integration Tests 297
    Implementing End-to-End Tests 302
    Conclusion 304
    Notes 305

How to Leverage Mermaid and ChatGPT for Writing Tests 306
    Simple Example 307
    Writing Unit Tests 313
    Implementing Integration Test 318
    Implementing End-to-End Test 324
    Conclusion 328
    Notes 329

TABLE OF CONTENTS

Chapter 9: Summary 331
Types and Methods of Testing 331
Product Stage and Testing Ratio 331
Common Types of Testing 331
Testing Methods and Tools 332
Testing Strategies at Different Stages of Product Development 332
Leveraging AI to Improve Testing Efficiency 333
Conclusion 333

Index 335

About the Author

Hsin-Hao Tang (Summer) is passionate about front-end development, with a strong focus on creating products that deliver excellent user experiences and high performance. She is also a skilled SEO expert. She is an active blogger and writer. Her technical books in Chinese have been very well received by developers.

About the Technical Reviewer

Eric Lee is a Senior Software Engineer with nine years of experience focusing on front-end development and has worked in ecommerce and electric vehicle industries. Passionate about maintainable code and developer experience, Eric believes testing is not only a crucial step to ensure great user and developer experiences but also to ensure the success of your product. As a technical reviewer, he hopes this helps developers understand testing's importance and use it to build confidence between releases.

Acknowledgments

I would like to express my heartfelt gratitude to Alex Liu, Eddie Kao, Hunter Liu, Kent Chen, Leslie Liu, Sean Chou, and Yvonne Huang for their invaluable support and contributions. Your insights, encouragement, and expertise have played a crucial role in the creation of this book. Thank you!

Introduction

Why I Wrote This Book

In the fast-paced and ever-evolving field of front-end development, one of the biggest challenges is maintaining high-quality code while producing work rapidly. This is why testing has become so crucial. Deciding on the right testing approach and how to write and execute tests is a key issue every developer must consider. Code without tests is difficult to guarantee in terms of quality, and the solution lies in developing a solid testing strategy. This book shares the practical experience I've accumulated in front-end testing, with the hope of inspiring and helping others.

Whom This Book Is For

If you

- Want to dive deep into the types and implementation of front-end testing
- Are looking to build flexible, maintainable test code
- Wish to write test code efficiently
- Face challenges when writing tests and are seeking solutions

INTRODUCTION

this book will provide you with

- Detailed explanations, supported by visuals and code examples, to help you learn, practice, and apply various front-end tests, while seeing the effectiveness of writing tests in real-world applications
- Clear principles and viewpoints to guide you in evaluating testing strategies and costs, so you can make the best choices
- Tips on effectively using AI tools to generate test code and boost productivity
- A clear and thorough explanation of various challenges through easy-to-understand examples, helping you tackle testing obstacles with ease

How This Book Is Structured

The book is divided into eight chapters:

- Getting Started with Testing: A deep dive into the fundamental concepts, techniques, and various types of front-end web testing
- Unit Testing: In-depth exploration of how to validate logic at the smallest scope, emphasizing the importance of component testing, and a comparison of popular testing frameworks to ensure foundational tasks are done correctly
- Integration Testing: Verifying specific features from the user's perspective, with guidance on how to simulate real-world scenarios and use snapshots to improve the stability of your codebase

- End-to-End Testing: Testing the entire workflow, focusing on simulating real user behavior to achieve comprehensive coverage
- Visual Testing: Ensuring visual accuracy, detailing how to precisely compare UI elements across different browsers and viewports to accelerate the UI testing process
- What to Do After Writing Tests: When and How to Run Them: Discussing different testing methods and timings, such as pre-commit hooks, manual triggers, pre- and post-merge tests, and continuous integration, as well as how to deduce usage case coverage from code coverage
- Frequently Asked Questions: Practical solutions to common challenges, helping developers overcome the hurdles of testing
- Leveraging AI for Writing Tests: How to leverage AI tools to enhance the efficiency of writing tests and increase productivity

You can read the chapters in sequence or choose individual sections based on your needs.

Code examples from this book can be found at the following links:

- Chapters 1, 2, 4, 5, 7: `https://bit.ly/49wKbrC`
- Chapter 3: `https://bit.ly/3SZw2xL`
- Chapter 5: `https://bit.ly/3MB2xxn`

INTRODUCTION

Conventions Used in This Book

// ... indicates that part of the code has been omitted.

This is a key concept. Important concepts will be highlighted in bold. Example file paths will be noted above the code blocks.

```
// Example file path src/sayHi.js
const sayHi = () => console.log('Hi!');
```

About Me

I'm Summer, an engineer, speaker, and writer, and the author of the technical blog *Summer* (https://www.cythilya.tw/) and the book *Speed Up Your App with Web Vitals*. My expertise includes SEO, front-end performance, and testing.

Forewords

Foreword by Joey Chen
Common Issues and Decision Points in Testing Practice

In today's software industry, everyone agrees on the value of automated testing, but it's easier said than done. Many teams understand the concept but struggle with implementation. Even after becoming familiar with testing frameworks and writing some automated tests, teams often encounter decision-making challenges such as

- Should tests simulate reality or use mock data?
- Should tests verify implementation details or focus on external behaviors?
- For front-end testing, should rendering be included? Should tests focus on shallow rendering or full rendering?
- When should snapshot testing be used, and when is visual testing more appropriate? What are the use cases and limitations of each?
- Should visual tests cover specific component combinations or entire web pages?
- How much test coverage is enough?
- How should naming conventions be defined and aligned with the team? What should the rationale be?

FOREWORDS

These questions are common in real-world practice, and this book can help readers understand the practicality of the topics discussed. To grasp the pros and cons of these technical decisions and the scenarios they're best suited for, readers must first understand the underlying implementation methods and framework characteristics. The book provides well-sized, concise, and easy-to-understand examples that allow readers to learn and follow along to turn knowledge into skill. By following the content and building a solid foundation, readers will gain a clearer understanding of various approaches and their context, enabling them to make informed, "just right" decisions when working with their team.

Content Overview

I categorize the book's chapters into three main areas. The first is to help readers make the right decisions with the highest return on investment in different situations. Investing in testing is like buying insurance—it involves considering costs and identifying the risks to mitigate. When resources are limited, the goal is to maximize user experience and save valuable team resources by focusing on the most critical areas based on product characteristics, team background, and constraints.

To make the best decisions with the highest ROI, you need a variety of solutions at your disposal. The second category is testing classifications and how different types of tests can complement each other for greater synergy. The book explains different types of tests based on granularity, scope, and goals and how frameworks and features can be used to achieve the most appropriate testing.

For front-end testing, several key types are discussed, such as unit testing, which focuses on functions or classes and ensures code logic and consistency. Integration testing focuses on components, isolating only system boundaries or third-party libraries and services. However, integration testing comes with challenges, and the book offers suggestions: Should child components be isolated or included? What is the right way to test state, rendering, and dependencies? When should certain aspects be tested, and when should they not? The book also delves into using framework features for testing, including how to test state machines provided by frameworks. End-to-end testing, critical for front-end testing, focuses on user behavior, usage scenarios, and operational workflows to ensure the entire system's integrity and stability. Another challenge for front-end engineers is ensuring that the user interface works across different browsers, devices, screen sizes, and resolutions. The book covers available frameworks and services that automate visual testing to help maintain UI consistency without relying on manual testing or visual inspection.

The third category, after understanding the goals, values, and strategies of various tests, is lowering the cost of writing tests to maximize ROI. The book provides valuable advice on selecting suitable frameworks and libraries based on specific objectives, avoiding reinventing the wheel, and leveraging existing tools. It also explains how to integrate CI pipelines into the product development lifecycle to maximize the value of testing. The book highlights how to save time using AI tools like Copilot, which can rapidly generate test code based on comments, leaving developers to verify, refactor, and adjust the output.

I'm personally a fan of Kent Beck's principle in software development: *Make it work. Make it right. Make it fast.* Summer's book reflects these three phases, making it easier for software engineers to read, understand, and apply.

Recommendation

The different types of tests mentioned in this book are not mutually exclusive but should complement each other for maximum efficiency. Most testing-related books focus on back-end testing, while front-end testing resources often focus solely on framework learning. Few touch on the practical considerations and trade-offs engineers face. This book is

FOREWORDS

perfect for front-end engineers looking for a comprehensive foundation. It covers more than just how to write front-end tests; it helps readers make well-rounded, informed decisions. Though my expertise leans toward the back end, this book taught me a lot about front-end testing, providing valuable insights and practical tips, making it an excellent resource for any back-end engineer looking to learn more about front-end testing.

What I appreciate about this book is its clear structure, comprehensive approach, and easy-to-follow pace. The examples are well sized and practical and encourage hands-on learning. I recommend that readers start by reviewing the FAQ chapter, reflect on how they typically handle similar issues, and then compare their thoughts with Summer's insights and recommendations. Three examples that I think will resonate with teams include

- Tests break whenever the UI or functionality changes.
- How best to test scenarios involving timers or intervals.
- How to identify which part of the process or rendering failed when a test breaks.

My acquaintance with Summer stems from Trend Micro's annual corporate training. Despite her focus on front-end development, her questions in class and discussions about real-world problems were insightful. She then systematized what she learned and shared her knowledge clearly through her blog, designing examples in her own language to explain concepts. Great authors and teachers often start as excellent learners. I'm honored that Summer invited me to write this foreword. Reading this content was refreshing and filled gaps in my front-end testing knowledge.

I believe this book will help many front-end engineers and even back-end engineers save valuable time, allowing them to spend more time learning and expanding their skills and careers. I'm grateful to Summer for pouring her time and effort into helping readers save time, build high-quality products, and create better experiences for users.

Joey Chen, Odd-e Taiwan Agile Coach

Foreword by Eddie Gao

Summer is a very diligent person in every aspect. Although I'm a few years older than her, she always seems surprised when I say I grew up reading her blog, but I genuinely learned a lot about JavaScript from it. Thanks to her meticulous personality, she ensures every article or book she writes is thoroughly researched before she begins. Sometimes, when our students are searching for front end–related information and come across her blog, I always recommend it by saying, "Yes, you can trust what this person writes."

Testing is a subject that many people know is important, yet don't quite know how to approach—especially front-end testing. Most people (including myself) tend to open a browser to see if the page layout is off or if there are any red error messages in the console. But in more complex front-end projects, this kind of testing only scratches the surface. The logic hidden beneath the surface often depends on luck and the developer's experience to work correctly. The challenge is that even if you want to start introducing test-driven development (TDD) into your project, choosing the right testing tools or frameworks isn't too difficult, but there are many questions: Should you write the tests first, or finish the features and then add tests later? What should be tested and what shouldn't? What level of test coverage is sufficient? While writing tests may rely on a developer's experience, there are methodologies established by industry experts that can serve as valuable guides.

FOREWORDS

For those using React or similar front-end frameworks, many tutorials teach component decomposition for reusability. However, the real purpose of breaking down components isn't just reuse—it's like writing functions. The key is to assign a piece of logic or code an easily identifiable name. Once a component is broken down, it can be unit tested, just like Lego blocks. As long as each block works perfectly, assembling them together should result in a functioning system.

I often hear concerns about how to test third-party payment services or external APIs. Should we test these non-self-written services or just ensure the workflow passes?

Summer's book covers these topics. Moreover, in the era of AI dominance, the book introduces how to use AI tools to assist in writing tests, which can be a great starting point for those who are less familiar with testing.

Learning front-end testing through Summer's book is essentially learning how to write more confident front-end code!

Eddie Gao, 5xcampus

Foreword by PJCHENder

Have you ever had this experience?

The designer asks you to enlarge the CTA (call-to-action) button text on the home page to make it more noticeable and increase the click-through rate. You think this is an easy task, and you know to be extra careful when editing CSS so you don't accidentally affect other components. Soon, you submit a pull request, and your colleague quickly approves it, efficiently pushing it live.

The next day, the designer notices that the button styles on the product page have changed, and you start feeling a bit anxious and uneasy. Could it be that my changes yesterday unintentionally broke something?

FOREWORDS

The story ends here, but regardless of whether or not you caused the issue, one thing remains the same: you lack confidence in the code you modified.

Writing tests is a way to boost that confidence. If tests had been in place, you might have caught the issue where changing A affected B before it went live. If there weren't any tests, at least after discovering the problem, you could add them to avoid making the same mistake next time.

In Summer's book, a variety of testing types are introduced in a clear and accessible way. From unit testing, integration testing, and end-to-end testing to visual testing, which is especially important for front-end development, all areas are covered. It also demonstrates how to run tests in CI and provides rich practical insights on why front-end testing focuses more on behavior rather than code implementation. The book systematically organizes different testing methods and tools for use at various stages.

If you're looking for a comprehensive understanding of front-end testing—from types to tools to execution—this is definitely a book worth reading.

PJCHENder, web developer and author of *Get Reacting with Your Website: Starting from Hooks*

Foreword by Eric Lee

You're tasked with making a change to a complex application, but after deploying, a seemingly unrelated feature breaks. Sound familiar? It's time to start writing tests for your code. Testing not only boosts your confidence with each change but also helps you write more maintainable and readable code.

Summer, a leading expert in testing, demystifies the often-intimidating world of front-end testing in *Practical Front-End Testing: Strategies and Best Practices for Developers*, providing clear explanations and practical guidance for creating well-tested applications.

FOREWORDS

Practical Front-End Testing: Strategies and Best Practices for Developers covers a wide range of topics, from the importance of testing to different testing strategies and how to test common features. One of my favorite sections is on conducting visual tests using tools like Storybook and Cypress. This approach is logical for front-end developers but not as widely adopted as I'd hoped. Design inconsistencies directly impact user experience, but users might not always report them. By combining this with the section on running tests in CI/CD, you'll create a robust pipeline that automatically catches bugs and visual regressions early.

I wish I had this book when I started my career. It covers theory, concepts, and real-world examples that engineers actually encounter. You'll learn how to design effective test cases, identify potential edge cases, and automate your testing workflow for maximum efficiency. With this book, you'll be productive from day one, have peace of mind knowing you have a solid development process, and ultimately become a better front-end developer.

Eric Lee, Senior Software Engineer at Rivian

CHAPTER 1

Getting Started with Testing

You will learn the following in this chapter:

- Front-end testing basics—their importance, challenges, test types, and effective strategies

- Various front-end testing types—unit, integration, end-to-end, and visual—as well as their scopes, benefits, and applicable scenarios to optimize testing strategies

- Various testing techniques such as Agile, Scrum, TDD, BDD, and DevOps and their application in development processes, particularly UI development

- Test naming conventions like Given-When-Then and it should, along with the 3A pattern for clarity

- The concepts of mock, spy, and double in testing, along with their differences, use cases, and examples

CHAPTER 1   GETTING STARTED WITH TESTING

What Is Front-End Web Testing?

Front-end web testing refers to the process of testing the front end of web applications. The front end is the part of the website that users interact with directly, including the interface, styles, animations, and functionalities.

Why Write Tests?

Imagine you are a developer. Have you ever experienced the following?

- Developing new features and being unsure whether all scenarios are covered. A feature often has many considerations and possible paths.

- Modifying or refactoring functionality and being uncertain if the original intent has been unintentionally altered. This can lead to new features or bug fixes that introduce new issues, creating a cycle of fixing and refixing.

- Testing involves too many variables, and manual testing is time-consuming and labor-intensive. Factors such as resolution (desktop vs. mobile), browsers (Chrome, Firefox, Safari), and various process combinations make manual testing impractical and exhaustive.

- Many front-end details are hard to detect manually and require automated tools for effective inspection.

CHAPTER 1   GETTING STARTED WITH TESTING

Now, imagine you are a user. Have you experienced the following?

- New features on a website breaking or being poorly designed, forcing you to switch to alternative products
- Some website features being supported only on specific browsers or platforms, such as working on Chrome or desktop but not on Safari or mobile
- The display or interaction feeling off or laggy, leading you to seek out other products
- Difficulty reading the website after changing languages, resulting in a poor user experience

How should developers address these issues? Especially in the front-end domain, where development environments evolve rapidly and technologies continually advance, maintaining high-quality code amid tight development schedules is indeed a significant challenge. The best way to tackle these challenges is through frequent testing and attention to various details. Take the first step and start writing tests!

How to Start Writing Tests?

The main goals of front-end web testing are

- To ensure that the front-end functionality of the website or application operates correctly and meets various scenarios and workflows, instilling greater confidence in adding, modifying, and refactoring features in the future
- To provide a good user experience by checking for performance bottlenecks and compatibility across different browsers and platforms

Thus, the focus of front-end testing should be to achieve the following:

- Ensure that core functionalities and integrations with other services operate correctly.
- Ensure that the interface displays and interacts smoothly.
- Increase productivity and reduce the cost of manual testing.

Developers can plan corresponding test types based on these goals, including unit tests, integration tests, end-to-end tests, and visual tests. Unit tests, integration tests, and end-to-end tests effectively check if core functionalities and integrations work properly, while visual tests ensure smooth user interface display and interaction. By combining different testing methods and tools, you can significantly enhance product quality and developer productivity while reducing the costs of manual testing.

This book will provide a detailed introduction to various types and methods of testing, helping you plan a testing structure, process, and test writing suited to your product. Follow the guidance in this book to upgrade your product!

Types of Front-End Testing

Front-end testing can be categorized into various types, as depicted in Figure 1-1, which shows the well-known Testing Pyramid model. This model includes unit testing, integration testing, end-to-end testing, and visual testing. The purpose of testing is to verify whether the current results match the expected outcomes. The main distinction among these types of tests is usually the scope of verification: from bottom to top, the scope ranges from small to large, the quantity decreases, the cost increases, and the confidence provided to developers increases. Generally, lower-level tests should be performed first and in greater numbers, but adjustments

CHAPTER 1 GETTING STARTED WITH TESTING

can be made depending on the product or project type (Note 1). However, tests cannot always be strictly categorized into a single type; there may be some gray areas. For example, testing larger components may be closer to integration testing, but unit tests might still be needed to ensure the correctness of the component's functionality.

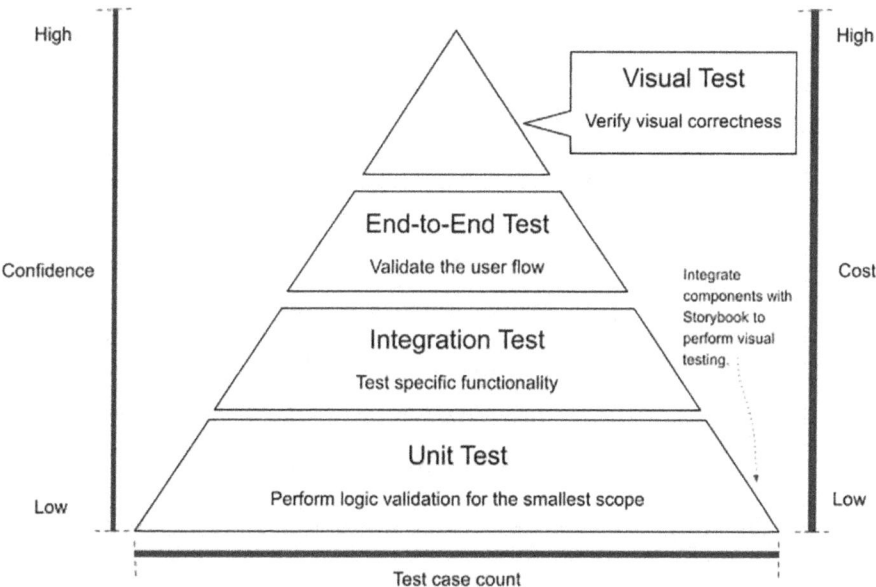

Figure 1-1. Testing Pyramid

In the following chapters, this book will explain, exemplify, and compare the different types of tests to provide a deeper understanding of their characteristics. This section will provide a brief overview of each test type to give developers an initial concept.

Unit Testing

Unit testing refers to testing the "smallest unit" or "independently testing specific code snippets" (Note 2). This type of testing primarily validates whether the inputs and outputs of functions, methods, or class instances

CHAPTER 1 GETTING STARTED WITH TESTING

meet expectations. It focuses on testing the smallest unit of code to ensure that it can operate independently and handle specific input and output scenarios correctly.

For example, the following code shows a function, `divideNumbers`, which divides two integers:

```
// src/utils/divideNumbers/divideNumbers.js

const divideNumbers = (num, den) => {
  if (den === 0) {
    throw new Error('Cannot divide by zero');
  }
  return num / den;
};
```

For the `divideNumbers` function, you can write tests for the following scenarios:

- Dividing two numbers evenly to get an integer.
- Dividing two numbers that do not divide evenly to get a fraction.
- When the numerator is zero, the result should be zero.
- When the denominator is zero, it should throw an error.

Here is an example of a unit test:

```
// src/utils/divideNumbers/divideNumbers.test.js

describe('divideNumbers', () => {
  // Dividing two numbers evenly to get an integer
  it('should return the correct integer when dividing two integers that are divisible', () => {
    expect(divideNumbers(8, 4)).toBe(2);
  });
```

```
// Dividing two numbers that do not divide evenly to get a
fraction
it('should return the correct fraction when dividing two
numbers that are not divisible', () => {
  expect(divideNumbers(7, 2)).toBe(3.5);
});

// When the numerator is zero, the result should be zero
it('should return zero when the numerator is zero', () => {
  expect(divideNumbers(0, 2)).toBe(0);
});

// When the denominator is zero, it should throw an error
it('should throw an error when dividing by zero', () => {
  expect(() => divideNumbers(10, 0)).toThrow('Cannot divide
  by zero');
});
});
```

Common unit testing frameworks include Vitest (https://vitest.dev/), Playwright (https://playwright.dev/), Jest (https://jestjs.io/), and Cypress (https://www.cypress.io/). For component testing, Jest is often used with Enzyme (https://enzymejs.github.io/enzyme/) or Testing Library (https://testing-library.com/).

The advantages of unit testing include the following:

- A smaller test scope allows for more focused testing, including happy path testing and edge cases, achieving the highest level of code quality assurance.

- Because unit tests focus on the smallest scope, they are generally the least costly in terms of time and effort to write and implement. This high cost-performance ratio makes unit testing highly recommended as the first line of testing.

CHAPTER 1   GETTING STARTED WITH TESTING

- Unit testing helps identify the root cause of issues; if an error occurs, you only need to review the related test cases to find the cause.

However, unit testing often lacks the integration between components and may differ significantly from real user interactions, necessitating other types of tests to achieve comprehensive and reliable test coverage.

For a detailed explanation and examples of unit testing, see Chapter 2.

Integration Testing

Integration testing, also known as functional testing, involves testing "combined code snippets." This type of testing is more comprehensive than unit testing and covers all aspects of specific features, including integrated components, related packages or libraries, and data presentation after fetching from APIs. Its purpose is to provide more thorough testing of the functionality, ensuring that integrated components work correctly and meet expectations in a real-world operating environment.

For example, the following code shows the `HelloWorld` component, where clicking the "Click!" button displays the message "Hello World!":

```
const HelloWorld = () => {
  const [message, setMessage] = useState('');

  return (
    <div>
      <button
        data-test-id="show-message-button"
        onClick={() => setMessage('Hello World!')}
      >
        Click!
      </button>
      <Text data-test-id="message">{message}</Text>
```

        </div>
    );
};
```

Here is an integration test example, testing the functionality of clicking the "Click!" button to display the message "Hello World!" In this test, to ensure complete functionality, two components <HelloWorld> and <Text> are integrated to test the button click and message display flow.

```
describe('HelloWorld component', () => {
    it('logs "Hello World!" when the button is clicked', () => {
        const { getByTestId } = render(<HelloWorld />);

        // Click the button
        fireEvent.click(getByTestId('show-message-button'));

        // Verify if the displayed message matches the
        expected outcome
        expect(getByTestId('message')).toHaveTextContent('Hello World!');
    });
});
```

Common integration testing frameworks include Jest with Enzyme or Testing Library and Cypress.

Compared to unit testing, integration testing is closer to actual user interactions, helping to verify the overall correctness and completeness of the functionality. However, it is harder to pinpoint the root cause of errors, which can be mitigated by using unit tests.

For detailed explanations and examples of integration testing, see Chapter 3.
```

End-to-End Testing

End-to-end testing (E2E testing) simulates the entire user interaction flow with the product. In the case of web interfaces, this testing simulates actions from opening a browser and entering a URL to navigating through specific features, browsing pages, and finally closing the window. Its purpose is to mimic real user behavior to ensure proper functionality in actual usage scenarios.

For example, the following code navigates to the "About Me" page of the "Summer" website (https://www.cythilya.tw/about/) and checks if the correct title text is retrieved (Note 3):

```
// cypress/e2e/cythilya.cy.js

describe('about page', () => {
  it('should get page title correctly', () => {
    cy.visit('https://www.cythilya.tw/about');

    cy.get('.page-title').should('have.text', 'About Me');
  });
});
```

Common end-to-end testing frameworks include Cypress (https://www.cypress.io/), Puppeteer (https://pptr.dev/), WebdriverIO (https://webdriver.io/), and Nightwatch (https://nightwatchjs.org/).

End-to-end testing's advantage is its ability to test the full functionality of the product, closely mimicking real user interactions. However, identifying the root cause of errors can be challenging and often requires tracing back to unit tests.

For detailed explanations and examples of end-to-end testing, see Chapter 4.

Visual Testing

Visual testing involves using tools to automatically detect changes in the user interface. It captures snapshots of what users see and compares them to identify any differences.

For example, the following code combines Cypress with Percy to capture snapshots of a page, using Mixtini as an example (Note 4):

```
// cypress/e2e/mixtini.cy.js

describe('Index page', () => {
  it('should update snapshot to Percy correctly', () => {
    cy.visit('https://mixtini-co.web.app/');
    cy.percySnapshot('index');
  });
});
```

After browsing the Mixtini home page, the cy.percySnapshot command captures a snapshot of the page and uploads it to Percy's service platform, where you can later view the comparison results.

Common visual testing tools include Chromatic (https://www.chromatic.com/), Percy (https://percy.io/), and end-to-end testing frameworks like Cypress (https://www.cypress.io/). These tools are effective for visual testing.

Visual testing's advantages include precise visual comparisons (pixel perfect) and the ability to test across various variables such as browsers and viewports. However, it may require third-party tools or services to implement, and it may not effectively detect dynamic changes on the screen.

For detailed explanations and examples of visual testing, see Chapter 5.

Whether it's unit testing, integration testing, end-to-end testing, or visual testing, this book will provide detailed explanations in the following chapters for each type.

I Only Have One Hour, Which Tests Should I Write?

In most project schedules, implementing functionality is always the most urgent task, followed by "possibly" writing tests. Testing often seems unimportant and is frequently overlooked, but tests are crucial for ensuring product and code quality. Issues such as breaking functionality or difficulty refactoring often stem from a lack of tests.

Testing is important, but what if I only have one hour to write tests? Of course, it's possible. But with only one hour, which tests should I write? How should I write them?

There are many types of tests; you can choose based on your testing goals:

- Core services of the product are suitable for unit testing, for example, verifying whether the inputs and outputs of functions, methods, or class instances meet expectations.

- Interfaces connecting the product with third-party services are suitable for integration testing, for example, integrating components, related packages or libraries, and data presentation from APIs.

- Testing the actual workflows of the product is suitable for end-to-end testing, for example, simulating the user flow from opening a browser, entering a URL, to navigating specific features and browsing pages.

- Emphasizing visual comparisons and testing various devices or browsers is suitable for visual testing, for example, different layouts on different devices, where visual testing can provide precise automated comparisons.

Next, consider how to write the tests.

First, consider where to write tests and how to conduct them. When selecting test locations, prioritize areas with a high return on investment, including important business logic, revenue-generating features, high-security areas, parts affecting reputation, and frequently modified or error-prone functionalities. Start with the main flow, then proceed to error handling and edge cases.

Additionally, testing should focus on meeting goals rather than the number of tests or coverage percentage. In other words, more tests aren't necessarily better; the ratio of tests should depend on the nature of the product and project. Code coverage is not an absolute indicator; assess the importance of functionality and usage scenarios to decide if writing tests is worthwhile (Note 5). Meeting user needs might be more important than having 1,000 tests or 90% coverage. A good practice is to add some tests with each code update, which helps improve code reliability and stability (Note 6).

Summary

Table 1-1 summarizes and compares the types of tests, applicable scenarios, advantages, and disadvantages.

Table 1-1. Summary and Comparison of Test Types, Scenarios, Advantages, and Disadvantages

Type	Description	Advantages	Disadvantages	Applicable Scenarios
Unit Testing	Testing the smallest unit	Focused testing within a small scope; lowest cost	Lacks integration between components; significantly differs from real user behavior	Core services of the product
Integration Testing	Testing combined code snippets	Integration helps detect overall correctness and completeness	Harder to identify root causes	Interfaces with third-party services
End-to-End Testing	Simulating user workflows	Closest to real user interactions	Harder to identify root causes	Testing actual product workflows
Visual Testing	Checking UI visual changes	Precise visual comparisons across various variables like browsers and viewports	Requires third-party tools or services; less effective for dynamic changes	Visual comparisons

Note that visual testing of components is tied to unit or integration testing. Compared to end-to-end testing, it has lower costs, shorter runtimes, and can be run more frequently, making it a valuable approach to reduce testing costs and time.

Once you've decided which tests to write, let AI assist in writing them. For more on using AI to write tests, see Chapter 8.

CHAPTER 1   GETTING STARTED WITH TESTING

Notes

- Note 1: For test structure planning strategies, besides the pyramid type, there are various variations such as ice cream cone, crab, trophy, diamond, and honeycomb. For related discussions, refer to Kent C. Dodds's "The Testing Trophy and Testing Classifications" (https://kentcdodds.com/blog/the-testing-trophy-and-testing-classifications) and "Pyramid or Crab? Find a testing strategy that fits" (https://web.dev/articles/ta-strategies).

- Note 2: For specific test terminology, if referring to the test code alone, use the noun "test"; if referring to the process, use the gerund "testing." For example, "unit test" refers to a single test case or test code, while "unit testing" refers to the process of executing a series of unit tests.

- Note 3: For more on this example, see Chapter 4.

- Note 4: For more on Mixtini and related examples, see Chapter 5.

- Note 5: For more on using usage scenarios to write tests, see Chapter 6, section "Inferring Use Case Coverage from Code Coverage."

- Note 6: For guidelines on reasonable coverage levels, refer to "JavaScript & Node.js Testing Best Practices" (https://github.com/goldbergyoni/javascript-testing-best-practices/), which suggests that "developers can gain confidence with sufficient code coverage; ~80% seems like a lucky number, 10% ~ 30% clearly cannot prove project correctness, but 100% might be overly time-consuming."

CHAPTER 1   GETTING STARTED WITH TESTING

Testing Techniques

What Are the Testing Techniques?

Developers can enhance code quality and productivity through various types of testing, and organizations also attempt to improve processes using different testing techniques, including

- Agile: Agile refers to the concept of allowing each stage of the development cycle to run concurrently, avoiding waiting times. By breaking down each phase into smaller increments, the operational cycle is shortened, providing the flexibility to adapt to rapidly changing requirements.

- Scrum: Scrum is an Agile development framework that emphasizes iteration, collaboration, and self-management. Development work is divided into cycles called sprints, each with a fixed duration. The team plans, develops, and reviews each sprint, delivering working software at the end of the sprint. Scrum manages the development process through product backlogs, sprint backlogs, and daily stand-up meetings.

- TDD (test-driven development): TDD is a development process where tests are written first, followed by code, and then refactoring. This workflow ensures code quality and helps developers better understand the requirements.

- BDD (behavior-driven development): BDD defines test specifications from the user's perspective and writes them in natural language. This approach helps developers better understand requirements and assists testers in writing effective tests.

- DevOps: DevOps combines development and operations culture, practices, and tools into a working model. Its goal is for engineers to take responsibility for the entire product lifecycle, including development, testing, deployment, and operations, rather than focusing solely on a single skill. This approach helps organizations seamlessly bridge development and operations, increasing team speed and productivity.

How Are These Testing Techniques Applied in Development?

Organizations attempt to apply various testing techniques to their development processes. Ideally, proper use of TDD and BDD can help developers ensure functional correctness and expected behavior during development. In contrast, Agile and DevOps provide a better collaborative and integrated environment, helping development teams test and deploy more efficiently.

How is this implemented in practice? In Scrum, for instance, the team decides what tasks to complete in each sprint during sprint planning and executes them accordingly. If requirements change, they are documented and discussed in the next sprint's planning session, allowing for continuous iteration with each sprint. For example, when developing a new feature, the team estimates the duration and the number of sprints needed to complete the feature and initially plans the work scope for each sprint. Changes such as requirement modifications or UI adjustments are logged in the backlog and reprioritized in the next sprint based on progress and priority. If tasks are independent, different developers can work on them simultaneously. During the sprint, developers can use daily stand-ups to sync information and discuss any issues. Features not yet fully implemented can be hidden using a feature toggle mechanism until completed, at which point the toggle can be turned on to make the feature available to users (Note 1).

When writing tests, the focus is on the function's performance and behavior and how users interact with the function or workflow. Specific test cases can be discussed with QA (Note 2), and test scripts can be written based on the minimum standards provided by the QA specifications.

Different testing techniques provide developers with varied workflows and experiences, but code quality is generally related to the amount of testing. More tests usually lead to better quality. Since code quality does not directly correlate with the process, it is recommended to start accumulating test cases from critical paths.

Are These Testing Techniques Suitable for UI Development?

How can developers apply these testing techniques to UI (user interface) development? We can plan and implement tests based on each sprint's output goals, with the following recommendations:

- Focus on how the functionality is presented and how users interact with it, such as when to click a button, when a modal appears, and what messages are displayed under specific conditions. Since functionality presentation or user interactions are related to function specifications and not visual details, minor visual adjustments will generally not affect the tests (Note 3).

CHAPTER 1   GETTING STARTED WITH TESTING

```
// src/Counter/Counter.enzyme.test.js

it('should get 1 when click the increment
button', () => {
  const wrapper = mount(<Counter />);

  wrapper.find('[data-test-id="increment-button"]').
  simulate('click');

  expect(wrapper.find('[data-test-id="counter-
  value"]').text()).toBe('1');
});
```

- Focus on whether integrations are correct, such as data flow or API connections, ensuring that events are triggered and responses are received correctly. Since integrations are related to functionality, not visual details, minor visual adjustments will generally not affect the tests (Note 4).

```
// src/Item.test.js

test('should show 2 items when click increment button',
async () => {
  // ...omitted...
  const spyDispatch = jest.spyOn(store, 'dispatch');

  // Click the "+" button to select the quantity
  fireEvent.click(getByTestId('add-to-cart'));

  // Click "+" again to add 1 more
  fireEvent.click(getByTestId('increment-button'));

  // Trigger action to add the item to the cart
  expect(spyDispatch).toHaveBeenCalledWith({
    type: ACTIONS.ADD_TO_CART,
```

```
      payload: { itemId: '999' },
    });
  });
```

These methods can be used to write tests before implementation. Common challenges include (1) unclear requirements and (2) tight development schedules that do not allow enough time for testing, but these challenges can be overcome to some extent (Note 5). Developers can still apply the above recommendations because these tests do not require knowledge of visual details—just the workflow and key components. It's important to note that visual details often change, especially as the product iterates. Teams may adjust and update the UI to improve quality, such as adding shadows to buttons for better aesthetics or repositioning elements for clearer content presentation. It's recommended not to write tests for visual details until the product stabilizes or to pay attention to element selection rules (Note 6) and consider using visual testing to assist.

Notes

- Note 1: Feature toggle is a software development technique used to dynamically enable or disable specific features in an application, enhancing the development team's flexibility and delivery of new features. This technique allows teams to control the application's behavior at runtime without redeploying or recompiling. The feature toggle decouples feature deployment from release, allowing features to be deployed in production even if incomplete or untested. It also enables dynamically turning features on or off in production to handle emergencies, test new features, or perform A/B testing. Feature toggles are typically implemented through conditional statements or configuration files in the code. When the application runs, it checks these conditions to determine whether to enable specific features, which can be based on various factors, such as user identity, environment variables, or date. The benefits of using feature toggles include increased deployment flexibility, risk reduction, continuous delivery and testing facilitation, and quicker feature delivery to users. However, excessive feature toggles can lead to increased code complexity and fragmented functionality, so careful consideration and management are necessary. Common feature toggle tools include LaunchDarkly (https://launchdarkly.com/).

- Note 2: QA refers to Quality Assurance Engineers responsible for reviewing outputs to ensure implementation according to specifications and meeting release quality standards. After product implementation specifications are completed, QA produces corresponding test specifications to test the outputs, ensuring the product meets expectations.

- Note 3: For more discussions on "how functionality is presented and how users interact with it," see Chapter 2, section "How to Write Tests for Components? A React Example," and Chapter 3, section "Testing Features from the User's Perspective and Maximizing Realism."

- Note 4: For discussions on how to write tests for data flows, see Chapter 3, section "How to Write Tests for State Management? A Redux Example."

CHAPTER 1   GETTING STARTED WITH TESTING

- Note 5: Using AI tools like Mermaid and ChatGPT can generate test scripts from flowcharts during the design phase, significantly aiding TDD adoption. For more on this, see Chapter 8.

- Note 6: For discussions on element selection rules, see Chapter 7, section "What to Do When UI Updates Cause Test Failures?"

Naming Conventions

When running tests, it's common to encounter test failures that require further investigation. When examining the cause of the test failure, the first step is usually to check the error message. For example, if a test case produces the error message `should get correct result`, the information is too vague to give developers a clear understanding of the issue, providing little help in resolving the problem.

```
FAIL  sample.js
  × should get correct result
```

Error messages are based on the descriptions written during test implementation. Therefore, before writing tests, it's essential to understand how to write effective descriptions—essentially how to name the tests. Currently, two mainstream test naming conventions are `Given-When-Then` and `it should`. Both conventions help developers clearly express the test's purpose, actions, and expected outcome. Additionally, they promote consistency and readability in test cases and, most importantly, assist developers in quickly identifying issues when tests fail.

CHAPTER 1   GETTING STARTED WITH TESTING

Given-When-Then

Given-When-Then, often abbreviated as GWT, is a well-known test naming convention commonly applied in testing techniques such as BDD and TDD to ensure clarity and consistency in test cases. It consists of three parts:

- Given: This step sets the preconditions for the test, describing the initial state needed before running the test. It is the preparation phase for the test case.

- When: This step describes the specific behavior or action being tested, detailing the action that triggers the test. It is the phase where the test behavior is executed.

- Then: This step verifies the result of the test, checking whether the outcome of the test action meets the expected result. It is the confirmation phase of the test.

For example, the test typically begins with a name and uses `describe` and `test` to separate the Given and When blocks, with Then subtly included within.

In this example:

- Given: The user is already logged in.
- When: The user submits the form.
- Then: The user should see a success message (Note 1).

```
describe('Login form', () => {
  describe('Given the form', () => {
    beforeEach(() => {
      setupLoginForm();
    });
```

```
    test('When the form is submitted', () => {
      submitForm();

      // Then ...
      expect(successMessage).toBeVisible();
    });
  });
});
```

Or, as shown in the following code, `describe` and `test` blocks clearly separate the Given, When, and Then sections:

```
describe('Login form', () => {
  describe('Given the form', () => {
    describe('When the form is submitted', () => {
      test('Then display a success message', () => {
        expect(successMessage).toBeVisible();
      });
    });
  });
});
```

it should

`it should` is another well-known test naming convention. It describes, in a single sentence, what is being tested, the expected outcome, and the conditions under which the outcome should occur. This convention is often paired with the 3A pattern to structure the test.

- should: Describes the expected result
- when: Describes the condition that triggers the result

For example, testing a function addNumbers that adds two numbers, the test case should return 3 when 1 + 2 indicates that when adding 1 + 2, the result should be 3.

```
// src/utils/addNumbers/addNumbers.test.js

describe('addNumbers', () => {
  it('should return 3 when 1 + 2', () => {
    expect(addNumbers(1, 2)).toBe(3);
  });
});
```

In this example:

- should: The expected result is 3.
- when: The condition is adding the numbers 1 and 2.

3A Pattern

The 3A pattern, also known as the AAA pattern, stands for Arrange, Act, and Assert. Arrange refers to setting up the test conditions, Act refers to executing the action being tested, and Assert refers to verifying the expected result. The 3A pattern corresponds to the Given-When-Then structure mentioned earlier.

For example, in the following code, the component is rendered, a button is clicked, and the text content is verified to be 1, in sequence:

```
// src/Counter/Counter.enzyme.test.js

// Arrange: Render the component (Given)
const wrapper = mount(<Component />);

// Act: Click the button (When)
wrapper.find('[data-test-id="button"]').simulate('click');
```

```
// Assert: Verify the text content is 1 (Then)
expect(wrapper.find('[data-test-id="value"]').text()).
toBe('1');
```

The 3A pattern offers a structured method for organizing and writing test cases. Its benefits include

- Clarity and readability: The test flow is easy to understand.

- Separation of concerns: The code is clearly divided into preparation, execution, and verification phases, helping maintain modularity.

- Consistency: The uniform structure of the code promotes consistency, making debugging and maintenance easier.

While the 3A pattern has many advantages, it may also be considered inflexible or burdensome in certain situations. Teams can discuss and adjust the pattern based on their specific needs.

Conclusion

Both `Given-When-Then` and `it should` are test naming conventions that clearly identify what is being tested, the expected result, and the conditions under which the test passes. These conventions help provide complete descriptions of test cases. Due to its simplicity and clarity, this book uses the `it should` convention along with the 3A pattern as the test naming model. Developers can choose either model based on their preferences and requirements.

The advantage of following a naming convention is that it clearly expresses the test's purpose, what it does, and the expected result. This approach makes collaboration with AI to write tests more effective and understandable (Note 2).

Notes

- Note 1: For more discussion and examples of using toBeVisible to check if an element is visible to the human eye, see Chapter 3, section "Snapshots."
- Note 2: For detailed explanations and examples of collaborating with AI to write tests, see Chapter 8.

Mock, Spy, and Double

Mock, spy, and double are three common concepts in testing. They are used to simulate, monitor, or replace real objects to facilitate testing. These tools are essential for handling dependencies in tests to ensure stability and reliability. The choice between them usually depends on the specific testing needs and code structure. This chapter will explain the differences between mock, spy, and double, provide examples, and describe their use cases in testing.

Mock

A mock is an object or function used to simulate or replace target components, third-party libraries, or API responses. By using mocks, developers can implement actual code during the testing process, replacing real implementation details. This method not only ensures that the code under test interacts correctly with its dependencies but also provides an isolated environment, making tests more reliable and easier to manage (Note 1). The core concept of mocking is that it allows developers to test parts of the code without relying on real dependencies. In other words, developers can focus on testing specific functionality or behavior without worrying about factors that may affect the test results. Mocks can be used in both unit and integration testing. Whether testing new features during development or checking the impact of changes during maintenance, mocks provide a simple and effective solution.

For example, in Jest, you can use `jest.mock` to mock components and their content from a specified path. In the following code, the component MyComponent.js from the src folder at the same level is mocked, returning `<div>Hello World!</div>`. In this test file, whenever the `<MyComponent>` component is rendered, it is replaced by `<div>Hello World!</div>`, bypassing the real implementation details.

```
jest.mock('./src/MyComponent', () => <div>Hello World!</div>);
```

Spy

A spy is an object that can monitor the behavior of a target object, recording the methods called, their parameters, and return values, without affecting the original behavior of the object. This method is useful for ensuring that the target being monitored is called and used correctly.

For example, suppose we have a `<Timer>` component that displays the remaining seconds as a countdown and shows a "Time's Up" message when the countdown ends. In this case, the `<Timer>` component calls the `clearInterval` method to clear the previously created timer when it is unmounted. We need to ensure that `clearInterval` is called at the appropriate time (Note 2).

```
// src/Timer/Timer.js

const Timer = () => {
  const [seconds, setSeconds] = useState(3);
  const intervalIDRef = useRef(null);
  const startTimer = useCallback(() => {
    intervalIDRef.current = setInterval(
      () => setSeconds((prev) => prev - 1),
```

```
      1000
    );
  }, []);

  const stopTimer = useCallback(() => {
    clearInterval(intervalIDRef.current);
    intervalIDRef.current = null;
  }, []);

  useEffect(() => {
    startTimer();
    return () => clearInterval(intervalIDRef.current);
  }, []);

  useEffect(() => {
    if (seconds === 0) {
      stopTimer();
    }
  }, [seconds]);

  return (
    <div>
      {seconds === 0
        ? `<span data-test-id="time-up">Time's Up</span>`
        : `Remaining seconds: <span data-test-id="remain-time">${seconds}</span>`}
    </div>
  );
};
```

We can wrap the clearInterval method as a spy and monitor it when the <Timer> component is unmounted, ensuring that clearInterval is called correctly and logging the parameters passed to it. Using Jest, we can use jest.spyOn to monitor whether clearInterval was called. As shown in the following code, spyOnClearInterval is an object that tracks calls to the clearInterval method, including the number of calls and the parameters passed. Here, the toHaveBeenCalledTimes assertion checks whether clearInterval was called. This monitoring mechanism not only helps developers ensure that clearInterval is called as expected but also provides rich information for debugging and testing. In the testing environment, spyOnClearInterval replaces the real clearInterval method to track its behavior during the test. This approach ensures the code runs correctly and provides detailed logs to assist with debugging and maintenance. By using spies, developers can test with greater confidence and ensure accurate results.

```
// src/Timer/Timer.test.js

it('should clean up the timer when unmount', () => {
  const { unmount } = render(<Timer />);
  const spyOnClearInterval = jest.spyOn(global, 'clearInterval');

  unmount();

  expect(spyOnClearInterval).toHaveBeenCalledTimes(1);
});
```

Double

Double is a term used in testing to refer to any mock object or function that replaces the real target. It includes both mocks and spies, and the choice of which to use depends on the specific testing needs.

Double refers to any object or function used to replace the real target during testing. It includes the two main forms: mocks and spies. As previously mentioned, they serve different purposes:

- Mocks are used to simulate the behavior of the target object, providing predefined responses without executing the real methods.

- Spies are used to monitor the behavior of the target object, recording methods called, parameters, and return values, without changing the object's behavior.

The choice between using a mock or a spy depends on the current test's goals and requirements. If the purpose of the test is to ensure that the code interacts correctly with the target object without executing the object's methods, mocks are the best option. However, if the goal is to ensure that the target object's methods are called correctly and to log the details of those calls, spies are the better choice.

Regardless of which form of double is used, the primary goal is to provide an isolated environment where tests can be run without relying on the real target object. This ensures that test results are reliable and repeatable. By using doubles, developers can test with greater confidence and ensure accurate results.

Notes

- Note 1: For more discussion on "mocks," see Chapter 3, section "Mocking Components, API Responses, and Third-Party Libraries."

- Note 2: For details about the <Timer> component, see Chapter 7, section "How to Test the Timer?"

CHAPTER 1   GETTING STARTED WITH TESTING

Chapter Review and Summary

- Front-end web testing refers to the process of testing the front-end part of a web application. The front end refers to the part of the website where users interact directly, including the interface, styles, animations, and functionality.

- The primary goals of front-end web testing are (1) to ensure that the front-end functions of the website or application work properly, covering various scenarios and workflows, and to provide confidence in adding, modifying, or refactoring features in the future; and (2) to deliver a good user experience by checking for performance bottlenecks, browser compatibility, and platform compatibility.

- To achieve the following goals for front-end testing: (1) core functions and integration with other services must work correctly; (2) the interface should display and operate smoothly; and (3) increase productivity while reducing the cost of manual testing. Developers can plan appropriate test types based on these goals, including unit testing, integration testing, end-to-end testing, and visual testing. Unit testing, integration testing, and end-to-end testing can effectively verify whether core functions and service integrations are working properly, while visual testing ensures that the user interface is displayed and operates smoothly. By combining different testing methods and tools, developers can significantly improve product quality and productivity while reducing manual testing costs.

CHAPTER 1   GETTING STARTED WITH TESTING

- Regardless of the testing technique used, code quality is generally related to the amount of testing conducted. The more tests there are, the better the quality.

- When applying testing techniques in UI development, the focus should be on functional correctness and service integration rather than visual details. Since it doesn't rely on visual specifics, tests can remain unaffected even if the UI changes. Visual changes are common, so developers should follow best practices for element selection and consider using visual testing tools to make tests more flexible.

- Currently, two mainstream test naming conventions exist: Given-When-Then and it should. Both approaches help developers clearly express the test's purpose, what actions are being tested, and the expected outcome. They also promote consistency and readability in test cases. Most importantly, when errors occur, these conventions help developers understand the cause and quickly identify the issue.

- Mock, spy, and double are three common concepts in testing, used to simulate, monitor, or replace real objects to facilitate testing. They are all tools used to handle dependencies in tests to ensure stability and reliability.

CHAPTER 2

Unit Testing

You will learn the following in this chapter:

- Unit testing benefits for code quality, early error detection, and the need for complementary testing methods
- The setup, installation, and comparison of Jest, Enzyme, and Cypress for effective unit testing of JavaScript applications
- Write unit tests with minimal scope validation by breaking down complex code and isolating dependencies for more focused and effective testing
- Write tests for React components by focusing on testing implementation vs. behavior, using examples like a counter and calculator component
- Shallow and full rendering techniques in React testing, explaining their benefits, limitations, and usage with Enzyme and React Testing Library

CHAPTER 2　UNIT TESTING

Unit Testing

Unit testing refers to testing the "smallest unit" or "independently testing specific code fragments" with the goal of verifying whether the input and output of a function, method, or class instance meet expectations. It focuses on examining the smallest functional units of the code to ensure they work independently and handle specific input/output scenarios correctly.

As shown in the code below, the addNumbers function provides the functionality to add two numbers:

```
// src/utils/addNumbers/addNumbers.js

const addNumbers = (a, b) => a + b;
```

Here's a sample unit test. Given two numbers as input, it verifies whether the output matches the expected result.

```
// src/utils/addNumbers/addNumbers.test.js

// Input two integers 1 and 2, expect to get 3
describe('addNumbers', () => {
  it('should return 3 when 1 + 2', () => {
    expect(addNumbers(1, 2)).toBe(3);
  });
});
```

During development, situations may arise due to code modifications or user actions under different scenarios. These issues can be prevented or adjusted through testing to avoid future problems, for example:

- A developer accidentally changes a + b to a - b. Running the test would throw an error, indicating to the developer that something broke and needs to be fixed.

- When users input 0.1 and 0.2, the result is not 0.3 but 0.30000000000000004. This happens because the calculation is converted to binary during the process. We need to adjust the addNumbers function to handle this correctly, which is particularly important for currency conversion or product discount calculations.

The code is modified as follows, using toFixed to round the decimal to a specified number of places (in this case, one decimal place), then converting the result back to a number. This avoids issues where the calculation result does not align with real-world use cases due to conversion limitations.

```
// src/utils/addNumbers/addNumbers.js

const addNumbers = (a, b) => Number((a + b).toFixed(1));
```

The following test case verifies that the addNumbers function correctly handles decimal addition. If any adjustments are made in the future, this test will effectively check if the function meets the specified use case.

```
// src/utils/addNumbers/addNumbers.test.js

it('should return 0.3 when 0.1 + 0.2', () => {
  expect(addNumbers(0.1, 0.2)).toBe(0.3);
});
```

These examples highlight the benefits and necessity of implementing unit testing, including

- Improving code quality: The smaller the testing scope, the more focused and detailed the tests can be, covering both happy path and edge cases, which ensures the highest level of code quality.

CHAPTER 2   UNIT TESTING

- Cost efficiency: Since unit testing targets the smallest scope, the time cost for implementation is typically the lowest. In this case, unit testing offers the best value in terms of cost and quality, making it the recommended starting point.

- Early detection of potential errors: Unit tests help identify the root cause of issues early. If errors occur, developers can quickly find the cause by examining the relevant test cases.

- Facilitating refactoring: When refactoring code, unit test cases can verify that functionality still works as expected.

- Providing excellent documentation: Each unit test case serves as a useful documentation tool, recording what functionality exists and how it operates. This helps the team understand the code more easily.

While unit testing is an essential testing method, it is not without limitations. Unit testing often differs significantly from real-world interactions between components and actual user behavior. Even if the unit test results are correct, other types of testing, such as integration testing, are needed to ensure data flow and interactions between components function properly.

Additionally, unit tests may pass, but that doesn't always guarantee alignment with real user interaction scenarios. There may be unforeseen interaction cases that result in unexpected outcomes. To ensure overall system quality, different types of tests, such as integration testing and end-to-end testing, are needed to complement one another and achieve comprehensive, reliable test coverage.

In summary, the primary goal of unit testing is to verify whether input and output meet expectations. Unit testing effectively improves code quality and quickly identifies core issues. However, because unit testing focuses on the functionality of individual components and differs significantly from real user interactions, it must be supplemented by other types of testing, such as integration testing and end-to-end testing, to ensure overall system quality.

Environment Setup, Installation, and Tool Comparison

In the field of software development, unit testing is an indispensable testing method. It focuses on testing individual units of code to ensure their functionality and behavior meet expectations. Jest and Cypress are two widely used testing frameworks in this domain. This section introduces the setup and installation process for both Jest and Cypress, allowing developers to choose the most suitable testing tool based on their needs and proceed with relevant testing. This will help developers more effectively test products and projects, ensuring their quality and stability.

Jest

Jest (https://jestjs.io/) is a testing framework for JavaScript that is known for its simple syntax, built-in assertions, and mocking capabilities. It integrates easily with other tools, making it simple for developers to write and run tests. As a result, Jest is widely used for unit testing and integration testing, making it a preferred testing framework for many JavaScript developers.

To install Jest, use the following commands, depending on your package manager, such as yarn (https://yarnpkg.com/) or npm (https://www.npmjs.com/) (Note 1):

```
yarn add --dev jest
npm install --save-dev jest
```

CHAPTER 2   UNIT TESTING

The `--dev` or `-D` option specifies that the package will be installed in the `devDependencies` section of the `package.json` file. This is because, during the development process, we use various testing tools and frameworks to run test scripts, which ensure the code operates as expected and helps identify and fix any potential issues. However, when the application is deployed to a production environment, these test scripts are not needed. Therefore, testing-related packages are installed in the `devDependencies` section rather than in `dependencies`.

Once installed, we can write a simple test to validate the code. Below is an example of an `addNumbers` function that provides functionality to add two numbers:

```
// src/utils/addNumbers/addNumbers.js

const addNumbers = (a, b) => Number((a + b).toFixed(1));
```

The unit test is written as follows. It provides two numbers as input and verifies that the output meets the expected result. The test is structured as follows:

- The first test case ensures that when the input parameters are integers 1 and 2, the result should be 3.
- The second test case ensures that when the input parameters are decimal values 0.1 and 0.2, the result should be 0.3. This checks how the function handles floating-point numbers.

The implementation of the test is as follows. This simple test helps confirm whether the `addNumbers` function performs its intended functionality correctly.

```
// src/utils/addNumbers/addNumbers.test.js

describe('addNumbers', () => {
  // Input 1 and 2, the result is 3
```

```
  it('should return 3 when 1 + 2', () => {
    expect(addNumbers(1, 2)).toBe(3);
  });

  // Input 0.1 and 0.2, the result is 0.3
  it('should return 0.3 when 0.1 + 0.2', () => {
    expect(addNumbers(0.1, 0.2)).toBe(0.3);
  });
});
```

Explanation:

- In the Jest testing framework, the describe function is used to group related test cases together, enhancing code modularity and readability. The describe function accepts two parameters: the first is a string that describes the test, and the second is a function that contains one or more test cases. This structure makes the test code more organized and easier to understand when reviewing results. For example, running the test code from this example will produce the following output, clearly showing the test results for the addNumbers.test.js file, with two test cases checking different scenarios:

```
PASS  src/utils/addNumbers/addNumbers.test.js
  addNumbers
    ✓ should return 3 when 1 + 2 (1 ms)
```
- ✓ should

CHAPTER 2   UNIT TESTING

Jest + Enzyme

Enzyme (https://enzymejs.github.io/enzyme/) is a JavaScript library designed specifically for testing React applications. It offers a rich API that allows developers to easily render, manipulate, and traverse React components. Enzyme supports rendering components and performing assertions for unit and integration tests. It also allows developers to simulate user interactions, test UI rendering, and verify behavior. These features make Enzyme a powerful tool that helps developers efficiently simulate and validate React application functionality. Its simple and understandable API enables developers to query and interact with rendered components, improving testing efficiency and accuracy.

To begin using Enzyme for testing React applications, you need to install Enzyme via a package manager. Additionally, since React's version updates may affect rendering and interaction methods, developers need to install the corresponding Enzyme adapter package based on the React version they are using (Note 6). These adapters act as an abstraction layer, providing a stable API interface that ensures testing reliability and compatibility when upgrading the framework. This method not only ensures the reliability of tests but also offers an easy and effective way to accommodate React version changes.

```
yarn add --dev enzyme @cfaester/enzyme-adapter-react-18
npm install --save-dev enzyme @cfaester/enzyme-adapter-react-18
```

Next, configure the settings file. `setupTests.js` is the default file that Jest reads for setting up the test environment. Here, Enzyme's adapter is configured to connect Enzyme with React 18.

```
// src/setupTests.js

import { configure } from 'enzyme';
import Adapter from '@cfaester/enzyme-adapter-react-18';

configure({ adapter: new Adapter() });
```

CHAPTER 2   UNIT TESTING

Once configured, you can begin writing test code. Below is an example of a <Counter> component that lets users increase or decrease a number by clicking buttons to implement a counting function. In this example, you'll see how to use Enzyme to render the component and simulate user interaction to ensure the component behaves as expected:

```js
// src/Counter/Counter.js

const Counter = () => {
  const [count, setCount] = useState(0);
  const increment = () => setCount(count + 1);
  const decrement = () => setCount(count - 1);

  return (
    <>
      <div data-test-id="counter-value">{count}</div>
      <button data-test-id="decrement-button"
      onClick={decrement}>
         -
      </button>
      <button data-test-id="increment-button"
      onClick={increment}>
         +
      </button>
    </>
  );
};
```

43

CHAPTER 2 UNIT TESTING

Explanation:

- The useState hook is used to create and manage the count state, initialized to 0.

- Two functions, increment and decrement, are defined to increase and decrease the count value. In the JSX return, the interface interacts with the user, displaying the current count value and two buttons ("+" and "-"). Clicking the buttons triggers the increment and decrement functions, respectively.

- Both the buttons and the displayed number have corresponding data-test-id attributes, which are used as selectors for testing purposes to find and interact with these elements in the test.

Using Jest and Enzyme to test the <Counter> component, the following code simulates clicking the "+" button and checks whether the count increases from 0 to 1. This test verifies how the component behaves on screen (Note 7).

```
// src/Counter/Counter.enzyme.test.js
describe('Counter component', () => {
  it('should get 1 when click the increment button', () => {
    const wrapper = mount(<Counter />);

    wrapper.find('[data-test-id="increment-button"]').simulate('click');

    expect(wrapper.find('[data-test-id="counter-value"]').text()).toBe('1');
  });
});
```

CHAPTER 2   UNIT TESTING

Explanation:

- Enzyme's mount method performs a full rendering, rendering the entire <Counter> component and all of its child components. This is particularly useful when testing the overall behavior of components in integration tests (Note 8).

- Enzyme's find method is used to locate target DOM elements within the rendered component by passing in a selector. In this case, it's used to find the DOM elements with the data-test-id attributes of increment-button and counter-value for further assertions.

- Enzyme's text method is used to retrieve the text content of the selected DOM element.

- Jest's expect assertion checks whether the actual text content retrieved matches the expected value "1." If they match, the test passes; otherwise, it fails with an error message.

To run the test:

```
yarn test src/Counter/Counter.enzyme.test.js
npm run src/Counter/Counter.enzyme.test.js
```

The test output shows that the <Counter> component behaves as expected:

```
PASS  src/Counter/Counter.enzyme.test.js
  Counter component
    ✓ should get 1 when click the increment button (35 ms)
```

CHAPTER 2   UNIT TESTING

Jest + Testing Library

Testing Library (https://testing-library.com/) is a tool designed specifically for testing JavaScript applications. Its core principle is to focus on testing user interface behavior rather than implementation details. It includes various versions tailored for different frameworks, such as React Testing Library, Vue Testing Library, and Angular Testing Library. These tools are designed to help developers test user interactions and behaviors. Testing Library is often used alongside testing frameworks like Jest, providing a simple and easy-to-understand API that makes test code more readable, maintainable, and comprehensible.

For React developers, to start using Testing Library, you can install it using a package manager from your project root.

```
yarn add --dev @testing-library/react
npm install --save-dev @testing-library/react
```

Since this guide prefers using `data-test-id` as the testing attribute rather than the default `data-testid`, the configuration can be adjusted by setting the `testIdAttribute`. This adjustment allows developers to customize the data attributes used for testing to match the project's coding style and consistency.

```
// src/setupTests.js

import '@testing-library/jest-dom';
import { configure as configureTestingLibrary } from '@testing-library/react';

configureTestingLibrary({ testIdAttribute: 'data-test-id' });
```

Once configured, you can start writing test code. For example, using Jest and React Testing Library, you can write test cases for the `<Counter>` component. The following code demonstrates how to simulate clicking the "+" button and check if the number increases from 0 to 1, just like in the previous example:

CHAPTER 2   UNIT TESTING

```
// src/Counter/Counter.rtl.test.js
describe('Counter component', () => {
  it('should get 1 when click the increment button', () => {
    const { getByTestId } = render(<Counter />);

    fireEvent.click(getByTestId('increment-button'));

    expect(getByTestId('counter-value')).
    toHaveTextContent('1');
  });
});
```

Explanation:

- React Testing Library's `render` method performs a full render, rendering the entire <Counter> component and all its child components. This is particularly useful when performing integration tests where you need to test the overall behavior of components.

- React Testing Library's `getByTestId` can be used to find the target DOM element by passing the testing attribute `data-test-id`. In this case, it looks for the `data-test-id` values of `increment-button` and `counter-value` to interact with these elements.

- The `@testing-library/jest-dom` library provides the Jest matcher `toHaveTextContent` to assert that the content of a DOM element matches the expected text.

- Jest's expect assertion checks if the actual text matches the expected value "1." If they match, the test passes; otherwise, it fails with an error message.

To run the test:

```
yarn test src/Counter/Counter.rtl.test.js
npm run src/Hello/Hello.enzyme.test.js
```

The test output shows that the <Counter> component behaves as expected:

```
PASS  src/Counter/Counter.rtl.test.js
  Counter component
    ✓ should get 1 when click the increment button (40 ms)
```

Cypress

Cypress (https://www.cypress.io/) is a comprehensive front-end testing framework that offers a range of powerful features, including real-time test feedback, a simple API, automatic waiting mechanisms, and support for screenshots and video recording. While Cypress was initially designed for integration or end-to-end testing, its powerful features and ease of use also make it a viable option for unit testing. This multipurpose testing framework not only helps developers ensure the overall quality of an application but also provides rich test feedback, leading to a more efficient development process.

To start using Cypress for testing, you can install it via a package manager from the project root.

```
yarn add --dev cypress
npm install --save-dev cypress
```

To ensure ease of use, consistency, and integration with other tools, you can add a `cypress:open` script in the `package.json` file as a preconfigured command (Note 9). This script acts as a shortcut for launching Cypress tests, so when testing is needed in the future, you can quickly start the Cypress test environment with a simple command. This approach not only simplifies the test initiation process but also ensures the consistency of the project's testing workflow with other development tasks, improving both efficiency and maintainability.

```
// package.json
{
  "scripts": {
    "cypress:open": "cypress open"
  }
}
```

To start Cypress, use the following commands:

```
yarn cypress:open
npm cypress:open
```

If this is your first time setting up the project, the Cypress setup interface will open in the browser. Since this chapter focuses on unit testing, choose the "Component Testing" option on the right, as shown in Figure 2-1. Follow the instructions on the screen to complete the setup. Once configured, Cypress will handle the necessary settings, unlike Jest, which requires manual configuration files for customization. This design allows developers to get started with writing test code quickly without spending much time on configuration.

CHAPTER 2   UNIT TESTING

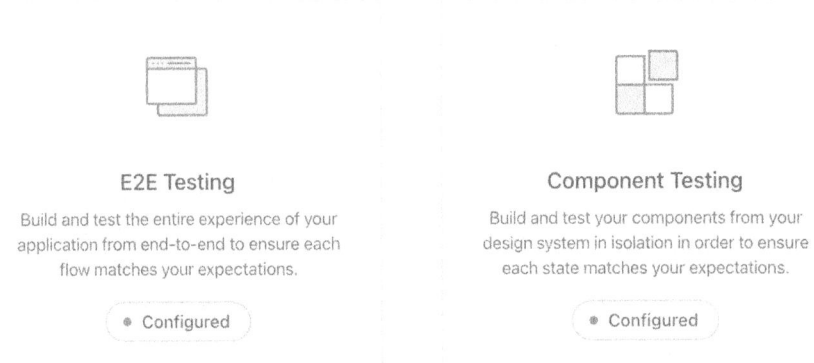

Figure 2-1. *Cypress setup interface*

Extend the mount command, which will help render components during testing.

// cypress/support/component.js

import { mount } from 'cypress/react18';

Cypress.Commands.add('mount', mount);

Once setup is complete, you can begin writing test code. For example, the following code shows how to use Cypress to test the <Counter> component. Like the previous examples, it simulates clicking the "+" button and checks if the number increases from 0 to 1.

// src/Counter/Counter.cy.js

```
describe('<Counter />', () => {
  it('should get 1 when click the increment button', () => {
    cy.mount(<Counter />);
```

```
    cy.get('[data-test-id="increment-button"]').click();
    cy.get('[data-test-id="counter-value"]').should('have.
    text', '1');
  });
});
```

Explanation:

- Cypress's mount method fully renders the <Counter> component and all its child components, just like in the previous examples. Full rendering is particularly useful for integration tests where the overall behavior of the component is tested.

- Cypress's get method is used to find target DOM elements in the rendered component by passing in the selector. In this case, it's used to find the DOM elements with data-test-id attributes increment-button and counter-value for further assertions.

- Cypress comes with a built-in assertion tool, Chai (https://www.chaijs.com/). Here, Chai's should function is used to assert that the actual text content matches the expected value "1." If they match, the test passes; otherwise, it fails with an error message.

It's important to note that since Cypress focuses on simulating real user interactions in a browser environment, it is primarily used for integration or end-to-end testing. Therefore, it does not offer shallow rendering functionality. Additionally, Cypress does not provide built-in mock component mechanisms, so for unit testing, Jest with Enzyme or Testing Library might be a better fit. However, if you want to switch between unit testing, integration testing, and end-to-end testing, or if you want to use a single testing framework for different types of tests, Cypress is a solid choice. Overall, Cypress is a comprehensive testing framework that, while less flexible for unit testing compared to Jest with Enzyme or Testing Library, meets the needs of developers for other types of tests depending on their preferences and use cases.

To run the test file, select `Counter.cy.js` for testing:

```
yarn cypress:open
npm run cypress:open
```

The test output shows that the `<Counter>` component behaves as expected:

```
Counter.cy.js 400ms
  <Counter />
    should get 1 when click the increment buttonpassed
    should get -1 when click the decrement button
```

As shown in Figure 2-2, during the testing process, developers can observe the effect of each line of code on the component in real time. This not only makes understanding the test results more intuitive but also provides developers with a powerful tool to quickly identify and resolve issues. If difficulties arise during the testing process, or debugging is needed, Cypress's time travel feature allows developers to rewind to any point in the test process and retrieve the component's state and related information at that moment, making debugging and issue resolution more convenient.

CHAPTER 2   UNIT TESTING

Figure 2-2. *Cypress test example*

In the following sections of this chapter, we will explore examples using these common frameworks to demonstrate how to write test code. However, developers can choose the framework they prefer based on their needs or preferences.

Notes

- Note 1: If you are using Create React App (https://create-react-app.dev/) as the project setup template, Jest and Testing Library are already built-in, so you don't need to install additional packages. Additionally, for the Node version, it is recommended to use the latest LTS (Long-Term Support) version.

- Note 2: Since Enzyme no longer supports React versions after 16, there is no official adapter. For React 17 and above, it is recommended to use unofficial adapters. This book uses React 18 and above, so it's recommended to install @cfaester/enzyme-adapter-react-18. For more information, see *Enzyme is dead. Now what?* (https://bit.ly/4bnIWNq).

53

- Note 3: For detailed explanations and examples of component testing, see the section "How to Write Tests for Components? A React Example" in this chapter.

- Note 4: For detailed explanations and examples of full rendering, see the section "Shallow Rendering and Full Rendering" in this chapter.

- Note 5: For more on pretest commands and examples, see Chapter 6, section "Pre-commands and Manual Test Invocation."

Minimal Scope Validation Logic

The purpose of unit testing is to test the smallest functional units of code to ensure they operate independently and correctly handle specific input and output scenarios as expected. This approach effectively improves code quality and helps identify core issues quickly. To achieve minimal scope validation logic in unit tests, two key principles must be followed:

- Break down overly complex code: Check whether the code block being tested only completes one task. If it performs multiple tasks or is too complex, refactoring is needed.

- Isolate dependencies: When writing tests, isolate dependencies and focus on testing only one function.

For example, the `checkValentinesDay` function checks whether today is Valentine's Day. If today is February 14, it returns the string "Happy Valentine's Day"; otherwise, it returns "Today is not Valentine's Day."

```
// src/utils/checkValentinesDay/checkValentinesDay.js
const checkValentinesDay = () => {
  const today = new Date();
  const month = today.getMonth() + 1;
  const day = today.getDate();
  return month === 2 && day === 14
    ? "Happy Valentine's Day"
    : "Today is not Valentine's Day";
};
```

The following test case assumes today is January 15 and checks whether it is Valentine's Day. In this test case, we expect that after calling the checkValentinesDay function, the result will be "Happy Valentine's Day."

```
// src/utils/checkValentinesDay/checkValentinesDay.test.js
describe('checkValentinesDay', () => {
  it('today should be Valentines Day', () => {
    expect(checkValentinesDay()).toBe("Happy Valentine's Day");
  });
});
```

When running this test using yarn test checkValentinesDay.test.js, the expected result is "Happy Valentine's Day," but we receive the message "Today is not Valentine's Day," causing the test to fail.

- checkValentinesDay › today should be Valentines Day
  Expected: "Happy Valentine's Day"
  Received: "Today is not Valentine's Day"

CHAPTER 2   UNIT TESTING

Breaking Down Overly Complex Code

Let's examine why the test fails. We assumed today is January 15, which is not Valentine's Day. However, what we are really trying to test is

- When today is January 15, it should correctly determine that it is not Valentine's Day and return the string "Today is not Valentine's Day."
- When today is February 14, it should correctly determine that it is Valentine's Day and return the string "Happy Valentine's Day."

Looking at the `checkValentinesDay` function, it does several things:

- Retrieves today's date
- Checks if today is February 14
- Returns "Happy Valentine's Day" or "Today is not Valentine's Day"

From this, it becomes clear that the `checkValentinesDay` function does too much. It not only checks if today is Valentine's Day but also retrieves today's date. This makes it difficult to ensure we are testing the minimal scope. Therefore, we need to refactor the `checkValentinesDay` function, simplifying its functionality to make it more focused.

Since the primary goal of `checkValentinesDay` is to "determine if today is Valentine's Day," we can break out the "retrieve today's date" part into a separate `getToday` function that can be reused. This allows the `checkValentinesDay` logic to focus solely on checking if today is Valentine's Day.

The refactored code looks like this: `checkValentinesDay` will call `getToday` to retrieve today's date and then return the appropriate string based on the result, either "Happy Valentine's Day" or "Today is not Valentine's Day."

CHAPTER 2 UNIT TESTING

```js
// src/utils/checkValentinesDay/checkValentinesDay.js
const checkValentinesDay = () => {
  const today = getToday();
  return today === '2/14'
    ? "Happy Valentine's Day"
    : "Today is not Valentine's Day";
};

const getToday = () => {
  const today = new Date();
  const month = today.getMonth() + 1;
  const day = today.getDate();
  return `${month}/${day}`;
};
```

Explanation:

- The getToday function retrieves today's date. First, it creates a Date object representing the current date and time. Then, the getMonth method is used to get the current month (note that getMonth returns months starting from 0, so we need to add 1 to get the correct month). For example, if today is January 15, the getMonth method will return 0 instead of 1. Then, the getDate method retrieves the current day. Finally, the month and day are combined into a string formatted as MM/DD and returned. In this case, it will return "1/15."

- The checkValentinesDay function checks if today is Valentine's Day by calling getToday to retrieve the current date in MM/DD format. It checks if today's date is the string "2/14," which is the defined date for Valentine's Day. If so, it returns "Happy Valentine's

Day"; otherwise, it returns "Today is not Valentine's Day." For example, if today is January 15, getToday will return "1/15," so checkValentinesDay will return "Today is not Valentine's Day."

After refactoring, the code structure and logic become clearer. Next, we will implement the test to ensure the functionality is correct and meets expectations.

Isolating Dependencies

After refactoring, each function does just one thing: checkValentinesDay only determines if today is Valentine's Day, and getToday only retrieves today's date. Now, we will write the test. It is important to "isolate dependencies" and test only one function at a time, ensuring the focus is on testing the specific functionality. Any functions outside the test's scope should be mocked to replace their actual implementation details (Note 1).

First, we mock getToday, which checkValentinesDay depends on. This allows us to focus solely on testing whether checkValentinesDay correctly determines if today is Valentine's Day.

```
// src/utils/checkValentinesDay/checkValentinesDay.test.js
jest.mock('./getToday', () => ({
  getToday: jest.fn(),
}));
```

Next, we implement the test to check two scenarios:

- When today is February 12, it should determine that it is not Valentine's Day and return the string "Today is not Valentine's Day."
- When today is February 14, it should determine that it is Valentine's Day and return the string "Happy Valentine's Day."

Since we have already mocked getToday, we can use mockReturnValue to set the return value of getToday, allowing us to test the logic of checkValentinesDay (Note 2).

```
// src/utils/checkValentinesDay/checkValentinesDay.test.js

describe('checkValentinesDay', () => {
  // When today is February 12, it should return "Today is not
  Valentine's Day"
  it('2/12 should not be Valentines Day', () => {
    getToday.mockReturnValue('2/12');
    expect(checkValentinesDay()).toBe("Today is not
    Valentine's Day");
  });

  // When today is February 14, it should return "Happy
  Valentine's Day"
  it('2/14 should be Valentines Day', () => {
    getToday.mockReturnValue('2/14');
    expect(checkValentinesDay()).toBe("Happy Valentine's Day");
  });
});
```

Running this test using yarn test checkValentinesDay.test.js will show that the test passes, with the following output:

```
PASS  src/utils/checkValentinesDay/checkValentinesDay.test.js
  checkValentinesDay
    ✓ 2/12 should not be Valentines Day (2 ms)
    ✓ 2/14 should be Valentines Day (1 ms)
```

CHAPTER 2   UNIT TESTING

Conclusion

Breaking down complex code into smaller parts and isolating external dependencies makes unit testing easier for developers. This method allows us to focus on validating the smallest possible scope, which in turn helps achieve testing goals. All test cases in this book are written according to this principle, enhancing both the efficiency and accuracy of testing.

Notes

- Note 1: For more on mocking, see Chapter 3, section "Mocking Components, API Responses, and Third-Party Libraries."

- Note 2: For explanations, comparisons, and examples of `mockImplementation` and `mockReturnValue`, see Chapter 3, section "Mocking Components, API Responses, and Third-Party Libraries."

How to Write Tests for Components? A React Example

When it comes to front-end testing, one of the main goals is to test the functionality and behavior of components. But how do you write tests for components? In this section, we will take React as an example to explain in detail how to write component tests, providing implementation examples to help understand and master the process.

Testing Implementation vs. Testing Behavior

When implementing unit tests for components, developers usually approach it from two perspectives: testing the "implementation" or evaluating the "behavior" of the component (Note 1). To illustrate these two approaches, we will implement a `<Counter>` component as an example. This component allows users to increment or decrement a number by clicking buttons, thereby achieving a counting function. The following example demonstrates how to use Enzyme to render the component and simulate user interactions to ensure that the component functions correctly. For a preview of the `<Counter>` component, refer to the previous section "Environment Setup, Installation, and Tool Comparison."

As shown in the code below, we implement the `<Counter>` component as a class component for the counter functionality. In the component's constructor, the initial state of `count` is set to 0. Next, we define two methods, `increment` and `decrement`, for incrementing and decrementing the counter's value, respectively. In these methods, we use the `setState` method to update the value of `count` by increasing or decreasing it based on the previous state. In the `render` method, we return JSX that contains the counter value, increment button, and decrement button, which serve as the user interface for interaction. Each element includes a `data-test-id` attribute for testing purposes, and both the increment and decrement buttons are bound to the corresponding click events, invoking the previously defined `increment` and `decrement` methods.

```
// src/Counter/Counter-class.js

class Counter extends Component {
  constructor(props) {
    super(props);
    this.state = { count: 0 };
  }
```

```
increment = () => {
  this.setState((prevState) => ({
    count: prevState.count + 1,
  }));
};

decrement = () => {
  this.setState((prevState) => ({
    count: prevState.count - 1,
  }));
};

render() {
  return (
    <>
      <p data-test-id="counter-value">Count: {this.state.count}</p>
      <button data-test-id="decrement-button" onClick={this.decrement}>
        +
      </button>
      <button data-test-id="increment-button" onClick={this.increment}>
        -
      </button>
    </>
  );
}
}
```

CHAPTER 2 UNIT TESTING

Testing Implementation

We will write the first test example to test the "implementation" of the component. This example will use Jest and Enzyme to write the test code.
Explanation:

- In the code, the describe function is used to define two test cases. In each test case, the beforeEach function is used to initialize the testing environment (Note 2). Then, the <Counter> component is shallow rendered (Note 3), and the result is stored as the wrapper variable. The advantage of this approach is that each test case uses a fresh, unaltered instance of the component, ensuring the accuracy and reliability of the test results (Note 4).

- The first test case checks that clicking the "+" button increases the number by 1. Using the test attribute data-test-id, the button with the value increment-button is found, and a click event is simulated. Then, the state of the <Counter> component is checked to see if it is correctly updated to 1.

- The second test case checks that clicking the "-" button decreases the number by 1. Similarly, the button with the value decrement-button is found using the test attribute data-test-id, and a click event is simulated. The state of the <Counter> component is then checked to ensure it is correctly updated to -1.

These tests ensure that the <Counter> component correctly increments or decrements the number when the user clicks the buttons. This not only guarantees that the component functions properly but also provides developers with a reliable way to verify and maintain the component's behavior.

63

```
// src/Counter/Counter-class.enzyme.test.js
describe('Counter component', () => {
  let wrapper;

  beforeEach(() => {
    wrapper = shallow(<Counter />);
  });

  // Check that clicking the "+" button increments the
  number by 1
  test('increments the counter value on button click', () => {
    const incrementButton = wrapper.find('[data-test-
    id="increment-button"]');

    incrementButton.simulate('click');

    expect(wrapper.state('count')).toBe(1);
  });

  // Check that clicking the "-" button decrements the
  number by 1
  test('decrements the counter value on button click', () => {
    const decrementButton = wrapper.find('[data-test-
    id="decrement-button"]');

    decrementButton.simulate('click');

    expect(wrapper.state('count')).toBe(-1);
  });
});
```

By checking the count state value of the <Counter> component after clicking the increment or decrement buttons, we are essentially testing how the component is implemented. This method allows us to examine the implementation details and confirm whether it works as expected. The advantage of this approach is that it ensures the component functions correctly; however, the downside is that it might make the test code fragile and unable to guarantee that the functionality is verified properly.

Testing Behavior

The next example will test the "behavior" of the component, and we will still use Jest and Enzyme to write the test code. The difference this time is that the test will focus on checking the change in the number displayed on the screen to evaluate the component's performance. First, in the first test case, we simulate the user clicking the "+" button and then check if the number increases from 0 to 1. Next, in the second test case, we simulate the user clicking the "-" button and check if the number decreases from 0 to -1. Through this approach, we can directly observe the change in the number on the screen after clicking the increment or decrement button, thus testing the "behavior" of the <Counter> component.

```
// src/Counter/Counter.enzyme.test.js

describe('Counter component', () => {
  // Check that clicking the "+" button increments the
  number to 1

  it('should get 1 when click the increment button', () => {
    const wrapper = mount(<Counter />);

    wrapper.find('[data-test-id="increment-button"]').
    simulate('click');

    expect(wrapper.find('[data-test-id="counter-value"]').
    text()).toBe('1');
  });
```

CHAPTER 2   UNIT TESTING

```js
// Check that clicking the "-" button decrements the
number to -1
it('should get -1 when click the decrement button', () => {
  const wrapper = mount(<Counter />);

  wrapper.find('[data-test-id="decrement-button"]').
  simulate('click');

  expect(wrapper.find('[data-test-id="counter-value"]').
  text()).toBe('-1');
});
});
```

We will use Jest along with Testing Library to write the third test example. The purpose of this example is the same as the second one above, which is to test the "behavior" of the component. First, using the render method provided by React Testing Library, we fully render the <Counter> component. Then, we use the getByTestId method to get the DOM element with the test attribute data-test-id of increment-button. Next, we simulate a click event and again use the getByTestId method to retrieve the DOM element with the test attribute data-test-id of counter-value. Finally, we check if its text content is "1," verifying that the number is correctly incremented after clicking the "+" button. This method not only tests the functionality of the component but also ensures that the behavior of the component meets expectations.

```js
// src/Counter/Counter.rtl.test.js

describe('Counter component', () => {
  // Check that clicking the "+" button increments the
  number to 1
  it('should get 1 when click the increment button', () => {
    const { getByTestId } = render(<Counter />);

    fireEvent.click(getByTestId('increment-button'));
```

```
    expect(getByTestId('counter-value')).
    toHaveTextContent('1');
  });

  // Check that clicking the "-" button decrements the
  number to -1
  it('should get -1 when click the decrement button', () => {
    const { getByTestId } = render(<Counter />);

    fireEvent.click(getByTestId('decrement-button'));

    expect(getByTestId('counter-value')).toHaveText
    Content('-1');
  });
});
```

Earlier, we mentioned implementing the <Counter> component as a class component. Now, we will refactor it to a functional component. The specification of the <Counter> component will remain unchanged, but the implementation details will be different. This situation is common during refactoring and is often encountered when fixing bugs or improving the code for efficiency.

Below is the reimplementation of the <Counter> component. This component uses the useState hook to create and set the count state, initializing it to 0. The <Counter> component defines two functions, increment and decrement, which are used to increase and decrease the count state value, respectively. In the JSX, we return a user interface that displays the current count value, along with "+" and "-" buttons to increment and decrement the value. When the user clicks these buttons, the increment and decrement functions are called. Each element has a data-test-id attribute for testing purposes, making it easier to find and interact with these elements in the tests.

```js
// src/Counter/Counter.js
const Counter = () => {
  const [count, setCount] = useState(0);
  const increment = () => setCount(count + 1);
  const decrement = () => setCount(count - 1);

  return (
    <>
      <div data-test-id="counter-value">{count}</div>
      <button data-test-id="decrement-button"
        onClick={decrement}>
        -
      </button>
      <button data-test-id="increment-button"
        onClick={increment}>
        +
      </button>
    </>
  );
};
```

What's the difference between testing "implementation" and testing "behavior"? After refactoring, we found that the first test example could not pass because Enzyme can only access state in class components. However, the second and third test examples, which test the behavior of the component, worked fine. Therefore, as long as the functionality remains the same, focusing on testing behavior—how the component performs or how the user interacts with it—allows test code to be more flexible. In contrast, focusing on testing implementation details can make the tests more fragile, failing to guarantee that functionality is correctly validated. As a result, testing "behavior" proves to be a better approach for both validating functionality and maintaining flexibility (Note 5).

In the early stages of writing test code, developers typically choose Jest with Enzyme to conduct tests. These early test codes mainly focus on testing the "implementation" of components, such as checking the state changes of components after certain actions. React Testing Library, which was released later, offers a user-centric testing perspective, focusing on the changes in the UI seen by the user after specific interactions. In summary, Enzyme is more inclined to test the implementation of components, while Testing Library is geared toward testing user interactions. However, Enzyme also provides ways to simulate user-triggered events to test component performance and user behavior, as demonstrated in the second test example of this section.

Moreover, from the perspective of snapshots, Enzyme's snapshots focus on the internal structure of the component, including props, state, and child components, monitoring the internal changes. On the other hand, Testing Library's snapshots focus on the appearance seen by the user, i.e., the final rendered UI, not the internal structure of the component (Note 6). This difference reflects the different focuses and advantages of these two testing approaches.

Splitting Logic and Presentation

When testing components, separating logic from the presentation allows for more efficient testing. To illustrate this, we will implement a calculator `<Calculator>` component as an example. The `<Calculator>` contains two input fields for entering numbers, a drop-down for selecting the +, -, *, or / operator, and a button to perform the calculation. The following code uses the `useState` hook to store the user's input and operator, defines the `handleChange` function to handle changes in the input fields and drop-down, and defines the `calculateResult` function to compute the result of the two numbers. Finally, the input fields, drop-down, calculate button, and result display are rendered, with corresponding `data-test-id` attributes added for easy element selection during testing.

CHAPTER 2 UNIT TESTING

```js
// src/Calculator/Calculator.advenced.js
const Calculator = () => {
  const [num1, setNum1] = useState('');
  const [num2, setNum2] = useState('');
  const [operator, setOperator] = useState('+');
  const [result, setResult] = useState('');

  const handleChange = (e) => {
    const { name, value } = e.target;
    if (name === 'num1') {
      setNum1(value);
    } else if (name === 'num2') {
      setNum2(value);
    } else if (name === 'operator') {
      setOperator(value);
    }
  };

  const calculateResult = () => {
    const parsedNum1 = parseFloat(num1);
    const parsedNum2 = parseFloat(num2);

    switch (operator) {
      case '+':
        setResult(parsedNum1 + parsedNum2);
        break;
      case '-':
        setResult(parsedNum1 - parsedNum2);
        break;
      case '*':
        setResult(parsedNum1 * parsedNum2);
        break;
```

```
      case '/':
        setResult(parsedNum1 / parsedNum2);
        break;
      default:
        setResult('Invalid operator');
  }
};

return (
  <div>
    <input
      data-test-id="number1"
      type="number"
      name="num1"
      value={num1}
      onChange={handleChange}
    />
    <select
      data-test-id="operator"
      name="operator"
      value={operator}
      onChange={handleChange}
    >
      <option value="+">+</option>
      <option value="-">-</option>
      <option value="*">*</option>
      <option value="/">/</option>
    </select>
    <input
      data-test-id="number2"
      type="number"
      name="num2"
```

```
      value={num2}
      onChange={handleChange}
    />
    <button data-test-id="calculate"
    onClick={calculateResult}>
      Calculate
    </button>
    <div data-test-id="result">{result}</div>
  </div>
 );
};
```

This code is generally fine, but there are a few points worth discussing:

- First, this component handles the UI, calculation logic, and state management all at once, making it difficult to separate parts for reuse.

- Second, without breaking the component into smaller pieces, the code can become overly lengthy, which should be avoided to keep it more understandable and maintainable.

- Similarly, lack of separation can make testing too complex, causing the test code to become brittle and harder to maintain.

- Lastly, without breaking it up, it becomes challenging to achieve division of labor or phased development, potentially leading to a disorganized and inefficient development process. Therefore, it's recommended to split this component, separating the UI, calculation logic, and state management to enhance reusability, testability, and maintainability.

The issues mentioned above can be resolved through refactoring. The goal of refactoring is to break the code into smaller units, making it easier to maintain, test, and reuse. It also facilitates phased development and better teamwork. Before refactoring, we will first write tests for the <Calculator> component using React Testing Library. In the following test case, we will verify that the result of 5 * 3 is 15. The test simulates user interaction by inputting numbers, selecting an operator, and clicking a button to get the result. This method is appropriate because it tests from the user's perspective, making the test more comprehensive and flexible and less prone to failure due to changes in implementation details, thus reducing the maintenance effort for the tests.

```
// src/Calculator/Calculator.advenced.test.js
describe('Calculator', () => {
  it('should get 15 when 5 multiplied by 3', () => {
    const { getByTestId } = render(<Calculator />);

    // Enter numbers
    fireEvent.change(getByTestId('number1'), { target: { value: '5' } });
    fireEvent.change(getByTestId('number2'), { target: { value: '3' } });

    // Select operator
    fireEvent.change(getByTestId('operator'), { target: { value: '*' } });

    // Click calculate button
    fireEvent.click(getByTestId('calculate'));

    // Verify the result
    expect(getByTestId('result')).toHaveTextContent('15');
  });
});
```

Next, we will refactor the <Calculator> component by encapsulating the business logic and state management related to calculations in a custom hook, useCalculatorHook, while keeping only the UI-related parts within the <Calculator> component. This approach has many benefits, including making the code easier to maintain, test, and reuse, as well as simplifying collaboration and phased development.

```js
// src/Calculator/useCalculatorHook.js
const useCalculatorHook = () => {
  const [num1, setNum1] = useState(0);
  const [num2, setNum2] = useState(0);
  const [operator, setOperator] = useState('+');
  const [result, setResult] = useState(0);

  const handleChange = (e) => {
    const { name, value } = e.target;
    if (name === 'num1') {
      setNum1(value);
    } else if (name === 'num2') {
      setNum2(value);
    } else if (name === 'operator') {
      setOperator(value);
    }
  };

  const calculate = () => {
    switch (operator) {
      case '+':
        setResult(num1 + num2);
        break;
      case '-':
        setResult(num1 - num2);
        break;
```

```
    case '*':
      setResult(num1 * num2);
      break;
    case '/':
      setResult(num1 / num2);
      break;
    default:
      setResult(0);
    }
  };

  return {
    calculate,
    handleChange,
    num1,
    num2,
    operator,
    result,
  };
};
```

In this refactoring, we extracted the business logic and state management related to calculations from the <Calculator> component and moved them into the custom hook useCalculatorHook. This hook handles all the logic and state for the <Calculator> component, including number inputs, operator selection, and calculation results. In the future, if you need to reuse the calculator's logic, you can simply reuse the useCalculatorHook. By refactoring this way, the <Calculator> component is now focused solely on the UI display, making it easier to understand, test, and maintain.

```
// src/Calculator/Calculator.advenced-refactor.js

import useCalculatorHook from './useCalculatorHook';
```

```jsx
const Calculator = () => {
  const { calculate, handleChange, num1, num2, operator,
  result } =
    useCalculatorHook();

  return (
    <>
      <input
        data-test-id="number1"
        type="number"
        value={num1}
        onChange={handleChange}
      />
      <select data-test-id="operator" value={operator}
      onChange={handleChange}>
        <option value="+">+</option>
        <option value="-">-</option>
        <option value="*">*</option>
        <option value="/">/</option>
      </select>
      <input
        data-test-id="number2"
        type="number"
        value={num2}
        onChange={handleChange}
      />
      <button onClick={calculate}>Calculate</button>
      <div data-test-id="result">{result}</div>
    </>
  );
};
```

CHAPTER 2   UNIT TESTING

Since we've split the calculator into the <Calculator> component and the useCalculatorHook, we can now test each part separately. We've already written tests for the <Calculator> component, and now we will write tests for the useCalculatorHook. The following example tests the scenario where 5 + 3 equals 8. Notice that the test works by calling the exported functions to input numbers, select an operator, and trigger the calculation to get the result.

```
// src/Calculator/useCalculatorHook.test.js

describe('useCalculatorHook', () => {
  test('should get 8 when add 5 and 3', () => {
    const TestComponent = () => {
      const {
        calculate,
        handleNum1Change,
        handleNum2Change,
        handleOperatorChange,
        num1,
        num2,
        operator,
        result,
      } = useCalculatorHook();

      return (
        <div>
          <input
            data-test-id="number1"
            value={num1}
            onChange={handleNum1Change}
          />
          <select
            data-test-id="operator"
```

```
          value={operator}
          onChange={handleOperatorChange}
        >
          <option value="+">+</option>
        </select>
        <input
          data-test-id="number2"
          value={num2}
          onChange={handleNum2Change}
        />
        <button data-test-id="calculate" onClick={calculate}>
          Calculate
        </button>
        <div data-test-id="result">{result}</div>
      </div>
    );
};

const { getByTestId } = render(<TestComponent />);

// Enter numbers
fireEvent.change(getByTestId('number1'), { target: { value: '5' } });
fireEvent.change(getByTestId('number2'), { target: { value: '3' } });

// Select operator
fireEvent.change(getByTestId('operator'), { target: { value: '+' } });

// Click calculate button
fireEvent.click(getByTestId('calculate'));
```

```
  // Verify the result
  expect(getByTestId('result')).toHaveTextContent('8');
 });
});
```

This code is used to test the behavior of the custom useCalculatorHook. The scenario being tested is that when adding 5 and 3, the result should be 8. In the test code, we first render the test component <TestComponent>, which uses the useCalculatorHook to return states and functions. Then we simulate entering numbers, selecting an operator, clicking the calculate button, and finally verifying that the result is 8. This testing method simulates user interactions, ensuring that the calculator behaves as expected.

What are the differences after refactoring?

- Reusability: The logic and state have been extracted into useCalculatorHook, making it easy to reuse this custom hook elsewhere.

- Maintainability: The separation of logic and state makes the code more readable and understandable. The <Calculator> component focuses only on rendering the UI, making it easier to maintain.

- Collaboration: Breaking down the code facilitates division of work. Different functionalities can be implemented separately, tested, and submitted as smaller pull requests (PRs), which are easier to review (Note 7).

- Testability: The separation of logic and state allows us to test both parts individually. This makes the tests more comprehensive and flexible. When writing tests, it's best to minimize dependency on UI details. If the UI frequently changes or isn't finalized, testing the hook's functionality first ensures that the core features work properly. UI-related tests can be added later once the design is finalized. There are many ways to keep tests flexible regarding UI changes, such as using test attributes like `data-test-id` instead of relying on visible text to target elements. Additionally, tests that mimic actual user interactions tend to be more reliable and flexible (Note 8).

Splitting the code into smaller parts doesn't need to happen immediately in the early stages of development. Instead, consider refactoring and extracting features when encountering similar functionality that can be reused. This approach is known as the "refactor when needed" strategy. It allows developers to avoid overengineering during initial implementation and focus on solving real problems or meeting actual needs. This strategy also fosters discussions within the team, ensuring that the most suitable solution is chosen based on concrete examples. Ultimately, it improves development efficiency while maintaining code maintainability and scalability (Note 9).

Summary

When choosing a testing tool, Enzyme focuses on testing implementation, while Testing Library emphasizes testing behavior. The current trend in testing suggests that "behavioral testing" is a better approach. Therefore, whether you choose to use Jest with Enzyme or Testing Library, focusing on testing behavior is key. Cypress, because it allows real-time visibility into how each line of code affects the UI, better simulates actual user behavior, making it an excellent choice for testing behavior. This is especially beneficial for unit and integration testing of large components. Moreover, if you want a simple development environment that also supports end-to-end testing, Cypress is a solid option.

Regarding how to refactor components for better testability, a common approach is to encapsulate business logic and data state within a custom hook, while keeping the UI display part in the component. This method simplifies maintenance, testing, and code reuse while also making it easier to divide tasks or implement phased development.

Notes

- Note 1: Behavioral testing, also known as black-box testing, refers to testing the external behavior of a program rather than focusing on the internal implementation details.

- Note 2: For detailed explanations and examples of how to use the `beforeEach` function to initialize the test environment, see Chapter 7, section "How to Use Setup and Teardown? What Are beforeEach, afterEach, beforeAll, and afterAll?"

- Note 3: For more on "flaky tests" and examples, see Chapter 7, section "Why Do Some Test Cases Succeed Sometimes and Fail Other Times?"

- Note 4: For a detailed explanation and examples of full rendering, see the section "Shallow Rendering and Full Rendering" in this chapter.

- Note 5: For recommendations on how to test components, read Lily Scott's "The Right Way to Test React Components" (`https://bit.ly/3Sjqb6b`).

- Note 6: For detailed explanations and examples of snapshots, see Chapter 3, section "Snapshots."

CHAPTER 2   UNIT TESTING

- Note 7: For guidelines on how to handle code reviews, see Google's Code Review Guidelines (https://google.github.io/eng-practices/review/).

- Note 8: For more on how to avoid test failures caused by UI updates, see Chapter 7, section "What to Do When UI Updates Cause Test Failures?"

- Note 9: Refactor on Demand is a software development strategy that emphasizes refactoring code only when necessary. This approach, based on Donald Knuth's famous quote, "premature optimization is the root of all evil," highlights the importance of avoiding early refactoring or optimization without sufficient evidence. Instead, developers should focus on code readability, maintainability, and scalability during the early stages of development, waiting for real issues to arise before making improvements or optimizations. While this doesn't mean developers should never optimize, the key is to ensure that optimizations are truly needed and to proceed cautiously to avoid unnecessary mistakes.

Shallow Rendering and Full Rendering

In JavaScript and web development, rendering refers to the process of converting data into visual HTML elements. This process becomes more abstract and automated in JavaScript frameworks. In React, for example, JSX is used to implement the UI, and React converts this JSX into actual HTML elements, which are then inserted into the DOM. When testing, developers use "shallow rendering" or "full rendering" techniques to simulate this process to test the component's behavior.

Shallow Rendering

Shallow rendering is a technique that renders only the current component and does not render its child components. Since it only renders the component itself, it isolates unnecessary dependencies, reducing test complexity and making it ideal for writing unit tests. However, the limitation is that it cannot test the component's child components, which can be inconvenient for integration testing.

Common libraries like Enzyme or Testing Library provide APIs for shallow rendering and component interaction in testing.

Enzyme

Enzyme provides the `shallow` method to allow developers to perform shallow rendering. For example, the following code demonstrates the implementation of a `<Counter>` component, which allows users to increment or decrement a number by clicking buttons. The layout of the `<Counter>` component is presented in the earlier section, "Environment Setup, Installation, and Tool Comparison." The following code demonstrates how the `<Counter>` component is implemented as a class component. The constructor initializes the state `count` to 0. The `increment` and `decrement` methods are defined to increase and decrease the `count`. In the `render` method, JSX returns the UI with the count value, increment, and decrement buttons. Each element has a `data-test-id` attribute for testing purposes, and the buttons are bound to the corresponding methods.

```
// src/Counter/Counter-class.js
class Counter extends Component {
  constructor(props) {
    super(props);
    this.state = { count: 0 };
  }
```

```
  increment = () => {
    this.setState((prevState) => ({
      count: prevState.count + 1,
    }));
  };
  decrement = () => {
    this.setState((prevState) => ({
      count: prevState.count - 1,
    }));
  };
  render() {
    return (
      <>
        <p data-test-id="counter-value">Count: {this.state.count}</p>
        <button data-test-id="decrement-button" onClick={this.decrement}>
          +
        </button>
        <button data-test-id="increment-button" onClick={this.increment}>
          -
        </button>
      </>
    );
  }
}
```

Here's an example test using Enzyme's `shallow` method to implement shallow rendering. This test case verifies whether the shallow rendering correctly renders the `<Counter>` component. In the test, the `shallow` method is used to render the `<Counter>` component, and the `toJson` method from the enzyme-to-json package converts the rendered result into JSON format. The expect assertion compares the rendered result with the expected output. The toMatchSnapshot function captures a snapshot of the rendering, comparing it to previously generated snapshots. If the two snapshots differ, the test fails. Snapshot testing ensures that any unintended changes to the component are highlighted for the developer's review (Note 1).

```
// src/Counter/Counter-class-enhanced.enzyme.test.js
test('should shallow render component correctly', () => {
  const wrapper = shallow(<Counter />);

  expect(toJson(wrapper)).toMatchSnapshot();
});
```

The snapshot below shows the DOM structure produced by Enzyme's shallow rendering of the <Counter> component, including the component's attributes and event handlers. This structure contains only the first layer of the component and does not render the child components. The snapshot captures the component's rendered output in a specific state, and during future tests, it compares this output with previous results to ensure there are no unexpected changes in the component's rendering behavior.

```
// src/Counter/__snapshots__/Counter-class-enhanced.enzyme.test.js.snap

exports[`Counter component should shallow render component correctly 1`] = `
<Fragment>
  <CounterValue
    count={0}
  />
```

```
  <IncrementButton
    onClick={[Function]}
  />
  <IncrementButton
    onClick={[Function]}
  />
</Fragment>
`;
```

The next test case checks the `increment` method of the `<Counter>` component. It uses Enzyme's `shallow` method to shallow render the `<Counter>` component and calls the `increment` method, then checks whether the component's state has correctly updated from 0 to 1. This test case verifies the correctness of the `increment` method, but it only tests behavior directly related to this `<Counter>` component without involving its child components or external dependencies, focusing solely on the internal functionality.

```
// src/Counter/Counter-class-enhanced.enzyme.test.js

test('should increment the counter value to 1 when calling increment method', () => {
  const wrapper = shallow(<Counter />);

  wrapper.instance().increment();

  expect(wrapper.state('count')).toBe(1);
});
```

In this code, by checking the state value of `count` after clicking the increment or decrement button, the test is focused on testing the "implementation." As mentioned in previous chapters, if the `<Counter>` component is refactored later, tests that focus on implementation details may break. Therefore, it is generally recommended to test "behavior" instead. In other words, if the functionality remains unchanged, even if the implementation changes, testing behavior—how the component functions or how the user interacts with it—makes tests more flexible. On the other hand, focusing on testing implementation details makes tests more fragile and less reliable in validating the component's functionality. Testing behavior is a more robust and recommended approach (Note 2).

React Testing Library

Besides Enzyme, Jest can also be paired with React Testing Library to test components. React Testing Library provides a `shallow` method to perform shallow rendering. The following example still uses the `<Counter>` component, but it's slightly modified as a functional component using hooks. This updated `<Counter>` component uses the `useState` hook to manage the `count` state, initially set to 0. The component defines two functions, `increment` and `decrement`, to update the count value. The returned JSX includes three child components: `<CounterValue>`, `<DecrementButton>`, and `<IncrementButton>`. These components render the current count value, the decrement button, and the increment button, respectively, and contain relevant attributes and event handlers to interact with the `<Counter>` component.

```
// src/Counter/Counter-enhanced.js
const Counter = () => {
  const [count, setCount] = useState(0);
  const increment = () => setCount(count + 1);
  const decrement = () => setCount(count - 1);

  return (
    <>
      <CounterValue count={count} />
      <DecrementButton onClick={decrement} />
      <IncrementButton onClick={increment} />
    </>
  );
};
```

CHAPTER 2   UNIT TESTING

The following test case uses the createRenderer function from the react-test-renderer/shallow library to implement shallow rendering and generate a snapshot. It shallow renders the <Counter> component, only rendering the first layer, which includes the <CounterValue>, <IncrementButton>, and <DecrementButton> components, without rendering their child components. The rendered result is compared with the previously stored snapshot to check for any unintended changes.

```
// src/Counter/Counter.snapshot.rtl.test.js

import { createRenderer } from 'react-test-renderer/shallow';

describe('Counter component', () => {
  describe('shallowing rendering', () => {
    const renderer = createRenderer();

    it('should get snapshot correctly', () => {
      const counter = renderer.render(<Counter />);

      expect(counter).toMatchSnapshot();
    });
  });
});
```

The snapshot generated from the React Testing Library's shallow rendering of the <Counter> component shows only the direct child components. It does not render the nested child components. The snapshot is compared with previous snapshots to ensure consistency when no unexpected changes have occurred.

```
exports[
  `Counter component shallowing rendering should get snapshot
  correctly 1`
] = `
<React.Fragment>
```

```
  <CounterValue
    count={0}
  />
  <DecrementButton
    onClick={[Function]}
  />
  <IncrementButton
    onClick={[Function]}
  />
</React.Fragment>
`;
```

Full Rendering

Full rendering refers to rendering a component along with all of its child components. This approach allows testing the entire behavior of a component. However, the limitation is that it may increase test complexity and require more resources to execute the tests, making it more suitable for integration tests.

Popular libraries such as Enzyme and Testing Library offer APIs for full rendering and interacting with components during tests.

Enzyme

Enzyme provides the mount method to enable full rendering. Using the <Counter> component as an example, the following test case utilizes Enzyme's mount method to fully render the <Counter> component. It then uses the toJson method from the enzyme-to-json package to convert the rendered output to a JSON format. Finally, it applies Jest's snapshot testing to compare the rendered result with a previously generated snapshot to ensure that the <Counter> component is rendered correctly and has not changed unexpectedly. If the rendered result matches the previous

CHAPTER 2   UNIT TESTING

snapshot, the test passes; otherwise, it fails and displays the differences in rendering. Developers can use this to verify whether the changes are intentional or not. Since mount renders all components and includes DOM elements, it allows testing the complete lifecycle of the component and its child components, making it suitable for integration tests.

```
// src/Counter/Counter-class-enhanced.enzyme.test.js

import toJson from 'enzyme-to-json';

test('should mount component correctly', () => {
  const wrapper = mount(<Counter />);

  expect(toJson(wrapper)).toMatchSnapshot();
});
```

The snapshot below shows the fully rendered result of the <Counter> component using Enzyme's full rendering, including all the child components, attributes, and states. This snapshot is compared with the previously generated one to ensure consistency when no unexpected changes have occurred.

```
// src/Counter/__snapshots__/Counter-class-enhanced.enzyme.
test.js.snap

exports[`Counter component should mount component
correctly 1`] = `
<Counter>
  <CounterValue
    count={0}
  >
    <p
      data-test-id="counter-value"
    >
      Count:
```

```
        0
      </p>
    </CounterValue>
    <IncrementButton
      onClick={[Function]}
    >
      <button
        data-test-id="decrement-button"
        onClick={[Function]}
      >
        -
      </button>
    </IncrementButton>
    <IncrementButton
      onClick={[Function]}
    >
      <button
        data-test-id="increment-button"
        onClick={[Function]}
      >
        +
      </button>
    </IncrementButton>
  </Counter>
`;
```

The next test case evaluates the `increment` method within the `<Counter>` component. It uses Enzyme's mount function to fully render the `<Counter>` component in a complete DOM environment, allowing the interaction between the component and its child components to be tested. In this test, the `find` method locates the "+" button, and the `simulate` method mimics a click event. The test then checks if the component's state has been correctly updated from 0 to 1. This test case examines both the component's interaction behavior and its child components to confirm that the integration works as expected in a real use case. This example highlights the full rendering concept, but once again emphasizes that testing implementation details in this way is generally not recommended.

```
// src/Counter/Counter-class-enhanced.enzyme.test.js

test('should increment the counter value to 1 when clicking increment button ', () => {
  const wrapper = mount(<Counter />);

  const incrementButton = wrapper.find('[data-test-id="increment-button"]');
  incrementButton.simulate('click');

  expect(wrapper.state('count')).toBe(1);
});
```

React Testing Library

React Testing Library provides the render method to facilitate full rendering. The following test case fully renders the <Counter> component and captures a snapshot. During the test, the <Counter> component is first rendered into the DOM, and the toMatchSnapshot method verifies whether the rendered DOM structure matches the expected structure. It then compares the DOM structure with the previously stored snapshot to ensure consistency and detect any unexpected changes.

```
// src/Counter/Counter.snapshot.rtl.test.js

import { render } from '@testing-library/react';

describe('Counter component', () => {
  describe('full rendering', () => {
```

```
    it('should get snapshot correctly', () => {
      const counter = render(<Counter />);

      expect(counter.container).toMatchSnapshot();
    });
  });
});
```

The following snapshot shows the HTML structure rendered by React Testing Library's full rendering of the <Counter> component:

```
exports[`Counter component full rendering should get snapshot
correctly 1`] = `
<div>
  <p
    data-test-id="counter-value"
  >
    Count:
    0
  </p>
  <button
    data-test-id="decrement-button"
  >
    -
  </button>
  <button
    data-test-id="increment-button"
  >
    +
  </button>
</div>
`;
```

CHAPTER 2   UNIT TESTING

The next test case evaluates the `increment` method of the `<Counter>` component. It uses React Testing Library's `render` function to fully render the `<Counter>` component and simulate user interactions in a complete DOM environment. The test uses the `getByTestId` method to locate the "+" button and the `fireEvent.click` method to simulate a click. Finally, it verifies that the displayed result is updated to 1. This test case checks the component's interaction behavior and ensures that the `<CounterValue>`, `<IncrementButton>`, and `<DecrementButton>` components work correctly together in real use scenarios (Note 3).

```
// src/Counter/Counter.snapshot.rtl.test.js
describe('full rendering', () => {
  let counter;
  const renderCounter = () => <Counter />;

  beforeEach(() => {
    counter = render(renderCounter());
  });

  it('should get 1 when click the increment button', () => {
    const { getByTestId } = counter;

    fireEvent.click(getByTestId('increment-button'));

    expect(getByTestId('counter-value')).
    toHaveTextContent('1');
  });
});
```

Summary

The comparison between shallow rendering and full rendering is summarized in Table 2-1.

Table 2-1. Comparison of Shallow Rendering and Full Rendering

Rendering Method	Advantages	Disadvantages	Enzyme Method	Testing Library Method
Shallow rendering	Isolates unnecessary dependencies, making it ideal for unit testing	Cannot test child components, making it less convenient for integration tests	`shallow`	`shallow`
Full rendering	Renders the component and all its child components, enabling behavior testing	Increases test complexity and may require more resources, suitable for integration testing	`mount`	`render`

No matter which rendering method you choose, the selection should align with the test's objectives. For unit tests, shallow rendering should be used to isolate dependencies and focus on the component's behavior. For integration tests, full rendering should be employed to test the overall behavior of the component and its interactions with child components.

Notes

- Note 1: For more information on snapshots and examples, see Chapter 3, section "Snapshots."
- Note 2: For more discussion on testing implementation vs. behavior, see the section "How to Write Tests for Components? A React Example" in this chapter.

- Note 3: For more exploration on implementing integration testing, see Chapter 3, section "Testing Features from the User's Perspective and Maximizing Realism."

Chapter Review and Summary

- Unit testing refers to testing the "smallest unit" or "independently testing a specific piece of code." This type of testing primarily verifies whether the input and output of a function, method, or class instance meet expectations, focusing on testing the smallest unit of functionality to ensure that it operates independently and processes specific inputs and outputs correctly.

- Common unit testing frameworks include Jest paired with Enzyme or Testing Library and Cypress. Developers can choose the most suitable tools based on their product and project requirements.

- "Breaking down large chunks of code and isolating dependencies" allows developers to more easily implement unit tests, achieving the goal of testing minimal logic.

- Regarding how to write tests for components, when the functionality remains unchanged but the implementation may change, focusing on testing behavior allows tests to be more flexible. On the other hand, focusing on implementation details makes tests more fragile and less reliable for validating functionality. Therefore, "testing behavior" is the better approach for verifying functionality and ensuring flexibility.

CHAPTER 2   UNIT TESTING

- One common approach to refactoring components to be more test-friendly is to encapsulate business logic and state management in custom hooks, while leaving the UI in the component itself. This makes the code easier to maintain, test, and reuse and facilitates smoother collaboration and incremental development.

- In terms of choosing testing tools, Enzyme focuses on testing implementation details, while Testing Library emphasizes behavior testing. The current mainstream approach favors "behavior testing" as the better way to write tests. Therefore, whether using Jest with Enzyme or Testing Library, aiming for behavior testing is recommended.

- Since Cypress can immediately display the impact of every line of code on a component's UI, it excels at demonstrating actual user interactions, making it especially suitable for unit tests and integration tests of large components. If a simple development environment is needed along with end-to-end testing, Cypress is a good choice. However, Cypress does not offer shallow rendering or built-in mock component mechanisms, so for unit tests, Jest paired with Enzyme or Testing Library may be a better option.

- Comparing shallow rendering and full rendering: (1) Shallow rendering only renders the component itself, isolating unnecessary dependencies, making it suitable for unit testing. The limitation is that it cannot test child components, which can be inconvenient for integration testing. (2) Full rendering renders the component and all its child components, allowing the overall

97

behavior of the component to be tested. The downside is that it increases test complexity and may require more resources, making it better suited for integration testing.

- While unit testing can effectively verify whether code behaves as expected, it differs significantly from real user interactions. Therefore, it needs to be supplemented by other types of tests, such as integration testing and end-to-end testing.

CHAPTER 3

Integration Testing

You will learn the following in this chapter:

- Demonstrate how to test the interaction between combined components and ensure they function correctly in real-world environments.

- Write integration tests from the user's perspective and maximize realism by minimizing mocks and using real data.

- Mock components, API responses, and third-party libraries to improve testing by isolating dependencies and controlling variables.

- Snapshot testing ensures UI consistency by comparing component renders to saved snapshots, but it may not be suitable for dynamic data.

- Write tests for Redux actions and reducers by focusing on the expected state changes and user interactions.

Integration Testing

Integration testing, also known as functional testing, refers to testing "combined code segments." This type of testing is more comprehensive than unit testing, covering various aspects of a specific feature, including integrating components, related packages or libraries, and rendering

CHAPTER 3 INTEGRATION TESTING

data fetched from APIs. The goal is to perform a more thorough test of the functionality, ensuring that the integrated components work together properly and achieve the expected results in real operational environments.

Let's look at a simple example of an image list feature, with a structure as shown in Figure 3-1, implemented using two components: <ImageList> and <ImageItem>. The main purpose of this image list feature is to display image information visually.

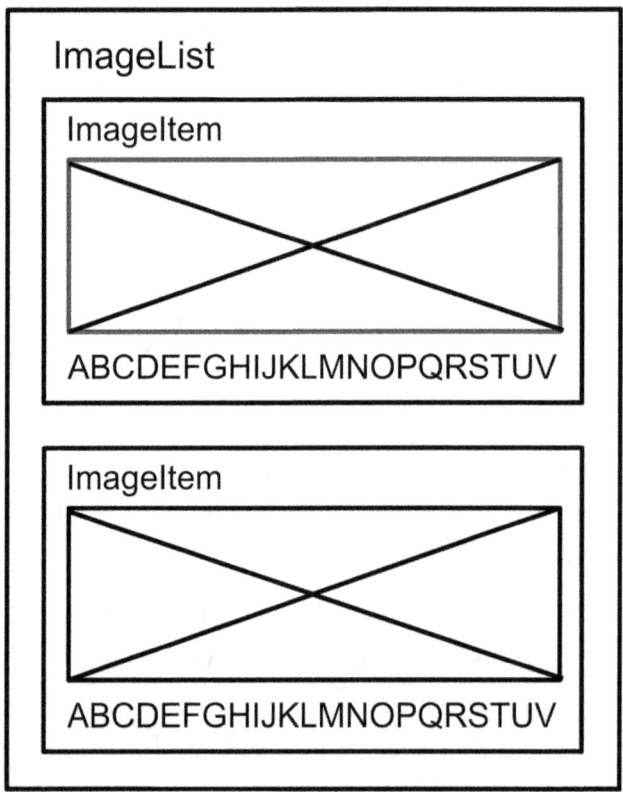

Figure 3-1. *Image list structure*

CHAPTER 3 INTEGRATION TESTING

Before implementing integration tests, let's observe the functionality and compare unit testing with integration testing. First, let's look at the larger component <ImageList>, as shown in the following code. This component is primarily responsible for determining how to display the image information received. If no image information is available, a prompt informs the user that no images are available; if there is image information, the <ImageItem> component displays the images.

```
// src/ImageList/ImageListMockData.js

const ImageList = ({ data }) => {
  // Render images
  const renderImages = () => {
    return data.products.map((({ id, title, images }) => (
      <ImageItem key={id} title={title} image={images[0]} />
    ));
  };

  // Render no data prompt
  const renderNoDataPrompt = () => {
    return <div data-test-id="no-data-prompt">No data to
    display.</div>;
  };

  return (
    <>
      {!!data.products.length ? (
        <div data-test-id="image-list">{renderImages()}</div>
      ) : (
        renderNoDataPrompt()
      )}
    </>
  );
};
```

101

CHAPTER 3   INTEGRATION TESTING

From a unit testing perspective, <ImageList> can be tested as follows:

- Check if the "No data to display" prompt appears when no data is available.
- Verify if the image section is displayed correctly when data is provided.

Here's the unit test implementation using Jest with React Testing Library:

```
// src/ImageList/ImageListMockData.shallow.jest.test.js
describe('ImageList', () => {
  // Check if the no data prompt appears when no images are
  available
  it('should render no data prompt when no images',
  async () => {
    const renderer = createRenderer();
    const mockedData = { products: [] };

    const wrapper = renderer.render(<ImageList
    data={mockedData} />);

    expect(wrapper).toMatchSnapshot();
  });

  // Check if the image section is displayed correctly when
  data is available
  it('should render correct image items when have data',
  async () => {
    const renderer = createRenderer();
    const mockedData = {
      products: [
        {
          id: '1',
```

CHAPTER 3 INTEGRATION TESTING

```
        title: 'Building a fast website: From metrics to user
        experience',
        images: ['https://bit.ly/4228ITo'],
      },
      {
        id: '2',
        title: 'Shimanami Kaido: A bike island-hopping
        adventure',
        images: ['https://bit.ly/4b5nLPO'],
      },
    ],
  };

  const wrapper = renderer.render(<ImageList
  data={mockedData} />);

  expect(wrapper).toMatchSnapshot();
  });
});
```

Explanation:

- The first test case checks whether the "No data to display" prompt is shown when there is no image data. We use react-test-renderer/shallow's createRenderer method to create a shallow renderer and use mock data for rendering. Then, we use toMatchSnapshot to verify the presence of the no data prompt snapshot.

- The second test case checks whether the image section is displayed correctly when image data is available. Similar to the first test, we use mock data and shallow rendering (Note 1), followed by checking the snapshot (Note 2) for the presence of the image section.

103

CHAPTER 3 INTEGRATION TESTING

These tests validate the rendering behavior of the `<ImageList>` component under various conditions to ensure the functionality works as expected.

Now, let's look at the unit test implementation for the child component `<ImageItem>`. Since `<ImageItem>` mainly displays an image and title, we can test whether the title text and image URL are correct. Here's the code for `<ImageItem>`:

```
// src/ImageList/ImageItem.js

const ImageItem = ({ title, image }) => {
  return (
    <div data-test-id="image-item">
      <img alt={title} data-test-id="image-item-src" src={image} />
      <p data-test-id="image-item-title">{title}</p>
    </div>
  );
};
```

Although Cypress is typically used for end-to-end testing, it can also be used for unit testing. Below is an example of how to implement unit tests for `<ImageItem>` using Cypress:

```
// src/ImageList/ImageItem.cy.js

describe('ImageItem', () => {
  // Verify if the title is displayed correctly
  it('should show image title correctly', () => {
    cy.mount(
      <ImageItem image={MOCK_IMAGE.images[0]} title={MOCK_IMAGE.title} />
    );
```

CHAPTER 3 INTEGRATION TESTING

```
    cy.get('[data-test-id="image-item-title"]').should(
      'have.text',
      'Building a fast website: From metrics to user
      experience'
    );
  });

  // Verify if the image URL is correct
  it('should show image url correctly', () => {
    cy.mount(
      <ImageItem image={MOCK_IMAGE.images[0]} title={MOCK_
      IMAGE.title} />
    );

    cy.get('[data-test-id="image-item-src"]').should(
      'have.attr',
      'src',
      'https://bit.ly/4228ITO'
    );
  });
});
```

Explanation:

- The first test case checks if the <ImageItem> component correctly displays the provided image title. We use Cypress's cy.mount to fully render the component and then use cy.get to find the element containing the title and verify if the text matches the expected string.

- The second test case checks if the image URL is displayed correctly. Similarly, we use cy.mount and then verify if the correct image URL is present using cy.get.

These tests ensure that <ImageItem> works correctly under different conditions and guarantees its functionality.

The above unit tests focus on individual components. For integration testing, we need to check whether the data passed from <ImageList> to <ImageItem> is correctly transferred and rendered.

In the following integration test, we use the cy.mount method to fully render the <ImageList> component. Then, we use the cy.contains method to check for the presence of specific text like "Building a fast website" and "Shimanami Kaido." If <ImageList> successfully passes the data to <ImageItem>, we should be able to retrieve these strings.

```
// src/ImageList/ImagesList.cy.js

it('should render correct image items when have data', () => {
  const mockedData = {
    products: [
      {
        id: '1',
        title: 'Building a fast website: From metrics to user experience',
        images: ['https://bit.ly/4228IT0'],
      },
      {
        id: '2',
        title: 'Shimanami Kaido: A bike island-hopping adventure',
        images: ['https://bit.ly/4b5nLP0'],
      },
    ],
  };
```

```
  // Render the component and pass in the data
  cy.mount(<ImageList data={mockedData} />);

  // Verify that the titles "Building a fast website" and
  "Shimanami Kaido" are present
  cy.contains('Building a fast website');
  cy.contains('Shimanami Kaido');
});
```

If the data from <ImageList> is not successfully passed to <ImageItem>, such as if the title field is renamed from title to heading, the test will fail.

```
// src/ImageList/ImageItem.js

const ImageItem = ({ heading, image }) => {
  return (
    <div data-test-id="image-item">
      <img alt={heading} data-test-id="image-item-src" src={image} />
      <p data-test-id="image-item-title">{heading}</p>
    </div>
  );
};
```

In this case, the test would fail, showing the following error message:

```
Timed out retrying after 4000ms: Expected to find content:
'Building a fast website' but never did.
```

Such data passing issues are not detectable with unit tests alone but can be caught with integration tests. Identifying side effects from integrations during testing helps reduce unexpected issues in real-world scenarios, which is the primary goal of integration testing.

CHAPTER 3   INTEGRATION TESTING

Notes

- Note 1: For more information on rendering, see Chapter 2, section "Shallow Rendering and Full Rendering."
- Note 2: For more details on snapshots, see the section "Snapshots" in this chapter.

Testing Features from the User's Perspective and Maximizing Realism

Since the goal of integration testing is to verify specific features to ensure that integrated components work together correctly and achieve the expected results in real operational environments, there are two principles to keep in mind when writing integration tests:

- Test features from the user's perspective.
- Maximize realism, minimizing the use of mocks, avoiding overly artificial data, and ensuring full component rendering.

Testing Features from the User's Perspective

Since integration testing aims to validate complete functionality, and ultimately, it is the user who verifies whether a feature works, it makes sense to test from the user's perspective. The focus should be on how the user interacts with the feature (Note 1). In plain terms, the test should specify what the user wants to see, open, or click.

For example, a correct test description might be

- Upon entering the home page, a red button is visible.
- By clicking the buttons "1", "+", "2", and "=", the input box displays "3."

In contrast, this is not written from the user's perspective:

- Add two numbers and get the result. The add(1, 2) function is expected to return 3.

If you want to test a simple calculator component, <Calculator>, you should write the test like this: the user clicks the buttons "1", "+", "2", and "=" and sees the result "3" on the screen. This type of description better reflects the user's workflow and expected outcome, meeting the purpose of integration testing more effectively.

```
it('get 3 when click button 1, button add, button 2, and button equal', () => {
  const wrapper = mount(<Calculator />);

  wrapper.find('[data-test-id="button-one"]').simulate('click');
  wrapper.find('[data-test-id="button-add"]').simulate('click');
  wrapper.find('[data-test-id="button-two"]').simulate('click');
  wrapper.find('[data-test-id="button-equal"]').simulate('click');

  expect(wrapper.find('[data-test-id="result"]').text()).toBe('3');
});
```

Explanation:

- Using Jest's `it` method, we define the purpose of the test case, describing that when the user clicks buttons "1", "+", "2", and "=", the expected result is "3."
- Enzyme's `mount` method is used to fully render the `<Calculator>` component for testing.
- Enzyme's `find` method locates button elements using the `data-test-id` attribute to target specific buttons, and `simulate('click')` mimics the user's button clicks.
- Jest's `expect` method checks if the result matches the expectation, and Enzyme's `text` method retrieves the text content of the selected DOM element.

The benefit of this testing approach is that it tests not only the user's interaction with the interface but also the corresponding functionality, such as the addition function. This method achieves the goal of integrating different components, related packages, or libraries.

Maximizing Realism

Since the purpose of integration testing is to verify that all components work together correctly, it's important to avoid excessive mocking and instead test with fully rendered components in as realistic a scenario as possible.

Let's revisit the image list feature, which is implemented using two components: `<ImageList>` and `<ImageItem>`. The main purpose of this feature is to visually display the retrieved image information. The `<ImageList>` component determines the display based on the image

CHAPTER 3   INTEGRATION TESTING

data received. If no image data is available, it shows a message to the user indicating that no images are available. If image data is present, the `<ImageItem>` component displays the images (Note 2). Here is the code for the `<ImageItem>` component:

```
// src/ImageList/ImageItem.js

const ImageItem = ({ title, image }) => {
  return (
    <div data-test-id="image-item">
      <img alt={title} data-test-id="image-item-src"
        src={image} />
      <p data-test-id="image-item-title">{title}</p>
    </div>
  );
};
```

Here's a mock implementation of the `<ImageItem>` component using `jest.mock`. This method replaces the real `<ImageItem>` component with a mock implementation (`<div data-test-id="image-item-title"> ImageItem</div>`). This allows the test to isolate the logic of `<ImageItem>`, avoiding its influence during testing. However, mocking `<ImageItem>` means reproducing the original implementation details. Any changes to the component require updates to the mock as well, which can easily be overlooked, leading to failed tests. Moreover, it's impossible to ensure that the mock fully represents the real component, making it difficult to confirm that the entire feature works correctly when integrated (Note 3). Therefore, for integration testing, we should remove the mock and fully render the `<ImageList>` component, including the real `<ImageItem>` (Note 4), to perform a more complete test and ensure integration quality.

```
// src/ImageList/ImagesList.mock.test.js
```

```
jest.mock('./ImageItem', () => () => (
  <div data-test-id="image-item-title">ImageItem</div>
));
```

Furthermore, since errors often occur in unforeseen circumstances, using overly simplified or fake test data is not effective in catching these types of issues. Developers tend to use small amounts of data in testing, whereas real-world environments typically handle much larger datasets. This discrepancy can lead to problems that are not detected during testing but emerge in production, such as layout issues, slow API responses, or exceeding the browser's local storage limits. Therefore, if possible, developers should test with data that closely resembles real-world conditions to ensure application stability and performance in actual environments.

Notes

- Note 1: Behavior-driven development (BDD) is a software development method that emphasizes describing software behavior in simple, natural language. By using scenarios to describe expected behavior and automated tests to ensure that the implementation meets these expectations, BDD fosters collaboration and ensures development aligns with user needs.

- Note 2: For information on the image list's UI, structure diagram, and examples, see the section "Integration Testing" in this chapter.

- Note 3: For more on mocking, see the section "Mocking

Components, API Responses, and Third-Party Libraries" in this chapter.

- Note 4: For details on full rendering, see Chapter 2, section "Shallow Rendering and Full Rendering."

Mocking Components, API Responses, and Third-Party Libraries

In testing, mocking is a technique used to simulate or replace target components, third-party libraries, or API responses. It allows the creation of simulated objects or functions that replace the real implementation details during tests to ensure the test code and its dependencies interact correctly.

The purposes of mocking are

- Isolating dependencies, focusing on testing and validating specific features: Mocks can replace the dependent objects or functions needed for interaction, allowing the test to focus on specific features without being affected by external dependencies.

- Controlling variables, effectively defining inputs or behaviors to produce specific outputs: This is useful for testing particular scenarios and edge cases or reducing uncertainty from external components and real environments.

- Reducing side effects, preventing the test from directly modifying data sources such as databases or issuing network requests, thus avoiding unnecessary work.

Because of these benefits, mocking provides consistent results,

CHAPTER 3   INTEGRATION TESTING

allowing developers to focus on testing specific features and accurately determining whether the functionality works as expected. Although previous chapters suggested aiming for realism and reducing the use of mocks (Note 1), mocking can still be used as a flexible solution when needed.

Mocking can be categorized into three main types: components, API responses, and third-party libraries. The following sections explain how to mock each of these types.

How to Mock Components?

In unit or integration tests, certain internal components may need to be mocked for reasons such as simplifying the test scenario. For example, Component A might use Component B internally, but Component B could be too complex or dependent on too many other elements, requiring refactoring to be fully tested. While this chapter, section "Testing Features from the User's Perspective and Maximizing Realism," encourages minimizing the use of mocks, mocking Component B can still be a reasonable compromise.

Let's revisit the image list feature, which is implemented using two components: <ImageList> and <ImageItem> (Note 2). The primary goal of this feature is to visually display the retrieved image information. The <ImageList> component decides how to display the images based on the received data. If there's no image data, a message informs the user that no images are available. If there is image data, <ImageItem> displays the images. The original implementation of <ImageList> is shown below. When <ImageItem> is needed, mocking it in tests can replace its real implementation.

```
// src/ImageList/ImageList.js
```

CHAPTER 3 INTEGRATION TESTING

```
const ImageList = () => {
  // ...code omitted...

  const renderImages = () => {
    return images.map(({ id, title, images }) => (
      <ImageItem key={id} title={title} image={images[0]} />
    ));
  };

  // ...code omitted...
};
```

In the following code, jest.mock is used to mock the <ImageItem> component. This method sets up a function that returns a mock implementation, such as <div>This is the ImageItem component</div>. This mock replaces the real <ImageItem> component during tests, isolating its logic to prevent it from affecting the test.

```
// src/ImageList/ImagesList.mock.test.js

jest.mock('./ImageItem', () => () => (
  <div>This is the ImageItem component</div>
));
```

Using @testing-library/dom's screen.debug to print the currently rendered output, we can see that the real implementation of <ImageItem> inside <ImageList> has been replaced with the mock implementation (Note 3).

```
<body>
  <div>
    <div>This is the ImageItem component</div>
    <div>This is the ImageItem component</div>
  </div>
</body>
```

115

CHAPTER 3   INTEGRATION TESTING

How to Mock API Responses?

In unit testing or integration testing, to comprehensively verify if a function works as expected, you often need to obtain data from an API to test whether the functionality operates correctly. However, obtaining data from an API involves network access and data stability concerns. Therefore, in unit or integration testing (rather than end-to-end testing), mocking the API response is a common practice to avoid making real network requests.

Let's revisit the image list feature. The <ImageList> component fetches image data from an API and displays it. When the API response contains no data, it shows a message indicating no images are available; otherwise, it displays the images using the <ImageItem> component.

```
const ImageList = () => {
  const [images, setImages] = useState([]);

  useEffect(() => {
    async function fetchData() {
      try {
        const response = await axios.get('https://dummyjson.
        com/products');
        setImages(response.data.products);
      } catch (error) {
        throw error;
      }
    }
    fetchData();
  }, []);

  const renderImages = () => {
    return images.map(({ id, title, images }) => {
      return <ImageItem key={id} title={title}
      image={images[0]} />;
```

```
    });
  };

  return (
    <>
      {images.length !== 0 ? (
        renderImages()
      ) : (
        <div data-test-id="no-data-prompt">No data to
        display.</div>
      )}
    </>
  );
};
```

Below is an example of a test case for verifying whether the <ImageList> component correctly renders the image data when received from the API. First, since the <ImageList> component fetches data using fetch, we use global.fetch = jest.fn().mockImplementation(...) to mock the implementation and provide mock data. Next, React Testing Library's act function is used to handle asynchronous rendering, ensuring that the component is fully rendered after the state has been updated. In this example, if render is not wrapped in act, the component might render prematurely, resulting in a snapshot indicating no data available. Finally, getAllByTestId is used to retrieve DOM elements with the test attribute data-test-id="image-item-title". Using Jest's expect assertion function, we verify that the <ImageList> component renders two elements with the image-item-title test attribute, meaning two image titles should be displayed (Note 4).

```
// src/ImageList/ImagesList.mock.test.js

describe('ImageList', () => {
  it('should render correct image items when have data',
```

```
  async () => {
    global.fetch = jest.fn().mockImplementation(() =>
      Promise.resolve({
        json: () =>
          Promise.resolve({
            products: [
              {
                id: '1',
                title:
                  'Creating a fast website: A comprehensive
                  guide to improving user experience and
                  traffic',
                images: ['https://bit.ly/4228IT0'],
              },
              {
                id: '2',
                title: 'Shimanami Kaido: An island-hopping
                cycling adventure',
                images: ['https://bit.ly/4b5nLPO'],
              },
            ],
          }),
      })
    );

    const { getAllByTestId } = await act(async () =>
    render(<ImageList />));

    expect(getAllByTestId('image-item-title')).toHaveLength(2);
  });
});
```

CHAPTER 3 INTEGRATION TESTING

mockImplementation and mockReturnValue are mocking methods provided by Jest to simulate function return values. The difference between these methods is that mockImplementation allows you to simulate the execution process of a function, while mockReturnValue only simulates the return value. Additionally, mockReturnValue is a simplified version of mockImplementation, used solely for setting the mock function's return value. Thus, if you're only simulating a return value, both can be used, but mockReturnValue is more intuitive and readable.

What exactly is the difference between mockImplementation and mockReturnValue? For example, in the following code, the getStatusById function returns the status corresponding to the id passed in based on the given list:

```
// src/utils/getStatusById/getStatusById.js

const getStatusById = (list, id) => {
  const { status } = filterList(list, id);
  return status;
};
```

Since the filterList function belongs to another module, we don't want to call it in this test. Therefore, we can use jest.mock to mock the return value of the filterList function, as shown below:

```
// src/utils/getStatusById/getStatusById.test.js

const mockList = [
  { id: 1, status: 'active' },
  { id: 2, status: 'inactive' },
  { id: 3, status: 'pending' },
];

jest.mock('./filterList', () => {
  return jest.fn().mockReturnValue({ status: 'active' });
});
```

```
describe('getStatusById', () => {
  it('should return active status when get element id
  1', () => {
    const id = 1;
    const result = getStatusById(mockList, id);
    expect(result).toBe('active');
  });

  it('should return inactive status when get element id
  2', () => {
    const id = 2;
    const result = getStatusById(mockList, id);
    expect(result).toBe('inactive');
  });
});
```

However, there's an issue. When searching for different `id` values, you need to simulate different return values. In such cases, you'll need `mockImplementation` to simulate the execution process of the `filterList` function, as shown below:

```
jest.mock('./filterList', () => {
  return jest
    .fn()
    .mockImplementation(
      (list, id) => mockList.filter((item) => item.id
      === id)[0]
    );
});
```

Thus, use `mockReturnValue` when return values don't need to change; use `mockImplementation` when return values need to be dynamic.

CHAPTER 3   INTEGRATION TESTING

An interesting issue worth discussing is whether the mock state affects other tests. For example, does mocking the return value of the `filterList` function affect other test cases? After slightly modifying the code and running the second test case, a message appears: `Number of calls: 1`. Although the first test case has already run, the second test case has not yet been executed, so you might expect the count to be `Number of calls: 0`. This happens because, in Jest, the mock state is global. The mock state from the first test case is not automatically cleared. Therefore, `mockClear` must be called manually to reset the mock state, ensuring that subsequent tests are unaffected by earlier mock calls.

```
// src/utils/getStatusById/getStatusById.test.js

it('should return inactive status when get element id 2', () => {
  expect(filterList).toHaveBeenCalledWith(mockList, 'fake-id');
});
```

In this test case, we use Jest's `toHaveBeenCalledWith` matcher to verify whether `dispatch` was called correctly, i.e., whether `filterList` was called with `mockList` and `fake-id`.

The test results show that the `filterList` function was called once.

```
Number of calls: 1
```

Here's the modification. Use `mockClear` in the `beforeEach` stage to reset the mock state. The `beforeEach` function runs before each test case, ensuring that all test cases start from the same initial state, reducing the likelihood of inconsistent test results (Note 5).

```
// src/utils/getStatusById/getStatusById.test.js

jest.mock('./filterList', () => {
  // code omitted...
});
```

121

```
describe('getStatusById', () => {
  afterEach(() => {
    jest.clearAllMocks(); // Clears all mock states
  });

  it('should return active status when get element id
  1', () => {
    const id = 1;
    const result = getStatusById(mockList, id);

    expect(result).toBe('active');
  });

  it('should return inactive status when get element id
  2', () => {
    const id = 2;
    const result = getStatusById(mockList, id);

    expect(result).toBe('inactive');
  });
});
```

During development or integration testing, you may not want to directly mock API responses within your project for various reasons: the API is not fully developed, you need to simulate different environments, or you don't want to add test data to the codebase. In such cases, MSW (https://mswjs.io/) is a recommended Chrome extension for simulating and managing HTTP/HTTPS network requests and responses, making it a useful tool to speed up development and validate code correctness.

How to Mock Third-Party Libraries?

Since whether third-party libraries function correctly is not a concern for developers, they are typically not mocked. However, when there's a need

CHAPTER 3 INTEGRATION TESTING

to define inputs or behaviors to produce specific outputs or test certain scenarios, mocking third-party libraries becomes a practical workaround.

Let's revisit the image list feature. In the previous example, the `<ImageList>` component fetched API responses using `fetch`. What if it used a library like `axios` instead (Note 6)?

```
// src/ImageList/ImageListAxios.js

const ImageList = () => {
  const [images, setImages] = useState([]);

  useEffect(() => {
    async function fetchData() {
      try {
        const response = await axios.get('https://dummyjson.
        com/products');
        setImages(response.data.products);
      } catch (error) {
        throw error;
      }
    }
    fetchData();
  }, []);

  // ...code omitted...
};
```

Here's the corresponding test. The goal is to verify whether the `<ImageList>` component correctly renders the received image data. Since the component uses `axios` to fetch data, `jest.mock('axios')` is used to mock the implementation, with `mockResolvedValue` providing mock data. This replaces actual network requests with mocked versions, making the test more stable and controlled by avoiding real network requests during the testing process.

CHAPTER 3   INTEGRATION TESTING

```
// src/ImageList/ImageListAxios.jest.test.js

jest.mock('axios');

describe('ImageList', () => {
  it('should render correct image items when data is available', async () => {
    const mockedData = {
      products: [
        {
          id: '1',
          title:
            'Creating a fast website: A comprehensive guide to
            improving user experience and traffic',
          images: ['https://bit.ly/4228IT0'],
        },
        {
          id: '2',
          title: 'Shimanami Kaido: An island-hopping cycling
          adventure',
          images: ['https://bit.ly/4b5nLPO'],
        },
      ],
    };
    axios.get.mockResolvedValue({ data: mockedData });

    const { getAllByTestId } = await act(async () =>
    render(<ImageList />));

    expect(getAllByTestId('image-item-title')).toHaveLength(2);
  });
});
```

Why Aim for Realism? Is Mocking Not Good Enough?

While "mocking" allows developers to test successfully, it does have certain limitations. For example, the results of mocking components, API responses, or third-party libraries may differ from real-world outcomes, making it harder to ensure proper interactions. Additionally, maintaining and updating both real and mock implementations can be challenging.

Mocks Can Diverge from Reality

Mocks are not real components or real API responses, which means they may deviate from actual results. For instance, if an API changes its data structure—adding new fields, renaming existing ones, or altering data types—mocks won't reflect these changes. Consequently, your UI may behave differently based on unexpected API responses, causing issues that go undetected during testing. Without reflecting real-world conditions, testing fails to ensure the functionality or product quality.

For example, in the test below, the `<ImageItem>` component is mocked, and the test checks if two `<ImageItem>` components are found based on the `data-test-id="image-item-title"` attribute:

```
// src/ImageList/ImagesList.mock.test.js

jest.mock('./ImageItem', () => () => (
  <div data-test-id="image-item-title">ImageItem</div>
));

// ...code omitted...

expect(getAllByTestId('image-item-title')).toHaveLength(2);
```

If the <ImageItem> component later updates its test attribute from data-test-id="image-item-title" to data-test-id="image-item-name", the test still passes, even though the real <ImageItem> no longer contains image-item-title. This shows how mocks can mask issues, preventing tests from reflecting the actual behavior of components, thus failing to safeguard the code effectively.

Mocking Cannot Guarantee Proper Interaction with Real Scenarios

Mocks cannot verify that actual interactions work correctly. For instance, does a real component transmit data properly when integrated with another component? Is the API still active? These limitations mean that testing doesn't fully validate the functionality or guarantee the product's quality.

As previously mentioned, the <ImageList> component's test simulates an API response rather than making a real network request. If the API changes its field names, data types, or goes offline, these issues would remain undetected. In practice, end-to-end testing is typically used to catch these kinds of problems.

```
// src/ImageList/ImageListAxios.jest.test.js

jest.mock('axios');

describe('ImageList', () => {
  it('should render correct image items when data is available', async () => {
    const mockedData = {
      products: [
        {
          id: '1',
          title:
```

```
          'Creating a fast website: A comprehensive guide to
          improving user experience and traffic',
        images: ['https://bit.ly/4228IT0'],
      },
      {
        id: '2',
        title: 'Shimanami Kaido: An island-hopping cycling
        adventure',
        images: ['https://bit.ly/4b5nLP0'],
      },
    ],
  };
  axios.get.mockResolvedValue({ data: mockedData });

  // ...code omitted...
  });
});
```

Difficulty in Maintaining and Updating Both Real and Mock Implementations

Mocked components, API responses, or third-party libraries require additional code. When features change, this test code also needs to be updated to stay in sync with the real-world implementation. Failing to update mocks undermines testing efforts and can lead to a failure in validating functionality or ensuring product quality.

As shown earlier, the <ImageItem> component is mocked in the test.

```
// src/ImageList/ImagesList.mock.test.js

jest.mock('./ImageItem', () => () => (
  <div data-test-id="image-item-title">ImageItem</div>
));
```

CHAPTER 3 INTEGRATION TESTING

The actual implementation of <ImageItem> contains a test attribute data-test-id="image-item-title".

```
// src/ImageList/ImageItem.js

const ImageItem = ({ title, image }) => {
  return (
    <div data-test-id="image-item">
      <img alt={title} data-test-id="image-item-src"
      src={image} />
      <p data-test-id="image-item-title">{title}</p>
    </div>
  );
};
```

If the <ImageItem> component updates its test attribute from data-test-id="image-item-title" to data-test-id="image-item-name", both the real and mock implementations need to be updated to maintain test accuracy.

```
// src/ImageList/ImageItem.js

const ImageItem = ({ title, image }) => {
  return (
    <div data-test-id="image-item">
      <img alt={title} data-test-id="image-item-src"
      src={image} />
      <p data-test-id="image-item-name">{title}</p>
    </div>
  );
};
```

The corresponding mock in the test must also be updated to reflect the change in the test attribute.

```
// src/ImageList/ImagesList.mock.test.js

jest.mock('./ImageItem', () => () => (
  <div data-test-id="image-item-name">ImageItem</div>
));
```

This approach, which involves maintaining and updating both real and mock implementations, relies heavily on manual detection and changes. It's challenging to ensure test effectiveness and manage code quality.

Can Testing Be Done Without Using Mock Data?

Unless the code is overly complex or dependent on too many external factors without plans for refactoring, testing can usually be done without mock data. In summary, unless absolutely necessary, it's best to aim for realism, minimize mocks, avoid overly simplified test data, and ensure components are fully rendered. This allows for more comprehensive testing of functionality, ensuring that integrated components work correctly together, ultimately delivering the expected results in real-world scenarios.

Notes

- Note 1: For more explanations and examples of "aiming for realism," see the section "Testing Features from the User's Perspective and Maximizing Realism" in this chapter.
- Note 2: For details on the image list structure and example, see the section "Integration Testing" in this chapter.
- Note 3: For more debugging techniques, see Chapter 7, section "How to Debug? What If an Element Can't Be Found? How Do You Trace the Data Flow?"

- Note 4: For verifying whether an element is present in the DOM, its count, and visibility, see the section "Snapshots" in this chapter.

- Note 5: For information on unstable tests and examples, see Chapter 7, section "Why Do Some Test Cases Succeed Sometimes and Fail Other Times?"

- Note 6: axios (https://axios-http.com) is a library for making HTTP requests that supports both browser and Node.js environments. It provides a simple API for handling asynchronous requests, processing HTTP responses, interceptors, request cancellation, and more. axios is a powerful and flexible tool that is widely applicable and convenient for many use cases.

Snapshots

Snapshot testing is a front-end testing method used to verify if the rendering of a component or page is consistent with previous results. It captures the rendered output of a component or page into a snapshot file, then compares future test results with this snapshot to ensure that updates to the code yield the expected results.

Let's revisit the image list feature, which is implemented with two components: `<ImageList>` and `<ImageItem>` (Note 1). The primary purpose of this feature is to display the retrieved image information visually. The `<ImageList>` component determines how to display the images based on the received data. If no image data is available, a message informs the user that no images can be displayed; if image data is available, the images are shown.

CHAPTER 3   INTEGRATION TESTING

```
// src/ImageList/ImageList.js
```

```
const ImageList = () => {
  // ...code omitted...
  return (
    <>
      {
        !!images.length
          ? renderImages() // Display images
          : renderNoDataPrompt(); // Prompt no images available
      }
    </>
  );
};
```

To generate a snapshot for the <ImageList> component, the following code is written. First, the <ImageList> component mocks an HTTP request using axios.get.mockResolvedValue, assuming the API returns mock data mockedData to render the component. Then, render is used to create the component and capture its snapshot, comparing it with the previously saved snapshot. If there is a mismatch, the test fails, ensuring that the rendered result is consistent with updates, maintaining UI stability. In this test case, mock data mockedData is used to render the component and generate a snapshot of the image list.

```
// src/ImageList/ImageListAxios.snapshot.jest.test.js
```

```
it('should render correct image items when data is available',
async () => {
  const mockedData = {
    // ...data omitted...
  };
  axios.get.mockResolvedValue({ data: mockedData });
```

```
  const wrapper = await act(async () => render(<ImageList />));
  expect(wrapper).toMatchSnapshot();
});
```

Jest's `toMatchSnapshot` method generates a snapshot of the element to verify its structure, while React Testing Library's act function synchronizes rendering asynchronous behaviors in the test. This ensures that the component's state is updated before rendering, resulting in the correct structure. Without wrapping the `render` method in `act`, the component would render before receiving data, resulting in a snapshot showing the "no data available" message.

The snapshot output looks like this. Here, the snapshot captures all DOM element attributes, including implementation details:

```
// src/ImageList/__snapshots__/ImageListAxios.snapshot.jest.test.js.snap

exports[`ImageList should render correct image items when data is available 1`] = `
Array [
  <div
    data-test-id="image-item"
  >
    <img
      alt="Creating a fast website: A comprehensive guide to improving user experience and traffic"
      data-test-id="image-item-src"
      src="https://bit.ly/4228IT0"
    />
    <p
      data-test-id="image-item-title"
    >
```

CHAPTER 3   INTEGRATION TESTING

```
      Creating a fast website: A comprehensive guide to
      improving user experience and traffic
    </p>
  </div>,
  <div
    data-test-id="image-item"
  >
    <img
      alt="Shimanami Kaido: An island-hopping cycling
      adventure"
      data-test-id="image-item-src"
      src="https://bit.ly/4b5nLPO"
    />
    <p
      data-test-id="image-item-title"
    >
      Shimanami Kaido: An island-hopping cycling adventure
    </p>
  </div>,
]
```

Another scenario occurs when no image data is available, in which case a message informs the user that no images can be displayed. This can be tested by simulating an API response with no data using mockResolvedValue, where the expected result is the display of a "no data" message.

```
// src/ImageList/ImageListAxios.snapshot.jest.test.js

it('should render no data prompt when no images', async () => {
  const mockedData = { products:   };
  axios.get.mockResolvedValue({ data: mockedData });
```

133

CHAPTER 3　INTEGRATION TESTING

```
  const wrapper = await act(async () => render(<ImageList />));
  expect(wrapper).toMatchSnapshot();
});
```

The snapshot for this scenario shows the "no data available" message.

```
// src/ImageList/__snapshots__/ImageListAxios.snapshot.jest.test.js.snap

exports[
  `ImageList should render correct image items when data is available 1`
] = `
<div
  data-test-id="no-data-prompt"
>
  No data to display.
</div>
`;
```

As demonstrated by the examples above, snapshot testing is a convenient method that allows developers to quickly implement tests while ensuring that the UI remains consistent and stable, avoiding unexpected changes.

Snapshot testing is a convenient testing method, but it's not suitable for every situation. Let's explore two examples to explain when snapshot testing is not ideal.

The first scenario is when data changes dynamically, making snapshots unsuitable for testing. For instance, when using `Date.now` to get a timestamp, the rendered output would constantly change. Here's an example where `Date.now` gets the current timestamp and renders it in a component:

```
it('should render now correctly', async () => {
  const now = Date.now();

  const testRenderer = renderer.create(<>{now}</>);

  expect(testRenderer).toMatchSnapshot();
});
```

If the current time is 2024/01/29 14:45, the timestamp will be 1706510752546, and this snapshot will serve as the basis for future comparisons.

```
exports[`ImageList should render now correctly 1`] =
`"1706510752546"`;
```

A second later, at 2024/01/29 14:46, the timestamp will be 1706510780376, which will no longer match the previous snapshot, causing the test to fail.

```
exports[`ImageList should render now correctly 1`] =
`"1706510780376"`;
```

Since the timestamp changes over time, it's unsuitable for snapshot testing. If there is mutable data in the test, it needs to be mocked so the test can compare fixed inputs and outputs, ensuring the expected results for specific scenarios. Additionally, if a snapshot conflict arises in version control, it's recommended to first resolve the code conflict before regenerating the snapshot.

The second scenario is when snapshots capture implementation details, like HTML structure changes, which lead to test failures with small updates, such as adding a `className` or changing a `data-*` attribute. Fixing these tests can become time-consuming, leading to wasted resources (Note 2). Thus, it's not recommended to use snapshots for recording implementation details. To test visual details, it's better to use visual testing tools specifically designed for visual comparisons. Visual testing captures snapshots of the actual UI, providing a more accurate representation. Also, since snapshots can't test user interaction with components, they should be supplemented with unit testing or other forms of testing.

So, when is snapshot testing appropriate? In unit or integration tests, shallow rendering can be used to test which components are rendered under specific conditions (Note 3). Alternatively, checking for the existence of specific components is another valid approach. For instance, the <ImageList> component decides whether to show a "no data" prompt or image blocks based on the API response. Using react-test-renderer/shallow for shallow rendering, only the first level of components is rendered, such as <ImageItem>.

```
// src/ImageList/ImageListMockData.shallow.jest.test.js

import { createRenderer } from 'react-test-renderer/shallow';

// ...omitted...

describe('ImageList', () => {
  it('should render no data prompt when no images',
  async () => {
    const renderer = createRenderer();

    const wrapper = renderer.render(<ImageList images={} />);

    expect(wrapper).toMatchSnapshot();
  });

  it('should render correct image items when data is
  available', async () => {
    const renderer = createRenderer();
    // ...omitted...

    const wrapper = renderer.render(<ImageList
    data={mockedData} />);
```

```
    expect(wrapper).toMatchSnapshot();
  });
});
```

The first test case checks the no-data scenario, producing the following snapshot where the "no data" message is displayed:

```
// src/ImageList/__snapshots__/ImageListMockData.shallow.jest.
test.js.snap

exports[`ImageList should render no data prompt when no
images 1`] = `
<React.Fragment>
  <div
    data-test-id="no-data-prompt"
  >
    No data to display.
  </div>
</React.Fragment>
`;
```

The second test case checks the scenario where data is available, resulting in a snapshot that displays the image blocks.

```
// src/ImageList/__snapshots__/ImageListMockData.shallow.jest.
test.js.snap
exports[
  `ImageList should render correct image items when data is
  available 1`
] = `
<React.Fragment>
  <ImageItem
    image="https://bit.ly/4228IT0"
```

```
      title="Creating a fast website: A comprehensive guide to
      improving user experience and traffic"
    />
    <ImageItem
      image="https://bit.ly/4b5nLPO"
      title="Shimanami Kaido: An island-hopping cycling
      adventure"
    />
  </React.Fragment>
`;
```

By rendering only the first layer of components, snapshots can help test conditional rendering while maintaining flexibility. This approach avoids recording excessive implementation details and reduces the chance of test failures, minimizing maintenance costs.

Aside from using shallow rendering snapshots to test conditional rendering, checking for the presence of specific components is also an effective method. For example, the `<ElementList>` component contains two elements that can either be visible or hidden on the screen, labeled with `data-test-id` as `visible-element` and `invisible-element`.

```
// src/ElementList/ElementList.js

const ElementList = () => {
  return (
    <>
      <div data-test-id="visible-element" style={{ display:
      'block' }}>
        This is a visible element
      </div>
      <div data-test-id="invisible-element" style={{ display:
      'none' }}>
```

```
      This is a hidden element
    </div>
  </>
);
};
```

The following test checks for the existence and visibility of these elements using getByTestId, along with toBeVisible, toBeInTheDocument, and toHaveLength to confirm that the elements are present in the DOM and visible or hidden as expected.

```
// src/ElementList/ElementList.test.js

describe('ElementList', () => {
  it('should display the elements correctly', () => {
    const { getByTestId, queryAllByTestId } =
    render(<ElementList />);

    // Check that the visible element is present
    expect(getByTestId('visible-element')).toBeVisible();
    expect(getByTestId('visible-element')).toBeInTheDocument();
    expect(queryAllByTestId('visible-element')).
    toHaveLength(1);

    // Check that the hidden element is present
    expect(getByTestId('invisible-element')).not.toBeVisible();
    expect(getByTestId('invisible-element')).
    toBeInTheDocument();
    expect(queryAllByTestId('invisible-element')).
    toHaveLength(1);
  });
});
```

Explanation:

- `toBeVisible` checks whether the element is visible to the user, considering CSS properties like `display`, `visibility`, `opacity`, and the `hidden` or `open` attributes. Elements may exist but not be visible, which is useful for checking the visibility state of elements. In this example, `visible-element` is shown, and `invisible-element` is hidden.

- `toBeInTheDocument` checks if an element exists in the DOM, even if it's not visible. In this case, both `visible-element` and `invisible-element` exist in the DOM.

- `toHaveLength` checks the number of elements returned by `queryAllByTestId`. Like `toBeVisible`, it's used to confirm the presence of elements in the DOM, regardless of visibility. In this example, both elements are present in the DOM.

In summary:

- Use `toBeVisible` to check whether an element is toggled between visible and hidden.

- Use `toBeInTheDocument` to check if an element is rendered in the DOM.

- Use `toHaveLength` to check how many times an element is rendered in the DOM.

Notes

- Note 1: For an explanation of the image list's structure and examples, see the section "Integration Testing" in this chapter.

- Note 2: For more details on avoiding test failures due to UI updates, see Chapter 7, section "What to Do When UI Updates Cause Test Failures?"

- Note 3: For a detailed explanation and examples of shallow rendering, see Chapter 2, section "Shallow Rendering and Full Rendering."

How to Write Tests for State Management? A Redux Example

While developers are often advised to focus on testing from the user's perspective and the behavior of components, avoiding deep testing of implementation details, it becomes crucial to test when core logic is stored in state management tools like Redux. This section will use Redux as an example to demonstrate how to write effective tests.

When testing Redux actions and reducers, the goal is to ensure that the state machine operates as expected. Since a reducer is a pure function, it will always produce the same output for the same input. Therefore, testing involves comparing the output to the expected result. In other words, given the previous state and an action, the reducer should output the expected next state.

```
(previousState, action) => newState;
```

Let's take an example of a dessert shop ordering system called "Summer's dessert shop." The interface is shown in Figure 3-2, where a user wants to order two "Chocolate Cream Rolls." The user clicks the "+" button to select the quantity, and now we will implement tests for this system.

CHAPTER 3   INTEGRATION TESTING

Figure 3-2. Summer's Dessert Shop Ordering System, Initial Screen

Users can modify the quantity by clicking the "+" and "-" buttons. Here, adding 1 more results in a total of 2, as shown in Figure 3-3.

Figure 3-3. Summer's dessert shop dessert shop ordering system, updated order quantity

To test the scenario where the user selects "Chocolate Cream Roll," clicks the "+" button to add one, and then clicks "+" again to add one more, the test implementation is as follows:

```
// src/Item.test.js
```

```
test('should show 2 items when clicking increment button',
async () => {
  // ...omitted...

  // Click the "+" button to select the quantity
  fireEvent.click(getByTestId('add-to-cart'));
  // Click "+" to add 1 more
  fireEvent.click(getByTestId('increment-button'));

  // Expect to display 2
  expect(getByTestId('item-quantity')).toHaveTextContent('2');
});
```

toHaveTextContent is a Jest matcher provided by @testing-library/jest-dom, used to check whether the text content of a DOM element matches the expected string. It is commonly used to verify that an element contains specific text. Here, toHaveTextContent retrieves the string "2" directly. If we used toBe, it would include more HTML details, which could make future adjustments more time-consuming when refactoring or maintaining the tests (Note 1).

//src/Item.js

```
<div data-test-id="item-quantity">2</div>
```

Since the "Add Quantity" functionality is a crucial logic, more detailed testing of the reducer's state can be performed for the following scenarios:

- The cart is empty, and the initial quantity of the item is 0.
- The cart already contains 1 item, and the initial quantity is 1.

Let's implement these two test cases.

The first test case involves an empty cart where the initial item quantity is 0. Triggering the action to add 1 results in a total quantity of 1.

```
// src/redux.test.js

test('should add 1 item to cart when dispatching action ADD_TO_CART from empty', () => {
  const initialState = { cart: {} };
  const action = {
    type: ACTIONS.ADD_TO_CART,
    payload: {
      itemId: 'item_id_998',
    },
  };

  expect(snackReducer(initialState, action)).toEqual({
    cart: {
      item_id_998: {
        quantity: 1,
      },
    },
  });
});
```

Explanation:

- `initialState` defines the initial state, which is an empty cart in this case.
- The action defines the `dispatch` action, which is ADD_TO_CART here, along with a payload specifying the item ID to add to the cart.

CHAPTER 3 INTEGRATION TESTING

- The expect function provided by Jest is used to assert whether the reducer's result matches the expected state for the given initial state and action.

- The toEqual method compares two values to see if they are equal. It's a strict comparison, performing deep comparisons for objects. In contrast, the more common toBe method does shallow comparison and cannot compare objects (Note 2).

- This test case expects that after the reducer receives the ADD_TO_CART action, the item should be added to the cart with a quantity of 1.

The second test case involves a cart with an initial quantity of 1 item. Triggering the action to add 1 more results in a total quantity of 2.

```
// src/redux.test.js

test('should get 2 items in cart when dispatching action ADD_
TO_CART from 1 item', () => {
  const initialState = {
    cart: {
      item_id_998: {
        quantity: 1,
      },
    },
  };
  const action = {
    type: ACTIONS.ADD_TO_CART,
    payload: {
      itemId: 'item_id_998',
    },
  };
```

145

```
  expect(snackReducer(initialState, action)).toEqual({
    cart: {
      item_id_998: {
        quantity: 2,
      },
    },
  });
});
```

Explanation:

- `initialState` defines the cart with 1 item having an ID of `item_id_998` and a quantity of 1.

- The action is defined as `ADD_TO_CART`, with a payload specifying the item ID to add.

- This test case expects that after the reducer receives the `ADD_TO_CART` action, the item quantity should increase to 2.

We've demonstrated how to test the scenario of ordering two "Chocolate Cream Rolls" from the user's perspective and the component's behavior. What if we want to verify that the action is called as expected? Here's the test implementation: we can use `jest.spyOn` to spy on the action's invocation and check whether it was called with the correct parameters. In this example, for the `ADD_TO_CART` action, we want to verify that after clicking the "+" button to select the quantity, and then clicking "+" again, the action is triggered with the specified item ID 999.

```
// src/Item.test.js

test('should show 2 items when clicking increment button',
async () => {
  // ...omitted...
  const spyDispatch = jest.spyOn(store, 'dispatch');
```

```
// Click the "+" button to select the quantity
fireEvent.click(getByTestId('add-to-cart'));
// Click "+" to add 1 more
fireEvent.click(getByTestId('increment-button'));

// Expect the action to be triggered with the
specified item ID
  expect(spyDispatch).toHaveBeenCalledWith({
    type: ACTIONS.ADD_TO_CART,
    payload: { itemId: '999' },
  });
});
```

Explanation:

- `jest.spyOn(...)` is used to spy on the action invocation, checking whether the correct parameters were passed.

- React Testing Library's `fireEvent.click` simulates user clicks on DOM elements. In this case, it clicks the element with the `data-test-id` of `add-to-cart` to add the item, followed by another click to increase the quantity to 2.

- Since simulating the user's actions triggers the `dispatch` to update the store, we can check whether the correct action was dispatched using Jest's `toHaveBeenCalledWith` matcher. It ensures that the ADD_TO_CART action was dispatched with the payload containing the specified item ID 999.

In summary, when adding or modifying functionality, such as adjusting the action sequence or updating naming conventions, testing implementation details can lead to test failures, which need to be balanced. Focusing on testing real user scenarios, rather than implementation details, provides more flexibility when features are added or modified, preventing test failures and the need to constantly fix tests. However, when core logic must be protected, or features are developed incrementally, duplicate tests may be necessary (Note 3). While these tests may seem repetitive, their goals differ. Unit tests provide more precise feedback for solving problems, while integration tests cover more user-level scenarios.

Notes

- Note 1: For more details on avoiding test failures due to UI updates, see Chapter 7, section "What to Do When UI Updates Cause Test Failures?"

- Note 2: For a comparison between `toEqual` and `toBe`, see Chapter 2, section "Environment Setup, Installation, and Tool Comparison."

- Note 3: For more on handling duplicate tests, see Chapter 7, section "How to Handle Duplicate Tests?"

Chapter Review and Summary

- Integration testing refers to testing the "combined pieces of code." Compared to unit testing, this type of testing is more comprehensive, covering various aspects of a specific feature, including integrated components, related libraries, and the presentation of data retrieved from APIs. The goal is to conduct

CHAPTER 3　INTEGRATION TESTING

more thorough testing of functionalities, ensuring that integrated components work correctly together and deliver expected results in real-world scenarios.

- Since the purpose of integration testing is to validate specific features and ensure that integrated components operate correctly in real-world scenarios, two principles should be followed when writing integration tests: (1) test the feature from the user's perspective, and (2) aim for realism by minimizing mocks that replace real-world situations, avoiding overly fake data, and rendering components as fully as possible.

- Mocking is a method used to simulate or replace target components, third-party libraries, or API responses. Mocks provide consistent results, allowing developers to focus on testing specific functionality and effectively verifying whether it works as expected. While tests should strive to be as realistic as possible by minimizing the use of mocks, they may still be necessary in some situations as a pragmatic compromise.

- Snapshot testing is a front-end testing method used to verify whether a component or page renders consistently with previous results. It outputs the rendered result as a snapshot file, then compares subsequent test results with this snapshot to ensure that changes in the code produce the expected results. Snapshot testing is a convenient method that not only enables rapid implementation but also helps maintain UI stability by preventing unintended changes.

CHAPTER 3 INTEGRATION TESTING

Shallow rendering is recommended for testing which components appear under certain conditions, offering flexibility by avoiding the recording of too many implementation details and reducing test failures and maintenance costs.

- Two scenarios where snapshot testing is unsuitable: (1) when the data is dynamic, as snapshots compare specific attributes and values; (2) it is not recommended to use snapshots to record implementation details.

- When testing Redux actions and reducers, the goal is to check whether the state machine operates as expected. Since a reducer is a pure function, it always produces the same output given the same input. Therefore, testing only requires comparing the output with the expected result.

- When core logic is stored in a state management tool, testing becomes crucial. Even though duplicate tests may be implemented, they serve different purposes and provide unique feedback. Unit tests provide more precise information to resolve issues, while integration tests are closer to user-level scenarios and cover more situations. These considerations should be used to determine whether to implement tests for state management.

- While integration testing aims to comprehensively verify functionality, there is still a slight gap between it and the real user workflow. This gap can be supplemented by other types of tests, such as end-to-end testing or visual testing.

CHAPTER 4

End-to-End Testing

You will learn the following in this chapter:

- End-to-end testing simulates real user behavior to ensure the product functions correctly, covering complete workflows and multiple functionalities.

- The installation and setup of Cypress for end-to-end testing, with configuration and usage examples.

- The principles and implementation of end-to-end testing, using an example to demonstrate user interaction simulations.

End-to-End Testing

End-to-end testing (often abbreviated as E2E testing) refers to simulating the actual user workflow when interacting with a product. For web interfaces, this type of testing can simulate actions such as opening a browser, entering a URL to navigate to a website, clicking specific features, browsing through pages, and finally completing the entire workflow and closing the window. The goal of this testing is to mimic real user behavior to ensure that the product functions correctly in real-world usage scenarios. It is typically the closest to the user level and covers the widest range of scenarios.

CHAPTER 4   END-TO-END TESTING

For example, we can use Cypress to create a test that simulates a user browsing the "About Me" page of the website "Summer's dessert shop" (https://www.cythilya.tw/about/). During this test, Cypress will automatically launch a browser, simulate user behavior, and finally verify if the page title is correctly retrieved. This test process covers the entire workflow of browsing a specific page, which consists of many small functionalities, including the individual components that make up the page, the utility functions used to retrieve the page title, and the mechanisms that link these functionalities together. In previous chapters, we focused on unit testing and integration testing to test these small functionalities individually. Those tests emphasized checking specific features, but now we enter the realm of end-to-end testing, which tests the entire feature workflow as a whole to ensure that the system operates smoothly and as expected.

```
// cypress/e2e/cythilya.cy.js

describe('about page', () => {
  it('should get title correctly when visit page', () => {
    cy.visit('https://www.cythilya.tw/about');

    cy.get('.page-title').should('have.text', 'About Me');
  });
});
```

Explanation:

- The `describe` function from Jest is used to group related test cases. Typically, the outermost `describe` indicates the page or component being tested, serving as the name of the test (Note 1). In this case, the test is for the "About Me" page.

CHAPTER 4   END-TO-END TESTING

- The `it` function from Jest describes the purpose of a specific test case. In this case, the test verifies whether the title is correctly retrieved when visiting the "About Me" page.

- Cypress's `cy.visit` function navigates the browser to the specified URL, here directing it to `https://www.cythilya.tw/about`.

- Cypress's `cy.get` function is used to select a DOM element with a specific selector. In this case, it selects the DOM element with the `.page-title` selector. Cypress, in combination with assertion tools like Chai, then uses the `should` function to assert whether the text content of this element matches the expected string "About Me." If they match, the test passes; otherwise, it fails.

Popular end-to-end testing frameworks include Cypress (`https://www.cypress.io/`), Puppeteer (`https://pptr.dev/`), WebdriverIO (`https://webdriver.io/`), and Nightwatch (`https://nightwatchjs.org/`). These frameworks effectively implement end-to-end testing, and in the following chapters, Cypress will be the primary framework for implementation examples.

There are many advantages to implementing end-to-end testing. First, since end-to-end testing simulates the entire user workflow from start to finish, it thoroughly tests product functionality and reflects real-world usage scenarios. Additionally, end-to-end testing covers multiple functionalities, expanding the scope of testing and helping to reduce the likelihood of errors in production environments. However, a challenge of end-to-end testing is that when errors occur, it can be difficult to quickly pinpoint the root cause, requiring a fallback to unit testing for adjustments. For scenarios that require detailed visual comparisons, visual testing is recommended to offload some of the burden from end-to-end testing and more effectively detect changes in the visual layout.

CHAPTER 4 END-TO-END TESTING

Notes

- Note 1: For discussions on naming tests, see Chapter 1, section "Naming Conventions."

Environment Setup and Installation

In the realm of end-to-end testing, there are several well-known testing frameworks such as Cypress, Puppeteer, WebdriverIO, and Nightwatch. These frameworks effectively implement end-to-end testing programs, allowing developers to choose the tool that best suits their product and project needs. Since this book primarily uses Cypress as the implementation example framework, this chapter will introduce the setup and installation process of Cypress for executing related tests.

To install Cypress in your project using a package manager like yarn or npm, use the following commands. The --dev or -D option specifies that the package will be installed under the devDependencies section of the package.json file, as Cypress is a testing tool required only during development and not needed in the production environment.

```
yarn add --dev cypress
npm install --save-dev cypress
```

After installation, Cypress can be used to implement and execute tests. To make the project easier to manage and integrate with other tools, you can add a custom script, cypress:open, to the package.json file to launch Cypress tests.

```
{
  "scripts": {
    "cypress:open": "cypress open"
  }
}
```

CHAPTER 4 END-TO-END TESTING

To launch Cypress, use the following command. The `cypress open` command will launch the Cypress interface, where developers can run test programs, view test results, check error messages, and monitor the testing process.

```
yarn cypress:open
npm cypress:open
```

If the project is being set up for the first time, the Cypress configuration interface will open in a browser. Since this chapter focuses on end-to-end testing, select the "End-to-End Testing" option (Note 1). Follow the instructions on the page to complete the setup step by step. Once the configuration is complete, Cypress automatically sets up the necessary configuration, allowing developers to start writing test programs without spending too much time on the setup process.

After the configuration is successful, developers can make additional adjustments based on their needs. For example, you can globally set the default viewport size for testing so that the web page opens with a size of 800x800 during each test run.

```
// cypress.config.js

e2e: {
  viewportWidth: 800,
  viewportHeight: 800,
},
```

Once the configuration is complete, you can start writing test programs. For example, you can use Cypress to create a test program that simulates a user visiting the "About Me" page of the "Summer's dessert shop" website (https://www.cythilya.tw/about/) and verify if the correct title string is retrieved (Note 2).

155

CHAPTER 4   END-TO-END TESTING

```js
// cypress/e2e/cythilya.cy.js

describe('about page', () => {
  it('should get title correctly when visit page', () => {
    cy.visit('https://www.cythilya.tw/about');

    cy.get('.page-title').should('have.text', '關於我');
  });
});
```

Regarding file structure, the main test programs are placed in the `cypress/e2e` folder, while related test data can be placed in the `cypress/fixtures` folder. Cypress will automatically read files from these folders and use them when executing tests. Cypress also provides many APIs for interacting with the browser, allowing developers to create test programs based on their specific needs.

Although this book primarily uses Cypress for the examples, developers can choose the framework that best suits their needs or preferences. Other frameworks, such as Puppeteer, have their own advantages and features. For example, Puppeteer is developed by Google and thus has strong support for Chrome (Note 3). Additionally, Puppeteer offers many APIs for interacting with the browser, giving developers more control when needed.

Notes

- Note 1: For an illustration of the Cypress setup interface, see Chapter 2, section "Environment Setup, Installation, and Tool Comparison."

- Note 2: For an explanation of this example, see Chapter 4, section "End-to-End Testing."

- Note 3: Cypress and Puppeteer have different design philosophies. Cypress is higher level, focusing more on the user perspective, while Puppeteer operates on a lower level, focusing on browser manipulation. For example, if you need to intercept a network request, Cypress provides the cy.intercept API, while Puppeteer uses page.setRequestInterception to achieve the same functionality.
- Below is an example of simulating a failed network request using Cypress. In this test case, cy.visit is used to navigate to a specific website, followed by cy.intercept to intercept the network request and return a custom response.

```
// cypress/e2e/network.interception.cy.js
describe('Network interception', () => {
  it('should intercept network request ', () => {
    cy.intercept('GET', 'https://www.cythilya.tw/about/', (req) => {
      // Intercept the network request and return a custom response
      req.reply({
        statusCode: 200,
        body: 'Connection refused',
      });
    });

    // Visit the website
    cy.visit('https://www.cythilya.tw/about');
  });
});
```

- Below is an example of simulating a failed network request using Puppeteer. First, launch Puppeteer using launch and create a new page with newPage to set up request interception. Use page.setRequestInterception(true) to enable interception, then use page.on('request', ...) to listen for request events. If a request's URL includes www.cythilya.tw/about, mark the request as connectionrefused and abort it. Finally, use page.goto(...) to visit the page that triggers the request, and close the browser afterward.

```
const puppeteer = require('puppeteer');

(async () => {
  const browser = await puppeteer.launch();
  const page = await browser.newPage();

  // Intercept network requests
  await page.setRequestInterception(true);

  // Listen to requests and simulate a failed network
  request for a specific URL
  page.on('request', (request) => {
    if (request.url().includes('www.cythilya.tw/about')) {
      request.abort('connectionrefused');
    } else {
      request.continue();
    }
  });
```

```
// Visit the website
await page.goto('https://www.cythilya.tw/about/');

await browser.close();
})();
```

- As demonstrated by these two examples, Cypress and Puppeteer differ in their design philosophies, leading to differences in how they interact with the browser. Developers can choose the framework that best meets their needs.

Verifying User Flow

Since the purpose of end-to-end testing is to simulate the real user's operation flow and ensure correct functionality in actual use cases, several principles must be observed when implementing it:

- Correctly simulate user interactions, such as clicking, typing, and scrolling.

- Accurately simulate the user environment, such as desktop or mobile devices, browsers, and platforms, to ensure consistent results across different environments.

- Provide comprehensive functionality coverage. Since end-to-end testing simulates the user's complete workflow, it thoroughly tests the product's features, making it the most accurate reflection of actual user interactions. Additionally, by spanning multiple features, it expands the testing scope, reducing the chances of errors in production. Therefore, end-to-end testing must cover all major application features to verify the overall functionality.

- Include testing for abnormal conditions to ensure that the application handles errors or unusual cases properly.

- End-to-end testing often incorporates performance and visual testing, and the decision to include or separate these tests depends on the product and project requirements.

When planning end-to-end testing, you should combine the user interaction flow with the expected outcomes to ensure that the entire application functions correctly while also providing extensive automated test coverage.

Memori

Memori (`https://memori-service.web.app/`) is a real-time sharing and interactive platform. It provides a user-friendly upload interface (Figure 4-1), allowing guests at social gatherings, weddings, or any events to take photos with their phones and immediately upload and share them. It enables easy photo sharing and browsing for all participants (Note 1). In this chapter, Memori will be used as the implementation example.

CHAPTER 4   END-TO-END TESTING

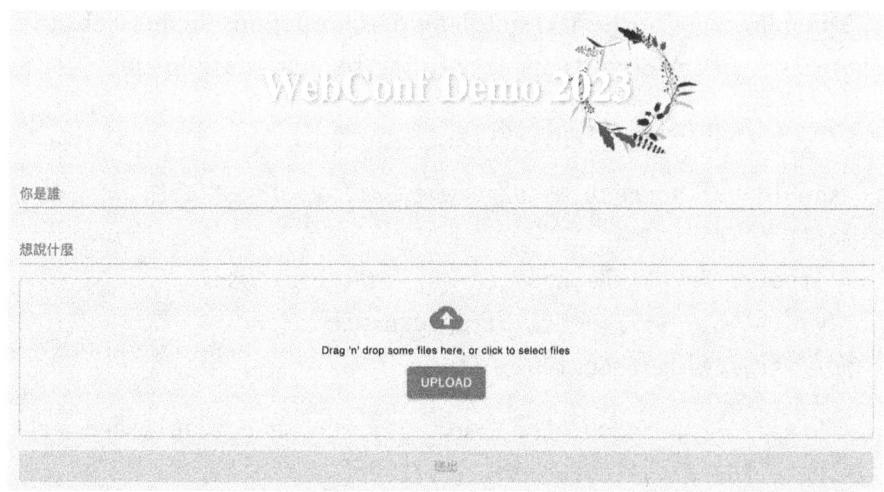

Figure 4-1. *Memori image upload (desktop version)*

For example, when testing the image upload functionality in a desktop environment, the user flow can be divided into two cases: Scenario 1 "Upload Success" and Scenario 2 "Upload Failure," with the following steps (Note 2).

Scenario 1: Successful Image Upload

- Step 1: Enter the website URL in the browser.
- Step 2: Input the username and message, and select an image file.
- Step 3: Click the submit button.
- Step 4: Display a success message for the image upload.

161

CHAPTER 4   END-TO-END TESTING

The following Cypress test simulates a user's actions on this website to ensure a success message is displayed after the image is uploaded.

```
// cypress/e2e/memori.upload.cy.js
```

```
it('should get success message when upload image with jpeg
format', () => {
  // Step 1: Enter the website URL in the browser
  cy.visit('https://memori-ui-upload.web.
  app/?serviceId=webconf2023');

  // Step 2: Input username, message, and select an image file
  cy.get('[data-cy="user-name"]').type('summer');
  cy.get('[data-cy="message"]').type('hello world!');
  cy.get('[data-cy="file-upload"]').selectFile('cycling.
  jpeg', {
    action: 'drag-drop',
    force: true,
  });

  // Step 3: Click the submit button
  cy.get('[data-cy="submit"]').click();

  // Step 4: Display success message for the image upload
  cy.get('[data-cy="success-message"]').should('exist');
});
```

Explanation:

- Jest's `it` function is used to describe the purpose of the test case (Note 3). In this case, the test checks whether a success message appears after a user uploads an image.

- Cypress's `cy.visit` function loads the specified URL in the browser, in this case, https://memori-ui-upload. web.app/?serviceId=webconf2023.

CHAPTER 4 END-TO-END TESTING

- Cypress's `cy.get` function is used to retrieve a specific DOM element by its selector. Here, it selects the `data-cy="user-name"` DOM element and simulates the user typing the username "summer." Then, it selects the `data-cy="message"` element and inputs the message "hello world!" The `selectFile` method is used to choose the image file `cycling.jpeg` and upload it. Finally, the `cy.get` method selects the DOM element with `data-cy="submit"` and simulates a click event to submit the form.

- The `cy.get` method selects the DOM element with `data-cy="success-message"` used to display the success message. Cypress uses assertion tools, such as Chai, and the `should` method checks whether the element exists. If it does, the test passes; otherwise, it fails.

Scenario 2: Failed Image Upload

- Step 1: Enter the website URL in the browser.
- Step 2: Input the username and message, and select a PDF file, which is an invalid image format.
- Step 3: Click the submit button.
- Step 4: Display a failure message for the image upload.

163

CHAPTER 4   END-TO-END TESTING

The following Cypress test simulates a user's actions on this website to ensure an error message is displayed when uploading an invalid image file format:

```
// cypress/e2e/memori.upload.cy.js

it('should get error message when upload file with pdf
format', () => {
  // Step 1: Enter the website URL in the browser
  cy.visit('https://memori-ui-upload.web.
  app/?serviceId=webconf2023');

  // Step 2: Input username, message, and select a PDF file,
  which is an invalid image format
  cy.get('[data-cy="user-name"]').type('summer');
  cy.get('[data-cy="message"]').type('hello world!');
  cy.get('[data-cy="file-upload"]').selectFile('cycling.pdf', {
    action: 'drag-drop',
    force: true,
  });

  // Step 3: Click the submit button
  cy.get('[data-cy="submit"]').click();

  // Step 4: Display failure message for the image upload
  cy.get('[data-cy="error-message"]').should('exist');
});
```

Explanation:

- Jest's it function is used to describe the test case, which checks whether an error message appears when the user uploads an invalid file format.

- Similar to Scenario 1, Cypress's `cy.visit` loads the URL. The `cy.get` function retrieves the DOM elements `data-cy="user-name"` and `data-cy="message"`, where the username "summer" and the message "hello world!" are entered. The `selectFile` method is used to upload the PDF file `cycling.pdf`. Finally, the `cy.get` method selects the `data-cy="submit"` element and simulates the submit action.

- The `cy.get` method then selects the DOM element with `data-cy="error-message"`, used to display the failure message. Cypress uses the `should` method to verify if the element exists. If it does, the test passes; otherwise, it fails.

Cross-Platform Testing

Since users will use different devices depending on their conditions, it is essential to conduct both cross-browser and cross-platform testing. For example, you can simulate a user going through the above process on an iPhone X. As shown in the code below, Cypress can use the `cy.viewport` command to set the desired screen size and orientation for testing. In addition to specifying width and height individually, you can directly set the device's name (e.g., `iphone-6` or `iphone-x`) to specify the viewport for that device.

Here is an example of Cypress test code that simulates user behavior on both desktop and iPhone X:

```
// cypress/e2e/memori.upload.cy.js
describe('upload page', () => {
  describe('desktop', () => {
    // ...other tests...
```

CHAPTER 4   END-TO-END TESTING

```
  });

  describe('mobile', () => {
    beforeEach(() => {
      cy.viewport('iphone-x');
    });

    it('should get success message when upload image with png
    format', () => {
      // Step 1: Enter the website URL in the browser
      cy.visit('https://memori-ui-upload.web.
      app/?serviceId=webconf2023');

      // Step 2: Input username, message, and select an
      image file
      cy.get('[data-cy="user-name"]').type('summer');
      cy.get('[data-cy="message"]').type('hello world!');
      cy.get('[data-cy="file-upload"]').selectFile('cycling.
      jpeg', {
        action: 'drag-drop',
        force: true,
      });

      // Step 3: Click the submit button
      cy.get('[data-cy="submit"]').click();

      // Step 4: Display success message for the image upload
      cy.get('[data-cy="success-message"]').should('exist');
    });

    it('should get error message when upload file with pdf
    format', () => {
      // Step 1: Enter the website URL in the browser
      cy.visit('https://memori-ui-upload.web.
      app/?serviceId=webconf2023');
```

```
    // Step 2: Input username, message, and select a PDF
    file, which is an invalid image format
    cy.get('[data-cy="user-name"]').type('summer');
    cy.get('[data-cy="message"]').type('hello world!');
    cy.get('[data-cy="file-upload"]').
    selectFile('cycling.pdf', {
      action: 'drag-drop',
      force: true,
    });

    // Step 3: Click the submit button
    cy.get('[data-cy="submit"]').click();

    // Step 4: Display failure message for the image upload
    cy.get('[data-cy="error-message"]').should('exist');
   });
  });
});
```

As seen in the examples above, end-to-end testing test cases simulate a user's entire interaction with the product, spanning multiple components and functionalities. In this case, the test verifies the entire image upload process, including browsing the page, form validation, image upload, and thumbnail preview. It ensures the functionality across different devices, such as desktops or mobile phones, works as expected in real-world scenarios.

Conclusion

When planning end-to-end testing, it is recommended to align the testing with user interaction flows and the intended outcomes. Based on the nature of the project or product, cross-browser and cross-platform tests should also be included. In other words, to implement a comprehensive end-to-end test, it's essential to have well-designed test cases that cover various aspects and scenarios. Collaborating with QA on testing strategies is also beneficial. In addition to writing tests during the development phase, it's common to gradually improve tests by first using end-to-end tests to check the happy path (ensuring the core functionalities work), followed by integration tests to handle edge cases, and finally unit tests to cover more complex business logic.

Given that end-to-end testing provides broader and more complete validation of functionality, why not rely solely on it? Here are several considerations:

- Since end-to-end testing simulates real user interactions to ensure correct behavior in real-world scenarios, the cost of setting up the environment (e.g., preparing realistic data and building the infrastructure) can be high.

- Writing tests that span across multiple pages or components increases the complexity, leading to higher costs in implementing tests.

- End-to-end testing focuses on validating user flows rather than individual functions or components, so when errors occur, it's not always easy to immediately identify the root cause.

- Due to the wide scope of end-to-end tests, even small errors can cause a single test case to fail. As the product evolves, the chance of test failure increases, making it hard to rely solely on end-to-end tests for quality assurance.

Thus, narrowing the scope of tests or combining different types of tests—such as increasing the number of unit and integration tests—will provide better quality assurance and confidence than trying to cover everything with large, all-encompassing end-to-end tests.

CHAPTER 4   END-TO-END TESTING

Finally, unit testing and integration testing focus on specific, isolated points, while end-to-end testing emphasizes process validation. By combining different types of testing, software can maintain stability throughout iterations without affecting existing functionality. Automation can further reduce the cost of manual testing, boosting productivity.

Notes

- Note 1: For more information about Memori, visit their Instagram page at `https://www.instagram.com/memori.service.tw/`.

- Note 2: Breaking down the steps in detail not only helps developers write test cases but also aids in collaborating with AI for test writing. See Chapter 8, section "Leveraging AI for Writing Tests," for more information and examples.

- Note 3: For a discussion on test naming conventions, refer to Chapter 1, section "Naming Conventions."

Chapter Review and Summary

- End-to-end testing (often referred to as E2E testing) is a process that simulates the real user journey while interacting with a product. In the context of a web interface, this type of testing mimics a user's actions from opening the browser, entering a URL, clicking specific features, navigating through pages, and completing the entire flow before closing the window. The goal of E2E testing is to replicate real user behavior, ensuring the product functions correctly in real-world scenarios. It is typically the most user-centric type of testing and covers the broadest range of use cases.

- Since the purpose of E2E testing is to simulate actual user operations and ensure proper functionality in real use cases, several principles must be observed when implementing E2E testing: (1) accurately simulating user interactions, (2) correctly replicating the user's operating environment, (3) covering functionality as comprehensively as possible, (4) including abnormal situation tests, and (5) optionally incorporating other types of testing based on the needs of the product or project.

- The advantages of E2E testing include the following: (1) Since it simulates the entire user journey, it thoroughly tests product functionality and best reflects real-world conditions. (2) Because it spans multiple functions, E2E testing broadens the scope of testing and helps reduce the likelihood of errors once the product is live in a production environment.

- While E2E testing effectively verifies the full product flow, identifying the root cause of issues can be challenging when errors occur. In such cases, unit testing may need to be used to isolate the problem. Additionally, for detailed visual comparisons, visual testing is recommended to lighten the load on E2E testing.

CHAPTER 5

Visual Testing

You will learn the following in this chapter:

- Visual testing uses tools to automatically capture UI snapshots and compare them, ensuring intuitive and precise detection of changes.

- Visual testing methods such as component-level testing with tools like Storybook, Chromatic, and Percy, ensuring UI consistency across different devices and interactions.

- Compare Percy, Chromatic, and Jest's toMatchSnapshot for visual testing, focusing on features, ease of use, and browser support.

Visual Testing

Visual testing is a type of testing that uses tools to automatically detect UI changes by capturing snapshots of what the user actually sees and comparing them to previous versions.

In the past, UI changes were often inspected using unit testing to generate text-based snapshots, which were then compared via version control or commands, or manually compared using screenshots to spot differences between the latest version and previous versions or mockups (Note 1). While these methods are simple and convenient, they do not

CHAPTER 5   VISUAL TESTING

clearly indicate what was updated. However, by generating real visual snapshots and highlighting the specific areas of change, developers can more intuitively identify what has changed, quickly locate problems, and make fixes more easily.

Mixtini

Mixtini (`https://mixtini-co.web.app/`) is an online service focused on promoting cocktails and bars, aiming to build a unified community around alcoholic beverages (Figure 5-1). The following end-to-end testing code example uses Mixtini as a demo (Note 2).

Figure 5-1. *Mixtini home page*

For example, the following code demonstrates how to use Cypress and Percy for visual testing, capturing and comparing a snapshot of a specific page (Note 3). After visiting Mixtini's home page, the `cy.percySnapshot` command is used to capture a snapshot of the home page and upload it to Percy's service platform. This allows viewing the comparison results on Percy to ensure the page's visual performance meets expectations.

CHAPTER 5   VISUAL TESTING

```
// cypress/e2e/mixtini.cy.js

describe('Index page', () => {
  it('should update snapshot to Percy correctly', () => {
    cy.visit('https://mixtini-co.web.app/');
    cy.percySnapshot('index');
  });
});
```

Explanation:

- Jest's `describe` function is used to define a group of test cases, typically specifying the page or component being tested (Note 4). In this example, it defines the tests for Mixtini's home page.

- Jest's `it` function describes a single test case, which, in this case, ensures that the snapshot is correctly uploaded to Percy.

- Cypress's `cy.visit` function directs the browser to the specified URL, which in this case is `https://mixtini-co.web.app/`.

- `cy.percySnapshot` is an extended method provided by the integration of Cypress and Percy. It captures a snapshot of Mixtini's home page and uploads it to Percy's service platform, where the comparison results can be viewed.

The snapshot comparison is shown in Figure 5-2, where Percy's platform highlights differences between the current version (right) and the previous version (left), making it easy to see what has changed.

CHAPTER 5   VISUAL TESTING

Figure 5-2. *Percy snapshot comparison*

How Snapshot Comparison Works

How does snapshot comparison work, and what does it mean to compare with a "previous version"? Snapshot differences stem from code changes, which can be explained from the perspective of version control. As shown in Figure 5-3, using Git as an example, when a developer first creates branch A from the main branch at commit x, the snapshot produced at commit x is the baseline for comparison between main and A. Over time, both main and A receive new commits, and each commit generates its own snapshot. If these snapshots are approved for updates, they become the new baseline. For example, main adds commits y and z after x, while A adds commits p and q after x, so the baseline for main is the snapshot generated at commit z, while the baseline for A is the snapshot generated at commit q.

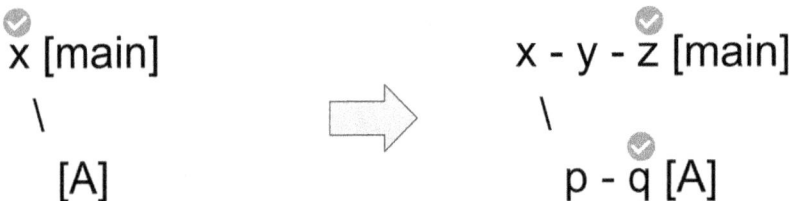

Figure 5-3. *Snapshot comparison principle—branch creation*

CHAPTER 5 VISUAL TESTING

When A submits a pull request (PR or MR for merge request) at commit q to merge back into main, the snapshots generated at z and q are compared. If the snapshot from q is accepted as the new baseline, it will become the baseline for main after A is merged into main (Figure 5-4).

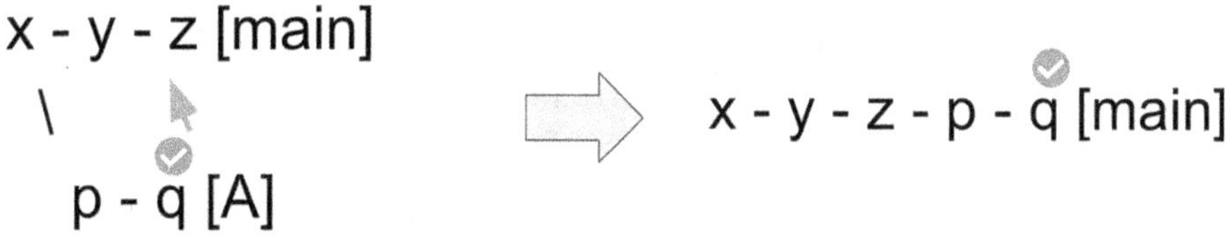

```
x - y - z [main]
 \
  p - q [A]
```
⟹
```
x - y - z - p - q [main]
```

Figure 5-4. Snapshot comparison principle—submitting pull request

What happens if the snapshot from q is rejected as the new baseline? This means the changes in q do not meet expectations, so the code must be modified, such as by adding commit r to meet the expected results, while maintaining z as the baseline (Figure 5-5). In short, snapshot comparison is based on Git commits.

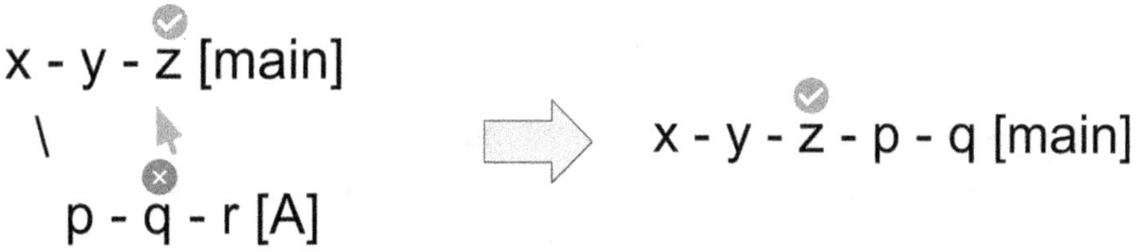

```
x - y - z [main]
 \
  p - q - r [A]
```
⟹
```
x - y - z - p - q [main]
```

Figure 5-5. Snapshot comparison principle—rejecting snapshot from q

Common visual testing tools include Chromatic (https://www.chromatic.com/), Percy (https://percy.io/), and end-to-end testing frameworks like Cypress (https://www.cypress.io/), all of which can effectively implement visual testing. In later chapters, these tools will be compared in more detail (Note 5).

CHAPTER 5   VISUAL TESTING

There are several advantages to implementing visual testing. First, visual testing captures real user views, not just the DOM structure, making changes immediately visible and solving the problem of non-intuitive text-based snapshots. Furthermore, compared to manual screenshot comparisons or manually comparing updates with the previous version or mockups, visual testing provides a more precise and flexible testing method. It can test across different browsers and viewports and enable pixel-perfect visual comparisons.

While visual testing offers significant benefits in providing stability and quality assurance, not all products are suitable for it. Consider other types of testing if the product meets any of the following criteria:

- Lack of version control: If code is not version-controlled, it is impossible to establish a baseline for comparison and manage the process effectively.

- Frequent UI updates: If the product is not in a stable state, visual comparisons become irrelevant, and visual testing may not be necessary.

Though visual testing has many advantages, it often requires third-party tools or services to implement and may not effectively capture dynamic changes on the screen. Additionally, when errors occur, the root cause may not be immediately clear, requiring further investigation through unit testing. To fully test a product, visual testing should be combined with other testing methods, which will be discussed in more detail in subsequent chapters.

Notes

- Note 1: Mockups refer to virtual prototypes or diagrams used in software development to simulate an interface, feature, or workflow, typically in the early design stages

CHAPTER 5 VISUAL TESTING

to facilitate discussion, validation, and determination of a product's look, feel, and functionality. They can be static sketches or interactive prototypes created with design or prototyping tools. Mockups provide early feedback and save time and costs.

- Note 2: Mixtini's Instagram is at `https://www.instagram.com/mixtini.co/` and its Facebook page is at `https://www.facebook.com/mixtini/`.

- Note 3: For information on how to integrate Cypress and Percy, please refer to the documentation "Integrate your Cypress tests with Percy" at this link `https://www.browserstack.com/docs/percy/integrate/cypress`.

- Note 4: For more on naming conventions for tests, refer to Chapter 1, section "Naming Conventions."

- Note 5: For a detailed comparison of commonly used snapshot tools, refer to the section "Tool Comparison" in this chapter.

Verifying Visual Accuracy

Visual testing is a specialized testing method used to detect changes in the user interface (UI) by capturing and comparing snapshots of what the user sees, ensuring visual consistency and accuracy. This method can be divided into two main types: testing individual components and testing entire web pages. Both approaches aim to maintain the visual quality and consistency of the UI, helping developers identify and fix any potential visual issues early on (Note 1).

CHAPTER 5   VISUAL TESTING

Component-Level Testing

When structuring projects, they are often built using shared components like building blocks. Therefore, when refactoring, testing these components helps detect unintended changes to existing business logic or avoid issues where fixing one feature breaks another. Since most projects consist of shared components, if you are implementing visual testing for the first time, it's recommended to start by testing shared components. Component-level testing can be combined with Storybook and visual testing tools to capture snapshots of each story, and continuous integration (CI) tools can automate these tests (Note 2).

Storybook (`https://storybook.js.org/`) is a tool for developing and showcasing UI components in various states and behaviors. It provides an environment for developers to quickly build, test, and document UI components. The core concept of Storybook is the story, which describes a component's behavior in different scenarios. Each story acts as a small example, showing how a component behaves in different states, helping teams understand and test UI components better. Moreover, Storybook integrates with tools like Chromatic and Percy to facilitate snapshot testing of components.

The steps to integrate Storybook with visual testing tools for snapshot testing are as follows:

- Step 1: First, use a package manager (like yarn) to install Storybook along with Chromatic or Percy. Choose one of these tools to install using the following command: `yarn add --dev chromatic storybook` or `yarn add --dev @percy/cli storybook`. Here, the `--dev` or `-D` flag indicates that the packages will be installed in the `devDependencies` section of the `package.json` file. This is because Chromatic and Percy are testing tools used during development, and they are not needed in the production environment.

- Step 2: Next, write your story and the `play` function. The `play` function is used to simulate user interactions in tests. It will be invoked during the test to mimic user actions on the web page, such as clicking buttons or entering text.

- Step 3: Run the tests and capture snapshots. Use the Chromatic or Percy commands to test and capture snapshots. For example, run the `chromatic` or `cy.percySnapshot` commands. Developers can choose to run tests manually on their local machine or automate the tests using CI tools.

- Step 4: Finally, view the snapshots on the Chromatic or Percy platform. After running specific commands, the snapshots will be uploaded to the service platform, allowing developers to view the comparison results on Chromatic or Percy.

Below are some test examples in different scenarios.

Testing Different Viewports

In component-level testing, it's possible to configure different variables in Storybook, such as setting parameters in the Storybook configuration file or in individual stories and then using tools like Chromatic or Percy. Here, we'll use an example of testing across different viewports.

With Chromatic, the first method is to set global configurations in the Storybook `preview.js` file. The following code shows Storybook's configuration options, where the `parameters` are used to configure settings for Chromatic. The viewport settings specify four viewport sizes: 320px, 576px, 768px, and 992px. This ensures snapshots are taken across different screen sizes, verifying that the UI layout and behavior function as expected on various devices.

```
const parameters = {
  chromatic: {
    viewports: [320, 576, 768, 992],
  },
};
```

The second method involves specifying the viewport list directly within individual stories. In the example below, we have a story named IntroStory, where the args define the story's parameters, and the chromatic section configures settings specific to Chromatic. The viewports parameter specifies the viewport sizes for testing—320px, 576px, 768px, and 992px—to simulate how the UI behaves on different devices, ensuring the layout and behavior are consistent with expectations.

```
IntroStory.args = {
  chromatic: {
    viewports: [320, 576, 768, 992],
  },
};
```

To execute the tests locally, use the following command to run the Chromatic CLI. The CLI will test all Storybook stories in the project and upload the results to the Chromatic platform for snapshot comparison.

```
npx chromatic --project-token <project-token>
```

npx is a Node.js command that runs locally installed packages. Here, npx runs the locally installed Chromatic package, and the test is executed using the project's token. While npm is a package management tool, npx is specifically designed to execute temporary commands without globally installing packages, avoiding versioning issues. If the package isn't found locally, npx will automatically install it, run the command, and delete it afterward, making the process simpler and more convenient for one-time tasks.

CHAPTER 5   VISUAL TESTING

Both methods—setting global configurations in Storybook's `preview.js` or specifying viewports within individual stories—achieve the goal of testing different viewports in Chromatic. The decision depends on whether it's a regular requirement (global configuration) or a rare, case-specific scenario (story-specific configuration). If using Percy, there are similar configuration options, which we'll cover later.

By using Chromatic to test specific components across various viewports, the resulting snapshots (as shown in Figure 5-6) demonstrate different layouts and behaviors across screen sizes. Developers can compare these snapshots with previous versions to ensure the changes are expected, maintaining consistency across devices, which is especially useful for websites supporting both desktop and mobile platforms.

Figure 5-6. Mixtini home page, testing different viewports

How does Percy handle this? You can configure viewports globally in the Percy configuration file or pass specific settings when running snapshot commands. The first method is to set viewports globally in Percy's `percy.json` configuration file. In the example below, the `snapshot` field defines related settings, and the `width` field specifies the viewport list. This allows snapshots to be captured at different screen sizes, ensuring consistent UI behavior across devices.

181

```
// percy.json
{
  snapshot: {
    widths: [320, 576, 768, 992];
  }
}
```

The second method involves passing parameters directly when calling the cy.percySnapshot command, typically for single tests. In the example below, the widths parameter is passed during the snapshot command, allowing snapshots to be taken at different screen sizes to ensure consistent layout and behavior across devices.

```
// Story
cy.percySnapshot('main page', {
  widths: [320, 576, 768, 992],
});
```

Explanation:

- cy.percySnapshot is a method provided by Cypress integrated with Percy, allowing snapshots to be captured for different components or pages. These snapshots are then uploaded to Percy's platform to compare differences between the current and previous snapshots.

- main page is the name of the snapshot, used to distinguish different screenshots in the project. This is typically used to identify the target of the test, such as the home page or product page.

- The widths field defines the different viewport sizes, with 320px, 576px, 768px, and 992px used here. As in the previous solution, the goal is to capture snapshots across different screen sizes to ensure consistent layout and behavior across devices.

Both methods allow Percy to test different viewports effectively, just as with Chromatic, and are particularly useful for websites supporting both desktop and mobile platforms.

Taking Snapshots After Specific Interactions

In addition to taking snapshots of a component's initial state, how do you capture snapshots after specific interactions? These interactions can generally be categorized into two types: those triggered by JavaScript and those triggered by CSS.

Interactions Triggered by JavaScript

The first type involves interactions triggered by JavaScript. For example, with Mixtini's search feature (Figure 5-7), we want to simulate a user typing "Irish Coffee" into the search bar, clicking the search button, and then capturing a snapshot of the search results for comparison (Note 3).

CHAPTER 5 VISUAL TESTING

Figure 5-7. *Snapshot of interaction triggered by JavaScript*

Here, we use Storybook combined with Chromatic to capture snapshots of the component. In the following code, we implement a play function within the story to simulate user interaction. Using the data-test-id attribute, we retrieve the DOM elements for the search bar and search button, simulate user actions by typing "Irish Coffee" and clicking the search button, and Chromatic automatically captures the snapshot after the interaction.

```
SearchService.play = async () => {
  const canvas = within(canvasElement);
  const Input = canvas.queryByTestId('input');
  const Button = canvas.queryByTestId('button');
  await userEvent.type(Input, 'Irish Coffee');
  await userEvent.click(Button);
};
```

Explanation:

- The `play` function is implemented for the `SearchService` story to simulate user interactions with the search feature.
- The `within` function from the `@storybook/testing-library` package wraps the `canvasElement` to facilitate querying and interaction.
- `queryByTestId` is used to find the DOM element with the `data-test-id` of `input` for the search bar and the `data-test-id` of `button` for the search button.
- `userEvent.type` simulates typing "Irish Coffee" into the search bar.
- `userEvent.click` simulates clicking the search button to submit the search query.
- After the `play` function completes, Chromatic automatically captures a snapshot, achieving the goal of capturing snapshots for interactions triggered by JavaScript.

Interactions Triggered by CSS

The second type involves interactions triggered by CSS. For example, with Mixtini's "Contact Us" feature, you may want to capture a snapshot of the button in its hover state (Figure 5-8).

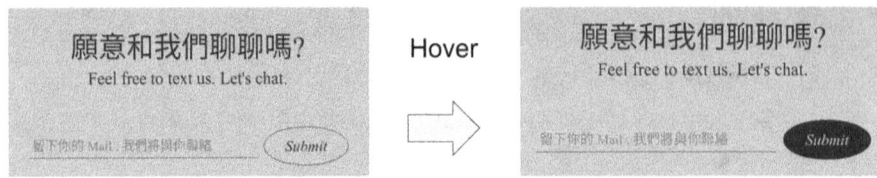

Figure 5-8. *Snapshot of interaction triggered by CSS*

The first approach is to create a .hover class representing the hover state, which will be added when capturing the snapshot to ensure the component reflects the hover state. Since the hover state is triggered by mouse events, and tests do not include real mouse interactions, we need to simulate this state by adding a .hover class.

```
&:hover,
&.hover {
  /* Styles for hover state */
}
```

Next, we add this class to the story when taking the snapshot. The following example shows a story for a <Button> component, where the hover class is added to capture the snapshot in the hover state:

```
import Button from './Button';

const Template = () => <Button className="hover" />;
```

The second approach is to use props and flags to capture snapshots of different states. Since we can't directly trigger the hover state, we can use a prop to simulate it. In the following code, the <Button> component uses a hover prop to determine its state. When hover is set to true, the component will appear in the hover state, allowing us to capture a snapshot.

```
const Button = ({ hover }) => {
  return <Button hover={hover} />;
};
```

In the story, we set the hover value to true to render the <Button> in the hover state and capture the snapshot. The following example shows a story for a <Button> component where the hover value is set to true, enabling the snapshot to be taken in the hover state:

```
import Button from './Button';

const Template = (args) => <Button {...args} />;

const ButtonStory = Template.bind({});

// Set hover value to true
ButtonStory.args = {
  hover: true,
};
```

Both of these methods allow you to capture snapshots of CSS-triggered interactions. You can choose the method that suits your specific use case.

Integrating CI Tools for Component-Level Testing

To automate component-level testing in CI tools, you can use GitHub Actions combined with Chromatic's chromaui/action@v1 tool. By creating a custom workflow, you can automatically test components and capture snapshots. The following code demonstrates how to trigger Chromatic to publish Storybook, test components, and capture snapshots whenever a pull request is submitted:

```
// .github/workflows/visual-testing.yml

name: 'Components Visual Testing'
on: [pull_request]
```

CHAPTER 5   VISUAL TESTING

```
jobs:
 chromatic-deployment:
   runs-on: ubuntu-latest
   steps:
     - uses: actions/checkout@v2
       with:
         fetch-depth: 0
     - name: Install dependencies
       run: yarn
     - name: Publish to Chromatic
       uses: chromaui/action@v1
       with:
         projectToken: ${{ secrets.CHROMATIC_TOKEN }}
```

Explanation:

- This GitHub Actions workflow, named "Components Visual Testing," triggers the `chromatic-deployment` job every time a pull request is submitted. The job runs on the `ubuntu-latest` environment, meaning it executes on the latest version of the Ubuntu operating system. It uses the `actions/checkout@v2` action to clone the project's code, with the `fetch-depth: 0` parameter ensuring the full commit history is retrieved. In a workflow, you can define multiple jobs, which run in parallel, and each job can contain several steps that run sequentially.

- In the `chromatic-deployment` job, the following steps are executed in order:

    - The `yarn` command installs the project's dependencies.

- Chromatic's GitHub Action, `chromaui/action@v1`, publishes the built components to the Chromatic service platform. The `projectToken` is the token specific to your Chromatic project, which can be obtained from their platform and stored securely in GitHub secrets. It is accessed using `${{ secrets.CHROMATIC_TOKEN }}`.

Since this component-level testing mechanism is integrated with unit testing or integration testing, it is more efficient and cost-effective compared to end-to-end testing. It can be run frequently, reducing the time and cost of executing tests, making it highly practical to use regularly.

Page-Level Testing

In addition to capturing snapshots of components, you can integrate end-to-end testing tools, such as Cypress, to capture snapshots of entire pages. The example below demonstrates how to use Cypress, Percy, and GitHub Actions to achieve this. Using Mixtini's home page as an example, after visiting the page, the `cy.percySnapshot` command is used to capture a snapshot of the home page and upload it to Percy's service platform. You can then view the snapshot comparison results on Percy's platform.

```
// cypress/e2e/mixtini.cy.js

describe('Index page', () => {
  it('should update snapshot to Percy correctly', () => {
    cy.visit('https://mixtini-co.web.app/');

    cy.percySnapshot('index');
  });
});
```

CHAPTER 5   VISUAL TESTING

On Percy's platform, you can view various details. The main features include the following:

- In the top-right corner, you can view snapshots based on different browsers and resolutions.
- Percy assists in comparing the current snapshot with previous versions and highlights any differences.
- If the changes are expected, you can click the "approve" button in the top-left corner to set this snapshot as the new baseline for future comparisons (Note 4).

Integrating CI Tools for Page-Level Testing

To automate page-level testing with CI tools, GitHub Actions can be used in conjunction with Percy's `percy-cli` tool. You can create a custom workflow to test specific pages and capture snapshots automatically. The following example sets up a workflow to run tests and capture snapshots every Monday at midnight:

```
// .github/workflows/regular-visual-testing.yml
name: Regular Visual Testing
on:
  schedule:
    - cron: '0 0 * * 1'
jobs:
  build:
    runs-on: ubuntu-latest
    steps:
      - name: Checkout
        uses: actions/checkout@master
      - name: Install packages
        run: yarn
```

CHAPTER 5   VISUAL TESTING

```
- name: Run visual testing
  run: npx percy exec -- cypress run --headless
  env:
    PERCY_TOKEN: ${{ secrets.PERCY_TOKEN }}
```

Explanation:

- This GitHub Actions workflow is named "Regular Visual Testing" and is set to run on a schedule. The cron expression determines the frequency of execution.

- The on field defines the trigger for the workflow. Here, a scheduled trigger is set using the cron expression '0 0 * * 1', which means the workflow will run every Monday at midnight.

- The build job runs on the latest Ubuntu version and executes the following steps:

  - actions/checkout@master is used to clone the project's code from the master branch, ensuring the latest version is tested.

  - yarn is used to install the project's dependencies.

  - The npx percy exec -- cypress run --headless command runs the tests. percy exec is a command provided by Percy's CLI to run tests in Percy's environment, and cypress run --headless runs the Cypress tests in headless mode. Running in headless mode means the tests execute without opening a browser, improving speed and making the tests suitable for CI environments.

- PERCY_TOKEN is the token for your Percy project, which can be obtained from Percy's platform. It is typically stored in GitHub Secrets and accessed using ${{ secrets.PERCY_TOKEN }}.

Workflow

The following workflow applies to both component- and page-level testing:

- Step 1: Run the tests. For component-level testing, you can use Storybook with Chromatic or Percy, and for page-level testing, tools like Cypress combined with Percy or other packages like cypress-image-diff-js can be used (Note 5).

- Step 2: Capture snapshots of the component or page.

- Step 3: Compare the snapshots using platforms like Chromatic, Percy, or other tools to identify differences.

- Step 4: Based on the snapshots, you can either update the code or refresh the snapshot baseline. This step may involve going back to Step 1 to rerun the tests, possibly multiple times.

- Step 5: Once changes are confirmed as expected, you can commit the code and schedule a release.

Summary

Here is a summary of when to use component-level testing vs. page-level testing:

- If you are implementing visual testing for the first time in a project or the project is primarily built from shared components, it is recommended to focus on component-level testing.

- If you are testing integration performance or the page consists mostly of custom features with fewer shared components, page-level testing would be a better choice.

Notes

- Note 1: For examples of component- and page-level testing, see https://bit.ly/3MB2xxn.

- Note 2: CI (continuous integration) and CD (continuous delivery/continuous deployment) are key concepts in software development and are part of automated workflows to improve software quality and speed of delivery. CI involves automatically testing and building code every time changes are made to a version-controlled repository, ensuring smooth integration of changes. CI helps teams discover and resolve integration issues early, reducing the cost of fixing errors later on. Common CI tools include Jenkins, GitHub Actions, Travis CI, CircleCI, and GitLab CI/CD. CD extends CI by automatically deploying tested code to production or testing environments. Continuous delivery involves delivering new software versions to a testing or pre-production environment for verification, while continuous deployment goes a step further by automatically deploying new versions to

CHAPTER 5   VISUAL TESTING

production without manual intervention. In summary, CI and CD aim to automate development processes, reduce human error, and improve delivery speed and software quality. CI focuses on integrating and testing code, while CD takes it further by deploying the tested code to production. Popular tools include AWS CodeDeploy, Azure DevOps Services, Google Cloud Build, GitLab CI/CD, and GitHub Actions.

- Note 3: For more information and examples on Mixtini, refer to the section "Visual Testing" in this chapter.

- Note 4: For the principles of snapshot comparison, see the section "Visual Testing" in this chapter.

- Note 5: `cypress-image-diff-js` (https://github.com/uktrade/cypress-image-diff) is a plug-in for the Cypress testing framework that provides snapshot and image comparison capabilities. It allows developers to compare two images within a Cypress test to detect visual differences, helping ensure that the visual presentation of a web page or application remains consistent after updates or changes.

Tool Comparison

When introducing visual testing into your workflow, which tool should you choose? Below is a comparison of Percy, Chromatic, and Jest's `toMatchSnapshot` (Note 1), covering different aspects.

CHAPTER 5 VISUAL TESTING

Snapshot File Types and Structure

Chromatic and Percy's snapshots are screenshots of what the user sees, whereas Jest's toMatchSnapshot stores snapshots of the DOM structure in a text format. Chromatic and Percy make changes more apparent, solving the problem of non-intuitive snapshots. These tools also provide built-in comparison functionality. As shown in Figure 5-9, Chromatic's platform compares the current snapshot with the previous version, highlighting differences, including both code and rendered output. This makes it easy for developers to understand what has changed and achieve pixel-perfect visual comparison. Moreover, Chromatic and Percy support tests across multiple browsers and viewports, making them more precise and flexible than manual checks or other tools.

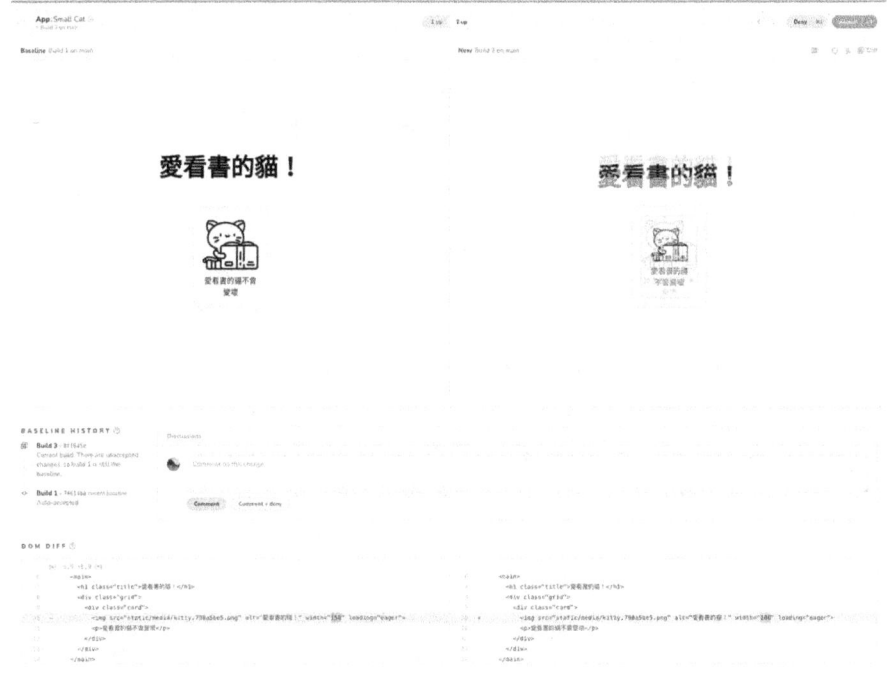

Figure 5-9. Chromatic marks the differences between snapshots, including code and rendered output

195

CHAPTER 5   VISUAL TESTING

Jest's `toMatchSnapshot` stores snapshots of the DOM structure in a text format, relying on version control tools or Jest's expect assertion to compare snapshot files.

```
// src/ImageList/__snapshots__/ImageListMockData.shallow.jest.test.js.snap

exports[`ImageList should render correct image items when have data 1`] = `
<React.Fragment>
  <ImageItem
    image="https://bit.ly/4228IT0"
    title="Improve website performance with key metrics to boost user experience and traffic"
  />
  <ImageItem
    image="https://bit.ly/4b5nLP0"
    title="Island-hopping bike trip along the Shimanami Kaido"
  />
</React.Fragment>
`;
```

However, when comparing source code with snapshots, Chromatic's built-in comparison tool helps developers easily identify how changes in the code affect the snapshots, while Percy lacks this feature. Jest's `toMatchSnapshot` relies on version control tools to manually compare snapshots with code, which can be less intuitive. In integration testing, while Jest's `expect(...).toMatchSnapshot()` can detect snapshot changes, developers still need to map changes back to the corresponding code, which can be challenging with complex files.

Reviewing Snapshots Based on Pull Requests or Branches

Once development is done, developers submit pull requests (PRs) for code review. At this stage, it's necessary to review snapshots for different PRs or branches to ensure that changes behave as expected. Chromatic provides a user-friendly tool for this, as shown in Figure 5-10, allowing developers to review snapshots by PR or branch. Percy offers this feature too, but it's not as easy to use, while Jest's toMatchSnapshot relies on version control tools. Although all three can accomplish this task, Chromatic offers the most convenient tools.

Figure 5-10. Chromatic shows snapshots by branch

Merge Checks

After submitting a PR, it is important to check if it meets the merge criteria so that reviewers and teams can decide whether to merge into the main branch (Note 2). By integrating GitHub Actions with Chromatic or Percy, the visual testing results can be part of the review process. If there are changes, they can be approved as the new baseline. If not, the PR can be merged directly. This streamlines the process and saves time, whereas with Jest's toMatchSnapshot, developers must manually update snapshots, check changes in version control, and resubmit PRs, leading to more time-consuming reviews.

CHAPTER 5   VISUAL TESTING

Component-Level Testing

Both Chromatic and Percy can integrate with Storybook for component-level testing, making them easy to implement in projects already using Storybook. Jest's `toMatchSnapshot`, on the other hand, requires developers to manually write tests for each component, as shown below:

```
// src/ImageList/ImageListAxios.snapshot.jest.test.js

it('should render no data prompt when no images', () => {
  // ...code...
  const wrapper = render(<ImageList />);

  expect(wrapper).toMatchSnapshot();
});
```

Page-Level Testing

For page-level testing, Percy can work with end-to-end testing frameworks, while Chromatic is limited to component-level testing. For example, Percy can integrate with Cypress to implement page-level testing and visual testing easily, while Jest's `toMatchSnapshot` cannot perform component- or page-level testing.

```
// cypress/e2e/mixtini.cy.js

describe('Index page', () => {
  it('should update snapshot to Percy correctly', () => {
    cy.visit('https://mixtini-co.web.app/');
    cy.percySnapshot('index');
  });
});
```

If Percy is not an option, is it still possible to do snapshot testing? Yes, tools like Cypress provide the `screenshot` method for snapshot testing on entire components or pages. However, comparing and storing snapshots would require additional setup, such as using third-party tools or services. For example, installing the `cypress-image-diff-js` package can be used for page comparison, but compared to Percy, this setup is more labor-intensive.

Browser Support

For browser support, Percy can test Chrome, Firefox, and Edge, while Chromatic only supports Chrome. Jest's `toMatchSnapshot` is browser independent.

Summary

The following table compares Percy, Chromatic, Cypress, Jest's `toMatchSnapshot`, and Cypress with the `cypress-image-diff-js` plug-in.

#	Percy	Chromatic	Cypress	Jest's `toMatchSnapshot`
Snapshot types and structure	Visual screenshot	Visual screenshot	Visual screenshot	Text-based DOM structure
Comparison tools	Platform tool	Platform tool	With `cypress-image-diff-js`	With version control or assertion

(continued)

CHAPTER 5   VISUAL TESTING

#	Percy	Chromatic	Cypress	Jest's `toMatchSnapshot`
Compare source code	No	Platform tool	With version control	With version control
Review snapshots by PR/branch	Platform tool	Platform tool	With version control	With version control
Merge checks	With `percy/exec-action`	With `chromaui/action`	No	Version control
Component-level testing	With Storybook	With Storybook	Built-in	No
Page-level testing	With e2e testing framework	No	Built-in	No
Browser support	Chrome, Firefox, Edge	Chrome	Chrome, Firefox, Edge	Browser independent
Features	Supports both component- and page-level testing	Focused on component-level testing, feature-rich	Integrates multiple testing methods	Easy to implement
Storage	Platform provided	Platform provided	Developer managed	Developer managed

Finally, for implementing visual testing, the recommended approach is

- Use Storybook with Chromatic for component-level testing, reviewing common components during PR reviews.

CHAPTER 5   VISUAL TESTING

- Use Cypress with the `cypress-image-diff-js` plug-in or, better yet, integrate Percy for page-level testing, regularly checking the status of specific pages in production.

Developers can choose the best option based on the specific needs and characteristics of their project or product.

Notes

- Note 1: Jest's `toMatchSnapshot` (https://jestjs.io/docs/snapshot-testing) is a method for comparing snapshots. It captures snapshots of rendered UI in tests and compares them with previous versions. If there are differences, the test fails, prompting developers to either update the code or the snapshot, helping to catch unintended changes.

- Note 2: For discussions about running tests during PR submissions, see Chapter 6, section "Run Tests Before Merging Code."

Chapter Review and Summary

- Visual testing is a type of testing that uses tools to automatically detect UI changes by capturing and comparing snapshots of what users actually see on the screen.

CHAPTER 5   VISUAL TESTING

- The benefits of implementing visual testing include the following: (1) Since the snapshots produced by visual testing represent the actual view users see rather than just the DOM structure, changes become more apparent, solving the problem of non-intuitive snapshots. (2) Compared to using manual screenshot comparisons or manually checking updates against previous versions or mockups, visual testing offers a more precise and flexible testing method. It can test across multiple browsers and viewports and achieve pixel-perfect visual comparisons.

- While visual testing can greatly enhance product stability and quality assurance, not all products are suited for this type of testing. Consider other types of testing if: (1) There is no version control: Without version control, there is no baseline for comparison or proper workflow management. (2) Frequent UI updates: If the product has frequent updates and lacks stability, comparisons may not provide meaningful insights, making visual testing unnecessary.

- When to use component- or page-level testing: (1) If you're introducing visual testing for the first time or the project heavily relies on shared components, it's recommended to focus on component-level testing. (2) If you are testing the effectiveness of integrations or working on customized pages with fewer shared components, page-level testing is a better choice.

- Recommended practices for implementing visual testing include the following: (1) Using Storybook with Chromatic for component-level testing to review shared components during PR reviews to ensure they function as expected. (2) Using Cypress with the third-party `cypress-image-diff-js` plug-in or integrating Percy for page-level testing, regularly checking specific pages in production environments.

- Although visual testing has many advantages, it requires third-party tools or services to function. In some cases, it may not effectively detect dynamic content changes. Additionally, when errors occur, it can be difficult to immediately identify the root cause, often requiring you to start with unit testing. To fully test product functionality, other testing methods should be used alongside visual testing.

CHAPTER 6

What to Do After Writing Tests: When and How to Run Them

You will learn the following in this chapter:

- Manual test invocation, pre-run commands, and monitoring file changes to efficiently execute tests during development

- Run tests before merging code, focusing on pre-commit, pre-push, and PR submission for quality assurance

- The importance of running tests regularly in CI to ensure stability, address gaps, and reduce test failures

- Use code coverage to infer use case coverage, ensuring comprehensive testing of product features and scenarios

CHAPTER 6   WHAT TO DO AFTER WRITING TESTS: WHEN AND HOW TO RUN THEM

Pre-commands and Manual Test Invocation

Automated tests can be executed manually through scripts or by using a test runner from a testing framework. By running tests in different ways, you can receive valuable feedback and support at various stages of the development lifecycle. This chapter explores pre-run commands, manually triggering tests, monitoring file changes to rerun tests, and how to add custom settings through configuration files.

Pre-commands

In most web projects, there is typically a configuration file (e.g., package.json) that contains the project's dependencies, information, and helper commands. These commands include how to build, run, and test the project. For running tests, a test command is usually defined in package.json to act as a pre-run command for the package manager to start the test runner.

If Jest is being used as the test runner, an example package.json file might look like this, where the --config option loads the relevant settings from a configuration file:

```
"scripts": {
  "test": "jest --config ./jest.config.js"
}
```

In this example, a test command is defined in the scripts section of package.json. It runs Jest tests using the configuration specified in the jest.config.js file, which customizes the behavior of Jest tests (Note 1).

You can run the test runner with a package manager like yarn or npm to execute the tests:

```
yarn test
npm run test
```

In some cases, multiple types of tests may be required, or specific execution contexts and conditions might need to be added. For instance, if you want to run visual testing for components using Percy with Storybook, you can add a command like `snapshot:storybook`, where `./storybook-build` is the directory containing the static files generated by Storybook. Pre-run commands help developers differentiate between various types of tests, making it easier to manually trigger the correct test or integrate with CI tools.

```
"scripts": {
  "test": "jest --config ./jest.config.js",
  "snapshot:storybook": "percy storybook ./storyDist"
}
```

Manual Test Invocation

Manual test triggering refers to developers manually running test commands (such as `yarn test` or `jest`) on their local development environment to start the test runner. During the development phase, manual test triggers provide quick feedback to help developers refine their code or test cases. Developers can also set specific configurations depending on the needs, such as rerunning updated tests based on file changes or adding custom settings to configuration files.

Monitoring File Updates and Rerunning Tests

Typically, you would use a package manager like `yarn` or `npm` to run the test runner. For example, when running `yarn test` or `npm run test`, these commands will look at the `package.json` file in the project and execute the script defined under the `scripts` section to start the test runner. This will run all the tests with files ending in `.test.js`.

CHAPTER 6 WHAT TO DO AFTER WRITING TESTS: WHEN AND HOW TO RUN THEM

```
yarn test
npm run test
```

If you want to continuously rerun tests as files are updated, you can use Jest's watch mode. With the `--watch` or `--watchAll` flags, Jest monitors file changes and reruns tests when updates occur.

```
jest --watch     # Rerun only modified files
jest --watchAll  # Rerun all tests
```

You can update the pre-run commands to make these options easier to access. For example, using `yarn`, you can create commands like `yarn test:watch` or `yarn test:watchAll` for rerunning modified files or all files, respectively.

```
"scripts": {
  "test": "jest --config ./jest.config.js",
  "test:watch": "jest --config ./jest.config.js --watch",
  "test:watchAll": "jest --config ./jest.config.js --watchAll"
}
```

The choice between rerunning modified files or all files depends on the project's size and the number of tests. For smaller projects or when the number of tests is low, running all tests may not take much time. However, in larger projects with more tests, rerunning all tests could take longer. It's recommended to rerun only modified files to reduce wait time.

Adding Custom Settings via Configuration Files

With Jest, you can customize which files should be tested or ignored by adding settings to a configuration file like `jest.config.js`. For instance, you can use `testPathIgnorePatterns` to skip files or directories that shouldn't be tested. In the following example, Jest is instructed to ignore any test files located in `node_modules` or `dist` directories. Since node_

CHAPTER 6   WHAT TO DO AFTER WRITING TESTS: WHEN AND HOW TO RUN THEM

modules contains third-party dependencies that don't need testing, and dist holds the project's build output, these paths are excluded from the testing process to improve efficiency.

```
module.exports = {
  testPathIgnorePatterns: ['/node_modules/', '/dist/'],
};
```

Summary

Setting up pre-run commands allows developers to execute tests with different scenarios and conditions quickly during development and makes it easier to integrate these tests with CI tools. Manual test triggering enables developers to get rapid feedback during development while allowing for customization, such as monitoring file changes and rerunning tests or using configuration files to add custom settings.

Manual test triggers are flexible and convenient during development but rely on manual execution, which can lead to human error or inefficiency. Therefore, automating the testing process is the best way to improve test efficiency and quality. The next chapter will explore how to implement automated testing.

Notes

- Note 1: For more information on Jest configuration, refer to the official documentation (https://jestjs.io/docs/configuration).

CHAPTER 6   WHAT TO DO AFTER WRITING TESTS: WHEN AND HOW TO RUN THEM

Run Tests Before Merging Code

To ensure that the codebase functions correctly before merging code back into the main branch, it is recommended to run tests as much as possible. There are a few key points in time when tests should be executed before code is merged: pre-commit, pre-push, and during PR submissions. These checkpoints help maintain code quality and prevent negative impacts on the existing codebase.

pre-commit

Pre-commit refers to running tasks before the git commit command, using Git's pre-commit hook to perform tasks such as code formatting checks and tests. As shown in Figure 6-1, if the checks pass, the git commit is executed; if they fail, the code remains in the staged phase (Note 1). The benefit is that it ensures all checks are completed before committing code, avoiding problems after the git push to a remote repository. This workflow can be improved by integrating tools like Husky (Note 2) and Lint-Staged (Note 3) to manage the process efficiently.

CHAPTER 6   WHAT TO DO AFTER WRITING TESTS: WHEN AND HOW TO RUN THEM

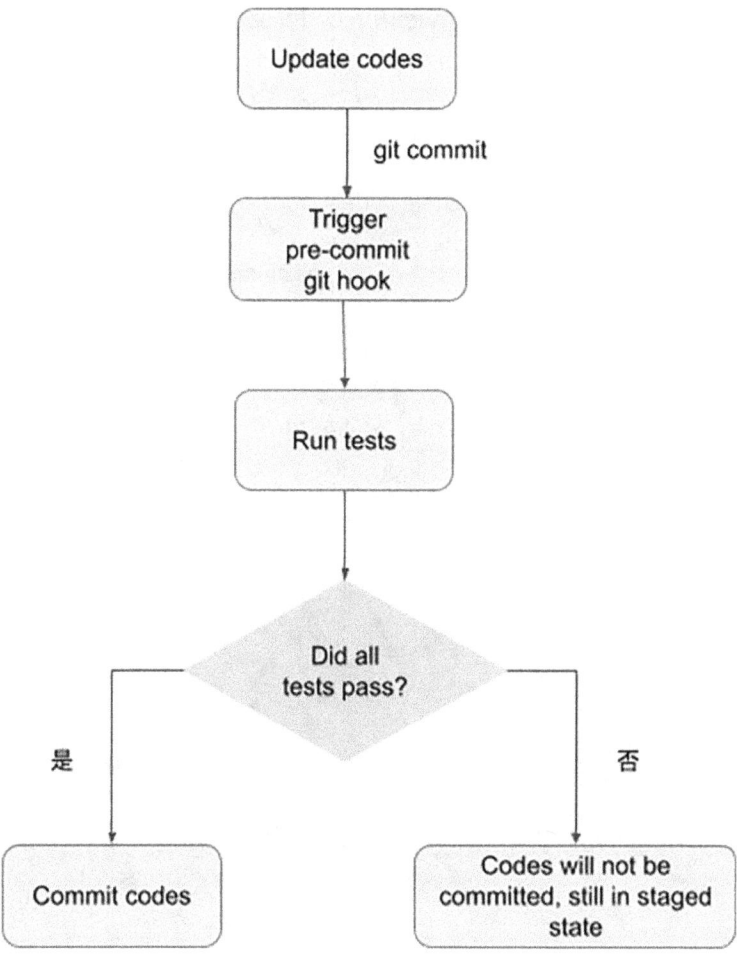

Figure 6-1. *pre-commit workflow*

pre-push

Pre-push refers to executing tasks before `git push`, using Git's pre-push hook. Similar to pre-commit, this checks code formatting and runs tests before pushing commits. As shown in Figure 6-2, if all checks pass, the git push is completed; if they fail, the commit stays local. This method ensures that all checks are done before pushing code, saving time and resources by avoiding errors being pushed to the repository, which can lead to multiple back-and-forth changes and wasted CI resources.

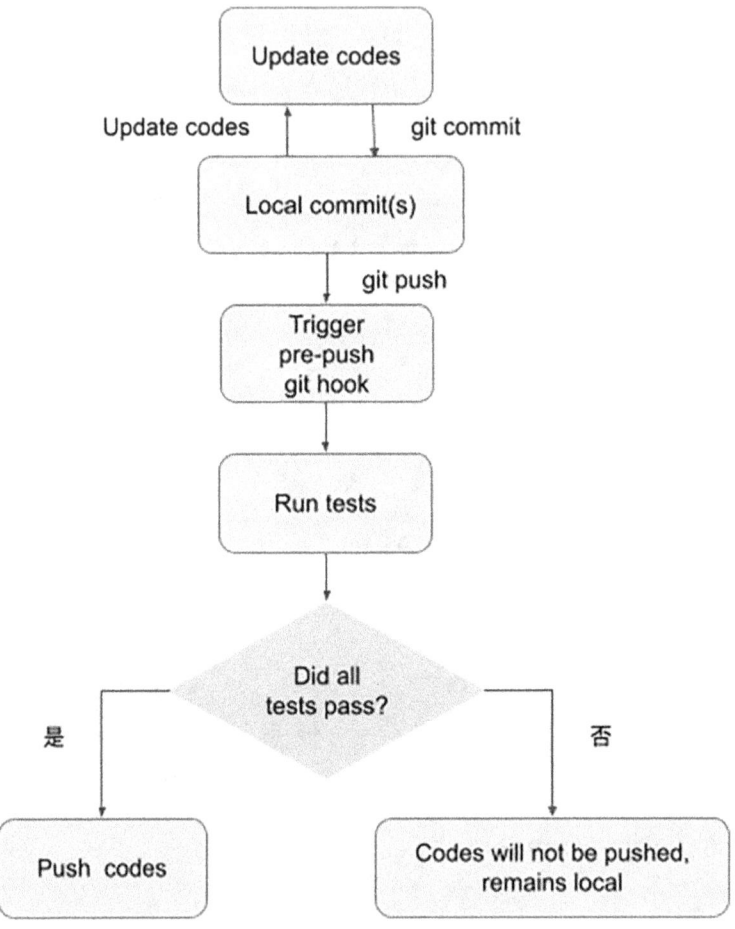

Figure 6-2. *pre-push workflow*

To summarize, both `pre-commit` and `pre-push` provide the following benefits:

- Early detection of issues to prevent problematic code from entering the codebase and causing confusion during code reviews or CI/CD pipeline failures

- Ensures CI/CD pipelines succeed, preventing unnecessary failures and errors, which saves resources

- Reduces wasted time and effort, increasing productivity

Since developers often commit frequently during development, pre-commit can lead to too many test executions or long execution times due to the large number of tests. This can disrupt development. Distributing some tasks to pre-push can be a good solution.

Running Tests During PR Submission

Many projects choose to verify the stability of the codebase before merging code into the main branch, meaning that tests are run during PR submission to check whether the merge passes all necessary checks. This ensures that new or modified code does not negatively impact the existing codebase. Additionally, it is a way to share information with the team. If a developer runs tests on their local environment, others working on the shared repository may not know that the changes have passed tests. Running tests during PR submission allows the team to better understand the status of development and engage in code review or discussions.

Popular code hosting services, like GitHub, enable status checks through GitHub Actions, which act as a form of testing. GitHub Actions execute each step and confirm whether they pass. Developers can require that PRs pass specific tests before merging the code back into the main branch.

For example, in Figure 6-3, a PR undergoes testing via GitHub Actions. If the tests pass, the PR is considered stable, and the team can proceed with code review.

CHAPTER 6   WHAT TO DO AFTER WRITING TESTS: WHEN AND HOW TO RUN THEM

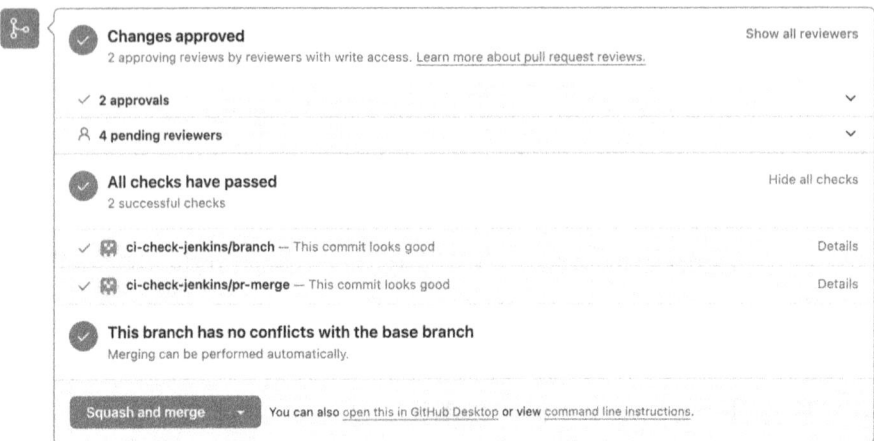

Figure 6-3. Merge checks

Summary

The key moments to run tests before merging code are `pre-commit`, `pre-push`, and during PR submissions. These checkpoints help ensure code quality and prevent code changes from negatively affecting the existing codebase. In addition to manually triggering tests during development or running tests before merging code, once a PR is merged into the main branch, continuous testing is essential to ensure long-term product stability. The next section will cover how to automate tests in CI.

Notes

- Note 1: In Git version control, the staged phase refers to changes that have been added to the index but not yet committed. Developers can use the `git add` command to stage changes and later commit them using `git commit`. More details about Git's file management process can be found in Gao Jianlong's book *Learn Git for Yourself* under the chapter "Working Directory, Staging Area, and Repository" (https://gitbook.tw/chapters/using-git/working-staging-and-repository#google_vignette).

- Note 2: Husky (https://typicode.github.io/husky/) is a tool that enables Git hooks to execute tasks like code formatting and testing before actions such as committing code to avoid polluting the codebase.

- Note 3: Lint-Staged (https://github.com/okonet/lint-staged) is used to specify the scope of checks by only running tasks on modified files instead of the entire project. It can also define different commands based on file types.

Running Tests Regularly in CI

In software development, testing is an essential part of ensuring product quality and reliability. Beyond manual testing during development and automated testing before merging code, most projects also schedule tests after PRs are merged into the main branch or set up regular testing (e.g., every night at 10 p.m.).

If comprehensive testing is done before merging code, why run tests again afterward? Here are the main reasons:

- Code interactions: Once merged, the code can interact in unexpected ways, causing issues that were not initially foreseen.

- Test instability: Some tests may be unstable, resulting in intermittent success or failure due to environmental or other factors (Note 1).

- Test cost or limitations: Certain high-cost end-to-end tests or tests requiring specialized environments may not be feasible in a developer's environment and thus need to be run in the CI environment.

Therefore, post-merge testing helps address potential gaps in pre-merge testing and further enhances product quality and stability.

Should Code Be Merged into the Main Branch When Tests Fail?

When tests fail, should the code still be merged into the main branch? This is a question worth considering from the following perspectives:

Can the root cause of the test failure be quickly identified and fixed?

- If yes, the issue should be fixed before continuing the code merge process.
- If not, the failing tests can be temporarily disabled and marked for future resolution, allowing time to fix the issues before re-enabling the tests.

Based on this, the potential risks of continuing to merge code when tests fail include the following:

- Failing to address issues may result in an accumulation of problems, making debugging and resolution more difficult later.
- Prolonged test failures can lead to fatigue among managers and developers, increasing the likelihood of overlooking the impact of test failures.

Considering these factors, it is recommended to pause code merges into the main branch when tests fail and resume merging only after the issues are fixed.

How to Reduce the Likelihood of Test Failures After Code Merges?

If test failures frequently occur after merging code, improvements can be made in the following areas:

- Identify and fix flaky tests: Flaky tests are prone to fail due to environmental or other factors, such as incomplete or incorrect test data or unstable test environments.

- Find better test implementation methods: Different products or teams may require different testing approaches. For example, for products that undergo frequent iterations, unit testing or integration testing, which focus on smaller scope tests, may be more suitable for quickly identifying and resolving issues.

- Narrow the scope of tests: Smaller tests make it easier to pinpoint issues. For instance, breaking a single end-to-end test case into multiple unit or integration test cases can help identify problems more efficiently, improving confidence and accuracy.

Implementing these strategies can effectively reduce the likelihood of test failures after merging code, ensuring greater product stability.

Notes

- Note 1: For more details and examples on "flaky tests," see Chapter 7, section "Why Do Some Test Cases Succeed Sometimes and Fail Other Times?"

Inferring Use Case Coverage from Code Coverage

Code coverage refers to the proportion of code that has been tested, while use case coverage refers to the proportion of test cases that cover all the features and scenarios of a project or product.

Traditionally, we have used code coverage to assess the quality of tests, but this approach has several limitations:

- Doesn't truly reflect product quality: Code coverage only shows how much of the code is tested, but it doesn't indicate whether the tests achieve their intended goals. For example, even if code coverage reaches 100%, there might still be important features or scenarios that are untested.

- Cannot provide effective testing recommendations: Code coverage can tell us which parts of the code need testing, but it doesn't tell us which parts are critical and should be prioritized for testing. Additionally, it doesn't indicate under which scenarios certain code is executed, making it ineffective in guiding test writing.

While code coverage is not a perfect metric, it can still serve as a helpful tool for identifying potential untested parts of the code. The following discussion explores how to use code coverage to infer use case coverage, improving testing effectiveness and achieving comprehensive feature coverage.

For example, let's consider a <Count> component where the number updates after 0.5 seconds when the user clicks the + or - button.

```
// src/Count/Count.js
const Count = () => {
  const [counter, setCounter] = useState(0);
```

CHAPTER 6 WHAT TO DO AFTER WRITING TESTS: WHEN AND HOW TO RUN THEM

```
  const delayCount = () => {
    setTimeout(() => {
      setCounter((prevCounter) => prevCounter + 1);
    }, 500);
  };

  return (
    <>
      <h1 data-test-id="counter">{counter}</h1>
      <button data-test-id="button-up" onClick={delayCount}>
        +
      </button>
      <button
        data-test-id="button-down"
        onClick={() => setCounter((prevCounter) =>
        prevCounter - 1)}
      >
        -
      </button>
    </>
  );
};
```

First, we test the current functionality with the following test for the `<Count>` component. The test simulates a user clicking the + button, then checks whether the `counter` value updates to 1 after 0.5 seconds.

```
// src/Count/Count.test.js
beforeAll(() => {
  jest.useFakeTimers();
});
afterAll(() => {
```

219

```
  jest.useRealTimers();
});

it('should get 1 when click + button', () => {
  const { getByTestId } = render(<Count />);
  fireEvent.click(getByTestId('button-up'));

  act(() => {
    jest.advanceTimersByTime(500);
  });

  expect(getByTestId('counter')).toHaveTextContent('1');
});
```

This unit test for the `<Count>` component fully renders the component using React Testing Library's render method and retrieves elements using getByTestId. The test simulates clicking the + button with `fireEvent.click`, and the act function ensures that asynchronous updates are properly handled. Finally, Jest's expect assertion checks whether the counter updates to 1 after the button is clicked.

Now, running the following command executes the tests and generates the test coverage report:

`yarn test Count.test.js --coverage`

The results for `Count.js` are shown below:

```
----------|---------|----------|---------|---------|-------------------
File      | % Stmts | % Branch | % Funcs | % Lines | Uncovered Line #s
----------|---------|----------|---------|---------|-------------------
All files |  77.77  |   100    |  66.66  |  85.71  |
 Count.js |  77.77  |   100    |  66.66  |  85.71  | 20
----------|---------|----------|---------|---------|-------------------
```

CHAPTER 6   WHAT TO DO AFTER WRITING TESTS: WHEN AND HOW TO RUN THEM

Explanation of each part of the report:

- `File`: The name of the file being tested, in this case, `Count.js`.

- `% Stmts` (statements coverage): The percentage of code statements that have been tested. In this example, `Count.js` has 77% statement coverage.

- `% Branch` (branch coverage): The percentage of code branches (e.g., `if` statements) that have been tested. Since `Count.js` has no branches, it shows 100% branch coverage.

- `% Funcs` (function coverage): The percentage of functions that have been tested. In this example, `Count.js` has three functions (the + button's onClick, the - button's onClick, and `delayCount`). Only two of them have been tested, giving a 66.66% function coverage.

- `% Lines` (line coverage): The percentage of lines of code that have been tested. In this example, `Count.js` has 28 lines of code (including blank lines), of which 24 are covered by tests, resulting in 85.71% line coverage.

- `Uncovered Line #s`: The specific line numbers not covered by tests. In this case, line 20 in `Count.js` is uncovered.

Next, use the test framework's report to analyze which parts of the code remain untested, and write corresponding test cases. Specifically, review the uncovered code, consider the scenarios where it would be executed, and implement tests for those scenarios. In this example, the uncovered line is line 20, which handles decrementing the counter.

CHAPTER 6   WHAT TO DO AFTER WRITING TESTS: WHEN AND HOW TO RUN THEM

```
// src/Count/Count.js
18  <button
19    data-test-id="button-down"
20    onClick={() => setCounter(prevCounter => prevCounter - 1)}
21  >
```

When would this line of code be executed? When the user clicks the - button to decrement the counter. Write a test case where clicking the - button results in the counter displaying -1. The test implementation is shown below:

```
// src/Count/Count.test.js
it('should get -1 when click - button', () => {
  const { getByTestId } = render(<Count />);

  act(() => {
    fireEvent.click(getByTestId('button-down'));
  });

  expect(getByTestId('counter')).toHaveTextContent('-1');
});
```

After modifying and adding the new test, run the tests again. The updated report will show full coverage:

```
----------|---------|----------|---------|---------|-------------------
File      | % Stmts | % Branch | % Funcs | % Lines | Uncovered Line #s
----------|---------|----------|---------|---------|-------------------
All files |   100   |   100    |   100   |   100   |
 Count.js |   100   |   100    |   100   |   100   |
----------|---------|----------|---------|---------|-------------------
```

CHAPTER 6   WHAT TO DO AFTER WRITING TESTS: WHEN AND HOW TO RUN THEM

While this improves code coverage to 100%, it also covers more usage scenarios. The benefit of this approach is that it helps developers identify untested code and implement tests based on the corresponding use cases, increasing the overall effectiveness of the tests.

Conclusion

When evaluating the application and determining what to test, code coverage does not provide deep insights into where most of the testing efforts should be focused. Therefore, it is essential to consider (1) the scenarios in which the code will be executed and (2) which tests can cover those scenarios. Use case coverage, which focuses on whether the tests cover all the features and usage scenarios of a project or product, is a better metric.

Chapter Review and Summary

- Automated testing can be performed manually via scripts or using a test runner within the testing framework. By leveraging different testing methods, assistance and feedback can be provided at various stages of the development lifecycle.

- To ensure that the codebase functions correctly before merging code back into the main branch, it is recommended to run as many tests as possible. Key moments for executing tests before merging include `pre-commit`, `pre-push`, and testing when submitting a pull request (PR). Since `git commit` can be triggered frequently during development, executing too many tests or lengthy tests during `pre-commit` can disrupt development or lead to excessive wait times. A more balanced approach is to allocate some tasks to `pre-push` instead.

- Whether tests are manually triggered during development or executed before merging, most projects also schedule tests after the code has been merged into the main branch or set up routine, periodic tests to ensure long-term, stable product performance. It's important to pause merging code into the main branch when tests fail and resume merging only after issues are resolved.

- As use case coverage focuses on whether tests cover all functionalities and scenarios of the project and product, it is considered a better metric. It's recommended to infer use case coverage from code coverage to write effective tests and achieve comprehensive functionality coverage.

CHAPTER 7

Frequently Asked Questions

What to Do When UI Updates Cause Test Failures?

Front-end developers often encounter a common issue after implementing tests: whenever the UI is updated, the tests fail, requiring corresponding adjustments, which can be time-consuming and labor-intensive. Is there a way to reduce the frequency or extent of these adjustments to save maintenance costs?

There are two main reasons why tests easily fail due to UI updates:

- The method for selecting elements is too loose, too strict, or lacks clear meaning.
- The test contains too many implementation details.

Let's break down each of these issues and provide solutions.

CHAPTER 7   FREQUENTLY ASKED QUESTIONS

The Element Selection Method Is Too Loose, Strict, or Lacks Clear Meaning

The Element Selection Method Is Too Loose

For example, consider the following code for the <Hello> component. How should we test that the string "This is test text" is correctly rendered?

```
// src/Hello/Hello.js

const Hello = () => {
  return (
    <div>
      This is a box
      <div>This is test text</div>
    </div>
  );
};
```

Let's try selecting the text directly for testing. Using React Testing Library's getByText to match the text can find the correct element. In this code snippet, the render method from React Testing Library fully renders the <Hello> component. Then, getByText is used to retrieve the corresponding DOM element based on the expected text. We can then use textContent to get the actual text and use an expect assertion to check if it matches the expected string "This is test text." Here, using toHaveTextContent is recommended for asserting the DOM element's text content because it provides a more readable and semantic way to verify the content. However, for demonstration purposes, we'll temporarily use the current approach and explain more later.

```
// src/Hello/Hello.test.js

it('should render the correct content', () => {
  const { getByText } = render(<Hello />);
```

```
expect(getByText('This is test text').textContent).toBe('This 
is test text'); // Recommended to use toHaveTextContent
});
```

Now, if the text changes to "This is not test text," two things need to be updated: the element selection and the comparison string, which doesn't seem ideal.

```
// src/Hello/Hello.test.js

it('should render the correct content', () => {
  const { getByText } = render(<Hello />);

  // Both places must be changed to "This is not test text"
  expect(getByText('This is test text').textContent).toBe('This 
is test text'); // Recommended to use toHaveTextContent
});
```

In this case, the line `expect(getByText('...').textContent).toBe('...')` should be changed to use `toHaveTextContent`. Why? When comparing the text content of a specific element, both `textContent` with `toBe` and `toHaveTextContent` can be used to assert the content.

Here's an example using `textContent` with `toBe`:

```
expect(getByTestId('sample-id').textContent).toBe('sample 
text...');
```

If the content doesn't match the expectation, the test will fail with an error message like

```
expect(received).toBe(expected)
    Expected: "sample text..."
    Received: "Hello World"
```

CHAPTER 7   FREQUENTLY ASKED QUESTIONS

An example using `toHaveTextContent`:

```
expect(getByTestId('sample-id')).toHaveTextContent('sample text...');
```

If the content doesn't match the expectation, the test will fail with an error message like

```
Expected element to have text content:
    sample text...
  Received:
    Hello World
```

Here are the differences between `textContent` with `toBe` and `toHaveTextContent`:

- `textContent` is a DOM element property that retrieves the text content. It directly accesses the element's text but doesn't provide semantic validation like `toHaveTextContent`. Using a matcher like `toBe` may compare more details than just text, including HTML details, which can lead to brittle tests and reduced flexibility.

- `toHaveTextContent`, from the `@testing-library/jest-dom` library, is a Jest matcher that checks if an element contains specific text. It offers a more readable and semantic way to verify text content. For example, error messages from `toBe` may not clearly indicate the root cause, while `toHaveTextContent` clearly states when the string differs from expectations. Using `toHaveTextContent` improves test readability and provides more useful error messages when tests fail, making it the recommended approach.

CHAPTER 7　FREQUENTLY ASKED QUESTIONS

Now, let's consider another case where the <Hello> component has two instances of the text "This is test text." Initially, we expected only one instance, but using getByText can only select one element, leading to test failures since multiple elements now contain the same text. If we want to select just one, using text content as the selection method will make it difficult to identify the correct instance. Essentially, when there are multiple elements with the same text, selecting based on text alone is too loose.

```
// src/Hello/Hello.js

const Hello = () => {
  return (
    <div>
      This is a box
      <div>This is test text</div>
      <div>This is test text</div>
    </div>
  );
};
```

If we really need to know how many elements contain "This is test text," we can use getAllByText and queryAllByTestId to select all matching elements and then make assertions. For example, the following code uses getAllByText to find elements with data-test-id="text-1" and queryAllByTestId to find elements with data-test-id="text-2". If these elements are not present, getAllByTestId('text-1') will throw an error like Unable to find an element by: [data-test-id="text-1"], while queryAllByTestId('text-2') will return an empty array [].

```
// src/Hello/Hello.test.js

// Will throw an error, useful for asserting the existence of a
specific number of elements
expect(getAllByTestId('text-1')).toHaveLength(0);
```

229

```
// Will return an empty array [], useful when retrieving
multiple elements under unknown conditions
expect(queryAllByTestId('text-2')).toHaveLength(0);
```

Both getAllByText and queryAllByTestId are matchers provided by Testing Library to retrieve elements with a specific data-test-id attribute. The difference is that getAllByText throws an error if it doesn't find the expected number of elements, making it useful for asserting exact counts, while queryAllByTestId returns an empty array and is useful for iterating over multiple elements.

The Element Selection Method Is Too Strict

Consider the following example where XPath /div/div is used to select the element containing the text "This is test text" (Note 1):

```
// src/Hello/Hello.js

const Hello = () => {
  return (
    <div>
      This is a box
      <div>This is test text</div>
    </div>
  );
};
```

If the component is updated and the tag is changed from <div> to <p>, the selection path must be updated to /div/p. This is common when refactoring or adjusting component structures. This scenario exemplifies how using an overly strict selection method can cause unnecessary test failures. Relying on XPath to select elements is rigid; any changes to the HTML structure require rewriting the selection rules, making it highly inflexible.

```
// src/Hello/Hello.js

const Hello = () => {
  return (
    <div>
      This is a box
      <p>This is test text</p>
    </div>
  );
};
```

The Element Selection Method Is Not Clear Enough

What if you use a class name to select the element, like using the `.text` selector?

```
// src/Hello/Hello.js

const Hello = () => {
  return (
    <div>
      This is a box
      <div className="text">This is test text</div>
    </div>
  );
};
```

The test might look like this. In this code, Cypress is used for testing. First, the `<Hello>` component is rendered into Cypress's testing environment using `cy.mount`. Then, the `cy.get` method selects the element with the class name `.text`. Finally, Cypress's built-in Chai assertion tool `should` checks if the element's text content is "This is test text."

CHAPTER 7   FREQUENTLY ASKED QUESTIONS

```
// src/Hello/Hello.cy.js

it('should show image title correctly', () => {
  cy.mount(<Hello />);

  cy.get('.text').should('have.text', 'This is test text');
});
```

Since class names are usually associated with styles, combining them with tests may lead to test failures when modifying the UI. For example, if the style class is changed from .text to .content, the developer must decide whether to remove .text and only keep .content or retain both. This requires developers to inspect the code carefully, making it unclear whether a class name is for styling or testing purposes.

```
const Hello = () => {
  return (
    <div>
      This is a box
      <div className="text content">This is test text</div>
    </div>
  );
};
```

In this example, if you remove .text, the test will fail. However, keeping both may seem redundant and could introduce maintenance issues later.

```
const Hello = () => {
  return (
    <div>
      This is a box
      <div className="content">This is test text</div>
    </div>
  );
};
```

The test must be updated as follows, changing .text to .content for it to work correctly. But if the class name is changed again in the future, the test will need updating again, still causing test failures due to UI changes.

```
// src/Hello/Hello.cy.js
it('should show image title correctly', () => {
  cy.mount(<Hello />);

  cy.get('.content').should('have.text', 'This is test text');
});
```

This unclear selection method not only causes test failures after code changes but also requires developers to carefully review the code for necessary adjustments, which can be time-consuming. It is recommended that element selection methods be clearly defined and not mixed. One approach is to use a data-* attribute, as discussed in the next section.

Using data-* attribute for Focused and Flexible Element Selection

When selecting elements, using data-* attributes (such as data-test-id) provides focus as it can be specifically named for testing purposes. Additionally, since this method is unrelated to HTML structure or styles, it offers greater flexibility.

```
// src/Hello/Hello.js
const Hello = () => {
  return (
    <div>
      This is a box
      <div data-test-id="text">This is test text</div>
    </div>
  );
};
```

Here's an example of a test. Regardless of future structural or styling changes, as long as the `data-test-id` remains as `text`, it will consistently provide access to the element's content or interactions. This avoids issues where the selector is too strict, too loose, or unclear in meaning. In other words, as long as the `data-test-id` remains unchanged, the test will work properly and won't easily fail.

```
// src/Hello/Hello.test.js
```

```
it('should render the correct content 2', () => {
  const { getByTestId } = render(<Hello />);

  expect(getByTestId('text')).toHaveTextContent('This is test text');
});
```

Tests with Too Many Implementation Details

Excessive Mocking

Mocking replaces real implementation details in tests with simulated code to ensure that the test code can correctly interact with the objects it depends on. However, when a feature changes, the test code using mocks also needs to be updated. If not, the test will fail.

For example, in a test, `<ImageItem>` is mocked to replace the real implementation.

```
// src/ImageList/ImagesList.mock.test.js
```

```
jest.mock('./ImageItem', () => () => (
  <div data-test-id="image-item-title">ImageItem</div>
));
```

CHAPTER 7   FREQUENTLY ASKED QUESTIONS

Here's the actual implementation of <ImageItem>:

```
// src/ImageList/ImageItem.js

const ImageItem = ({ title, image }) => {
  return (
    <div data-test-id="image-item">
      <img alt={title} data-test-id="image-item-src"
      src={image} />
      <p data-test-id="image-item-title">{title}</p>
    </div>
  );
};
```

If later <ImageItem> is updated, changing the test attribute data-test-id from image-item-title to image-item-name, both the real and mock code need to be updated to ensure the test's correctness.

```
// src/ImageList/ImagesList.mock.test.js

jest.mock('./ImageItem', () => () => (
  // Changed from image-item-title to image-item-name
  <div data-test-id="image-item-name">ImageItem</div>
));
```

Updated actual implementation of <ImageItem>:

```
const ImageItem = ({ title, image }) => {
  // Changed from image-item-title to image-item-name
  return (
    <div data-test-id="image-item">
      <img alt={title} data-test-id="image-item-src"
      src={image} />
      <p data-test-id="image-item-name">{title}</p>
    </div>
  );
};
```

CHAPTER 7   FREQUENTLY ASKED QUESTIONS

Excessive mocking in test implementation can lead to discrepancies between the mock and the real code, making it hard to ensure the test correctly interacts with the actual implementation. Maintaining both the real and mock code separately is difficult and relies heavily on manual updates, which makes it challenging to ensure the effectiveness of the tests and manage code quality. Therefore, unless necessary, tests should aim to be as real as possible, minimizing the use of mocks, avoiding overly fake data, and fully rendering components. This allows for more comprehensive testing of the functionality, ensuring that integrated components can work together correctly and achieve the expected outcomes in a real environment (Note 2).

Snapshots

Snapshots capture implementation details, so even small changes like adding a class name or updating a `data-*` attribute will cause tests to fail. Fixing these tests can be time-consuming and resource-intensive. Too many changes lead to wasted resources. Therefore, it is not recommended to use snapshots to capture implementation details (Note 3).

```
// src/ImageList/__snapshots__/ImageListAxios.snapshot.jest.test.js.snap

exports[`ImageList should render correct image items when have data 1`] = `
Array [
  <div
    data-test-id="image-item"
  >
    <img
      alt="Building a high-speed website, starting with web metrics! Key to enhancing user experience and traffic"
```

```
      data-test-id="image-item-src"
      src="https://bit.ly/4228ITO"
    />
    <p
      data-test-id="image-item-title"
    >
      Building a high-speed website, starting with web metrics!
      Key to enhancing user experience and traffic
    </p>
  </div>,
  <div
    data-test-id="image-item"
  >
    <img
      alt="Shimanami Kaido: Island-hopping cycling adventure"
      data-test-id="image-item-src"
      src="https://bit.ly/4b5nLPO"
    />
    <p
      data-test-id="image-item-title"
    >
      Shimanami Kaido: Island-hopping cycling adventure
    </p>
  </div>,
]
```

Comparing Details

When selecting elements for comparison, we often capture the entire DOM element and then extract its value. For example, getByTestId('item-quantity') will capture the following HTML structure:

```
<div data-test-id="item-quantity">2</div>
```

CHAPTER 7   FREQUENTLY ASKED QUESTIONS

To compare the content of this element, we can use either `getByTestId` with `toBe` or `toHaveTextContent` to extract the value. Which is better? Using `expect(getByTestId('item-quantity')).toHaveTextContent('2')` compares the string 2 extracted from the DOM element. As long as the `data-test-id` remains unchanged, the test will pass, and it won't fail due to changes in the structure. On the other hand, `expect(getByTestId('item-quantity')).toBe('2')` would compare the exact HTML structure `<div data-test-id="item-quantity">2</div>`, which would fail if the HTML structure changes. Therefore, using `toHaveTextContent` is more flexible and is the recommended approach.

Other similar examples include the following:

- Using `toHaveStyle` to check if the element a user hovers over in a list is highlighted with a specific color.

  `expect(selectItem).toHaveStyle({ backgroundColor: '#5e5e5e' });`

- Not all detailed checks are unreasonable. For instance, using `toHaveProperty` to ensure a submit button is disabled when a form is incomplete is valid because a form that hasn't passed validation should not be submitted. This test checks business logic, not just the UI display.

  `expect(button).toHaveProperty('disabled', true);`

- Using `toContainHTML` to verify if the `<TextBold>` component correctly bolds the text. Tests involving UI display are often fragile since they can involve many implementation details. However, in this case, it's reasonable because the component's purpose is to bold text using the `<strong>` HTML tag, so we need to ensure it works as expected.

```
    expect(textBoldComponent.getByTestId('bold-text')).
    toContainHTML(

      '<strong>test</strong>'

    );
```

Developers can find the most suitable testing method based on different scenarios. When writing tests, choosing the appropriate level of detail ensures that the tests are flexible and maintainable.

Splitting Logic, State, and UI Rendering

When testing components, separating logic and UI rendering can lead to more efficient testing. By appropriately splitting logic, state, and UI rendering—encapsulating business logic and data state in a custom hook and leaving only the display portion in the component—you can achieve more effective testing (Note 4).

For example, here's a calculator component <Calculator>, which includes two input fields for entering numbers, a drop-down menu for selecting the operator (+, -, *, /), and a button to perform the calculation. The following code uses the useState hook to store the user's input and operator, defines a handleChange function to handle changes in the input fields and drop-down menu, and defines a calculateResult function to compute the result based on the two numbers. Finally, the component renders the input fields, drop-down, calculate button, and result display, with corresponding data-test-id attributes for easy element targeting during testing.

```
// src/Calculator/Calculator.advanced.js
const Calculator = () => {
  const [num1, setNum1] = useState('');
  const [num2, setNum2] = useState('');
  const [operator, setOperator] = useState('+');
  const [result, setResult] = useState('');
```

CHAPTER 7   FREQUENTLY ASKED QUESTIONS

```
const handleChange = (e) => {
  const { name, value } = e.target;
  if (name === 'num1') {
    setNum1(value);
  } else if (name === 'num2') {
    setNum2(value);
  } else if (name === 'operator') {
    setOperator(value);
  }
};

const calculateResult = () => {
  const parsedNum1 = parseFloat(num1);
  const parsedNum2 = parseFloat(num2);

  switch (operator) {
    case '+':
      setResult(parsedNum1 + parsedNum2);
      break;
    case '-':
      setResult(parsedNum1 - parsedNum2);
      break;
    case '*':
      setResult(parsedNum1 * parsedNum2);
      break;
    case '/':
      setResult(parsedNum1 / parsedNum2);
      break;
    default:
      setResult('Invalid operator');
  }
};
```

```
return (
  <div>
    <input
      data-test-id="number1"
      type="number"
      name="num1"
      value={num1}
      onChange={handleChange}
    />
    <select
      data-test-id="operator"
      name="operator"
      value={operator}
      onChange={handleChange}
    >
      <option value="+">+</option>
      <option value="-">-</option>
      <option value="*">*</option>
      <option value="/">/</option>
    </select>
    <input
      data-test-id="number2"
      type="number"
      name="num2"
      value={num2}
      onChange={handleChange}
    />
    <button data-test-id="calculate"
    onClick={calculateResult}>
      Calculate
    </button>
```

```
      <div data-test-id="result">{result}</div>
    </div>
  );
};
```

In the above code, since the component handles the UI rendering, calculation logic, and state management, none of these parts can be easily reused. Ideally, we would refactor the component to encapsulate the calculation-related business logic and data state within a custom hook, useCalculatorHook, leaving only the UI rendering in the <Calculator> component. The benefit of this approach is that it makes the code more maintainable, testable, and reusable, and it simplifies collaborative and phased development. Here's how the refactored hook would look, making it easy to reuse the calculator logic by simply using useCalculatorHook in the future:

```
// src/Calculator/useCalculatorHook.js
const useCalculatorHook = () => {
  const [num1, setNum1] = useState(0);
  const [num2, setNum2] = useState(0);
  const [operator, setOperator] = useState('+');
  const [result, setResult] = useState(0);

  const handleChange = (e) => {
    const { name, value } = e.target;
    if (name === 'num1') {
      setNum1(value);
    } else if (name === 'num2') {
      setNum2(value);
    } else if (name === 'operator') {
      setOperator(value);
    }
  };
};
```

```
  const calculate = () => {
    switch (operator) {
      case '+':
        setResult(num1 + num2);
        break;
      case '-':
        setResult(num1 - num2);
        break;
      case '*':
        setResult(num1 * num2);
        break;
      case '/':
        setResult(num1 / num2);
        break;
      default:
        setResult(0);
    }
  };

  return {
    calculate,
    handleChange,
    num1,
    num2,
    operator,
    result,
  };
};
```

CHAPTER 7   FREQUENTLY ASKED QUESTIONS

Refactor the <Calculator> component as follows, focusing the <Calculator> component solely on UI rendering, making it easier to understand, test, and maintain:

```
// src/Calculator/Calculator.advanced-refactor.js

import useCalculatorHook from './useCalculatorHook';

const Calculator = () => {
  const { calculate, handleChange, num1, num2, operator,
  result } =
    useCalculatorHook();

  return (
    <>
      <input
        data-test-id="number1"
        type="number"
        value={num1}
        onChange={handleChange}
      />
      <select data-test-id="operator" value={operator}
      onChange={handleChange}>
        <option value="+">+</option>
        <option value="-">-</option>
        <option value="*">*</option>
        <option value="/">/</option>
      </select>
      <input
        data-test-id="number2"
        type="number"
        value={num2}
        onChange={handleChange}
      />
```

CHAPTER 7　FREQUENTLY ASKED QUESTIONS

```
      <button onClick={calculate}>Calculate</button>
      <div data-test-id="result">{result}</div>
    </>
  );
};
```

Since the calculator has now been split into the <Calculator> component and the useCalculatorHook, you can write separate tests for each part. The following test case checks whether the result of 5 * 3 is 15. In this example, the test simulates the user's actions, including entering numbers, selecting the operator, and clicking the button to get the result. This testing method is appropriate because it approaches testing from the user's perspective, making it more comprehensive and flexible. Additionally, it is less likely to fail due to implementation changes, which helps reduce the effort required to maintain the tests.

```
// src/Calculator/Calculator.advanced.test.js

describe('Calculator', () => {
  it('should get 15 when 5 is multiplied by 3', () => {
    const { getByTestId } = render(<Calculator />);

    // Input numbers
    fireEvent.change(getByTestId('number1'), { target: { value: '5' } });
    fireEvent.change(getByTestId('number2'), { target: { value: '3' } });

    // Select operator
    fireEvent.change(getByTestId('operator'), { target: { value: '*' } });
```

CHAPTER 7   FREQUENTLY ASKED QUESTIONS

```
    // Click calculate button
    fireEvent.click(getByTestId('calculate'));

    // Verify result
    expect(getByTestId('result')).toHaveTextContent('15');
  });
});
```

Now that the test for <Calculator> has been written, let's write the test for useCalculatorHook. The following test case is for the scenario where adding 5 and 3 results in 8. Notice that the test method involves using the exported function to input numbers, select the operator, and call the calculate function to get the result.

```
// src/Calculator/useCalculatorHook.test.js

describe('useCalculatorHook', () => {
  test('should get 8 when adding 5 and 3', () => {
    const TestComponent = () => {
      const {
        calculate,
        handleNum1Change,
        handleNum2Change,
        handleOperatorChange,
        num1,
        num2,
        operator,
        result,
      } = useCalculatorHook();

      return (
        <div>
          <input
            data-test-id="number1"
```

```jsx
      value={num1}
      onChange={handleNum1Change}
    />
    <select
      data-test-id="operator"
      value={operator}
      onChange={handleOperatorChange}
    >
      <option value="+">+</option>
    </select>
    <input
      data-test-id="number2"
      value={num2}
      onChange={handleNum2Change}
    />
    <button data-test-id="calculate" onClick={calculate}>
      Calculate
    </button>
    <div data-test-id="result">{result}</div>
  </div>
  );
};

const { getByTestId } = render(<TestComponent />);

// Input numbers
fireEvent.change(getByTestId('number1'), { target: { value: '5' } });
fireEvent.change(getByTestId('number2'), { target: { value: '3' } });

// Select operator
fireEvent.change(getByTestId('operator'), { target: { value: '+' } });
```

```
    // Click calculate button
    fireEvent.click(getByTestId('calculate'));

    // Verify result
    expect(getByTestId('result')).toHaveTextContent('8');
  });
});
```

When writing tests, the biggest issue is when changes to the UI break the tests. To avoid this, tests should not be too dependent on UI details. If the UI is constantly changing or is not yet finalized, it's a good idea to start by writing tests for the hooks, which will ensure functionality works correctly. Once the UI is stable, you can add component-related tests. Therefore, separating logic, state, and UI display by encapsulating business logic and data state in custom hooks, while leaving UI-specific parts in the component, leads to better testing outcomes.

Summary

To minimize the issue of tests breaking whenever the UI is updated, follow these principles when writing test code:

- Use `data-*` attributes to maintain focus and flexibility when selecting elements.
- Avoid testing with too much implementation detail, such as reducing mocks, avoiding snapshots for recording implementation details, and choosing test methods that do not involve comparing detailed UI structures.
- Separate logic, state, and UI display to simplify the scope of the tests and improve efficiency.

This approach will help reduce the cost of maintaining tests, saving both time and effort.

Notes

- Note 1: XPath (XML Path Language) is a query language used to locate nodes in an XML document. It uses path expressions to describe the relationships between nodes, allowing precise targeting of specific nodes within the XML structure. XPath is also commonly used for locating elements in HTML documents for automated web testing.

- Note 2: For more information on "mocking" and related topics, see Chapter 3, section "Mocking Components, API Responses, and Third-Party Libraries."

- Note 3: For more details on "snapshots," refer to Chapter 3, section "Snapshots."

- Note 4: For discussions on how to write tests for components, see Chapter 2, section "How to Write Tests for Components? A React Example."

How to Handle Duplicate Tests?

During software development, functionality is often developed in phases, and each phase typically involves implementing suitable tests to ensure product and code quality. For example, when developing a calculator's addition function, we can break down the implementation as follows.

In the first phase, we implement an addNumbers function:

```
// src/utils/addNumbers/addNumbers.js

const addNumbers = (a, b) => Number((a + b).toFixed(1));
```

CHAPTER 7 FREQUENTLY ASKED QUESTIONS

Here, we will examine three test cases:

- Test if 0.1 plus 0.2 equals 0.3 to check floating-point addition.

- Test if 5 plus -3 equals 2 to check negative number addition.

- Test if 5 plus 3 equals 8 to check positive number addition.

We write unit tests for addNumbers as shown below:

```
// src/utils/addNumbers/addNumbers.test.js

test('should return 0.3 when 0.1 + 0.2', () => {
  expect(addNumbers(0.1, 0.2)).toBe(0.3);
});

test('should get 2 when add 5 and -3', () => {
  expect(addNumbers(5, -3)).toBe(2);
});

test('should get 8 when add 5 and 3', () => {
  expect(addNumbers(5, 3)).toBe(8);
});
```

In the second phase, we implement a calculator component <Calculator>, which includes two input fields for numbers and a button to execute the calculation:

```
// src/Calculator/Calculator.js

const Calculator = () => {
  const [su, setSu] = useState(0);
  const [ad, setAd] = useState(0);
  const [result, setResult] = useState(0);
```

CHAPTER 7 FREQUENTLY ASKED QUESTIONS

```
const getResult = () => {
  const result = addNumbers(Number(su), Number(ad));
  setResult(result);
};

return (
  <>
    <input
      type="number"
      data-test-id="number-su"
      onChange={(e) => setSu(e.target.value)}
    />
    +
    <input
      type="number"
      data-test-id="number-ad"
      onChange={(e) => setAd(e.target.value)}
    />
    =<span data-test-id="result">{result}</span>
    <button data-test-id="get-result-button"
    onClick={getResult}>
      Get result!
    </button>
  </>
);
};
```

Now, let's write unit tests for the <Calculator> component as follows. In this code, we use React Testing Library's render method to fully render the <Calculator> component, use getByTestId to access elements on the page, simulate user input using fireEvent.change, and simulate button clicks using fireEvent.click. Finally, we use toHaveTextContent to compare the content of the result and use the expect assertion to check if the result equals the expected string "8."

CHAPTER 7 FREQUENTLY ASKED QUESTIONS

```js
// src/Calculator/Calculator.test.js
describe('Calculator', () => {
  test('should get 8 when add 5 and 3', () => {
    const { getByTestId } = render(<Calculator />);

    const suInput = getByTestId('number-su');
    const adInput = getByTestId('number-ad');
    const getResultButton = getByTestId('get-result-button');
    const result = getByTestId('result');

    act(() => {
      fireEvent.change(suInput, { target: { value: '5' } });
      fireEvent.change(adInput, { target: { value: '3' } });
      fireEvent.click(getResultButton);
    });

    expect(result).toHaveTextContent('8');
  });
});
```

At this point, both the addNumbers function and the <Calculator> component have unit tests to ensure the correctness of the addition functionality. However, upon reviewing the test code, we realize that the following test case is redundant with the UI component test for <Calculator>:

```js
test('should get 8 when add 5 and 3', () => {
  expect(addNumbers(5, 3)).toBe(8);
});
```

CHAPTER 7 FREQUENTLY ASKED QUESTIONS

So, how should we handle duplicate tests? Should we keep or remove them? This topic can be discussed from the following perspectives:

- As in this scenario, where features are developed in phases, and tests are written to ensure code quality at each step, duplicated tests may appear. Although the tests seem redundant, they serve different purposes and provide different insights. Unit tests offer precise problem-solving information, while integration tests are closer to user-level testing and cover more scenarios. Both types should be retained.

- If tests are written after feature development, the focus is typically on implementing integration tests. Depending on the product and development stage, the focus and types of tests may vary (Note 1). To speed up test execution, duplicate tests might be removed, such as the addNumbers test case in this case. Although the process may differ, the outcome remains the same. In practice, while unit tests can thoroughly test details and are less costly to implement, integration tests better reflect user scenarios and avoid resource waste, making them the preferred option.

Notes

- Note 1: For more on test structures, refer to Chapter 9, section "Summary."

CHAPTER 7   FREQUENTLY ASKED QUESTIONS

How to Test the Timer?

When testing time-related functionalities, it's impractical to actually wait for the specified duration. For example, if a countdown timer component is set to wait for 30 seconds, implementing a test that waits for 30 seconds would take too much time. Therefore, when testing time-related functions, we use fake timers to assist. What is a fake timer? It replaces the real timer in the test code with a substitute provided by the testing framework. In Jest, this is done using useFakeTimers.

Below is the implementation of the <Timer> component. It displays the remaining seconds and shows the message "Time's Up" after three seconds.

```js
// src/Timer/Timer.js

const Timer = () => {
  const [seconds, setSeconds] = useState(3);
  const intervalIDRef = useRef(null);
  const startTimer = useCallback(() => {
    intervalIDRef.current = setInterval(
      () => setSeconds((prev) => prev - 1),
      1000
    );
  }, []);

  const stopTimer = useCallback(() => {
    clearInterval(intervalIDRef.current);
    intervalIDRef.current = null;
  }, []);

  useEffect(() => {
    startTimer();
    return () => clearInterval(intervalIDRef.current);
  }, []);
```

CHAPTER 7   FREQUENTLY ASKED QUESTIONS

```
  useEffect(() => {
    if (seconds === 0) {
      stopTimer();
    }
  }, [seconds]);

  return (
    <div>
      {seconds === 0
        ? `<span data-test-id="time-up">Time\'s Up</span>`
        : `Remaining seconds: <span data-test-id="remain-
          time">${seconds}</span>`}
    </div>
  );
};
```

In the test code, we start by declaring the use of Jest's fake timers with useFakeTimers.

```
// src/Timer/Timer.test.js

jest.useFakeTimers();
```

We want to test that after one second, the message "Remaining seconds: 2" is displayed. In this test case, we fully render the <Timer> component using React Testing Library's render method (Note 1). Then, we use the jest.advanceTimersByTime function to fast-forward time, simulating the passage of one second. Finally, we use getByTestId to fetch the DOM element with the data-test-id attribute of remain-time, which holds the remaining time value, and assert using expect that it has correctly updated to two seconds. The act function is used to synchronize rendering with asynchronous behaviors in the test to ensure the component updates its state before rendering.

CHAPTER 7 FREQUENTLY ASKED QUESTIONS

```
// src/Timer/Timer.test.js
```

```
it('should show remaining 2 seconds after 1 second', () => {
  const { getByTestId } = render(<Timer />);

  act(() => {
    jest.advanceTimersByTime(1000); // Fast-forward time,
    simulating 1 second
  });

  expect(getByTestId('remain-time')).toBe('2');
});
```

Next, we test that the message "Time's Up" is displayed after three seconds. In this test case, we again fully render the <Timer> component and use jest.advanceTimersByTime to simulate the passage of three seconds. Finally, we retrieve the DOM element with data-test-id="time-up" and assert that the time-up message is displayed (Note 2).

```
// src/Timer/Timer.test.js
```

```
it("should show Time's Up after 3 seconds", () => {
  const { getByTestId } = render(<Timer />);

  act(() => {
    jest.advanceTimersByTime(3000); // Fast-forward time,
    simulating 3 seconds
  });

  expect(getByTestId('time-up')).toBeInTheDocument();
});
```

CHAPTER 7   FREQUENTLY ASKED QUESTIONS

Lastly, when testing time-related functionalities, it's important to verify that the timer is cleared when the component is unmounted. To check whether clearInterval is called when the component is removed, we use jest.spyOn to spy on clearInterval. The spyOnClearInterval object tracks the call (Note 3).

```
// src/Timer/Timer.test.js
it('should clean up the timer when unmounted', () => {
  const { unmount } = render(<Timer />);
  const spyOnClearInterval = jest.spyOn(global, 'clearInterval');

  unmount();

  expect(spyOnClearInterval).toHaveBeenCalledTimes(1);
});
```

This test ensures that the timer is correctly cleared when the component is unmounted. We fully render the <Timer> component using React Testing Library's render method and use jest.spyOn to listen for the global clearInterval method. The unmount method is called to simulate the component being removed. Finally, the test asserts that clearInterval was called once, ensuring the timer is properly cleared when the component is removed. Clearing timers is essential to avoid memory leaks and wasted resources. In JavaScript, if a timer is not cleared, it will continue running in memory, even after the related component is removed, potentially causing performance issues.

Using useFakeTimers allows developers to manipulate the timer like a time machine, freely moving forward or backward without waiting, making it much easier to test time-related functionalities.

CHAPTER 7   FREQUENTLY ASKED QUESTIONS

Notes

- Note 1: For more details on full rendering, see Chapter 2, section "Shallow Rendering and Full Rendering."
- Note 2: For detecting element presence in the DOM, quantity, or visibility status, see Chapter 3, section "Snapshots."
- Note 3: For the concepts of mock and spy testing, see Chapter 1, section "Mock, Spy, and Double."

How to Mock Only Part of a Module?

A module typically contains multiple methods, and developers may not always need to mock all of them when writing tests. Sometimes, only specific methods need to be mocked to produce desired inputs and outputs. How can we mock only part of a module? Let's use the bakeUtils module as an example to demonstrate how to mock just part of a module.

For example, the bakeUtils.js file contains several functions: bakeChocolatePudding, bakeLemonTart, bakeMatchaRoll, and bakeAllCakes, with bakeAllCakes being the default export.

```
// src/utils/bakeUtils/bakeUtils.js

const bakeChocolatePudding = () => 'Chocolate Pudding is baked.';

const bakeLemonTart = () => 'Lemon Tart is baked.';

const bakeMatchaRoll = () => 'Matcha Roll is baked.';

const bakeAllCakes = () =>
  'Chocolate Pudding, Lemon Tart and Matcha Roll are all baked.';

export default bakeAllCakes;
export { bakeChocolatePudding, bakeLemonTart, bakeMatchaRoll };
```

CHAPTER 7   FREQUENTLY ASKED QUESTIONS

Here's how to implement the test. Using jest.mock, we mock the bakeUtils module and use jest.requireActual('./bakeUtils') to get the real bakeUtils module. By passing in the functions that do not need to be mocked, we can preserve the implementation details we don't want to replace.

```
// src/utils/bakeUtils/bakeUtils.test.js

import bakeAllCakes, { bakeMatchaRoll } from './bakeUtils';

jest.mock('./bakeUtils', () => {
  const originalModule = jest.requireActual('./bakeUtils');

  return {
    __esModule: true,
    ...originalModule,
    default: jest
      .fn()
      .mockReturnValue('Chocolate Pudding and Matcha Roll are
      all baked.'),
  };
});
```

As a result, when bakeAllCakes is called, it executes the mocked version and returns the fake string "Chocolate Pudding and Matcha Roll are all baked" instead of the original result.

```
// src/utils/bakeUtils/bakeUtils.test.js

describe('bakeAllCakes', () => {
  it('should bake Chocolate Pudding and Matcha Roll', () => {
    expect(bakeAllCakes()).toBe(
      'Chocolate Pudding and Matcha Roll are all baked.'
    );
  });
});
```

However, when bakeMatchaRoll is called, since we preserved its original implementation, the output string remains unchanged.

```
// src/utils/bakeUtils/bakeUtils.test.js

describe('bakeMatchaRoll', () => {
  it('should bake Matcha Roll', () => {
    expect(bakeMatchaRoll()).toBe('Matcha Roll is baked.');
  });
});
```

This approach of mocking only part of a module allows developers to selectively control specific behaviors of a module while reducing unnecessary mocks, making the testing process more efficient.

How to Debug? What If an Element Can't Be Found? How Do You Trace the Data Flow?

When writing tests, you're often reviewing the results in the terminal without seeing the actual view in the browser. So what do you do when the test fails, and how do you debug it?

Let's explore the image list feature, which is implemented with two components: `<ImageList>` and `<ImageItem>` (Note 1). The purpose of this image list feature is to display the retrieved image data visually. The `<ImageList>` component is responsible for determining the display based on the fetched image data. If no image data is available, it shows a prompt to inform the user that no images are available; if there is image data, it uses the `<ImageItem>` component to display the images.

```
// src/ImageList/ImageListAxios.js

const ImageList = () => {
  const [images, setImages] = useState();
```

CHAPTER 7 FREQUENTLY ASKED QUESTIONS

```
  useEffect(() => {
    async function fetchData() {
      try {
        const response = await axios.get('https://dummyjson.
        com/products');
        setImages(response?.data?.products || );
      } catch (error) {
        throw error;
      }
    }
    fetchData();
  }, []);

  const renderImages = () => {
    return images.map(({ id, title, images }) => (
      <ImageItem key={id} title={title} image={images[0]} />
    ));
  };

  const renderNoDataPrompt = () => {
    return <div data-test-id="no-data-prompt">No data to
    display.</div>;
  };

  return <>{!!images.length ? renderImages() :
renderNoDataPrompt()}</>;
};
```

261

CHAPTER 7   FREQUENTLY ASKED QUESTIONS

Here's the test code:

```js
// src/ImageList/ImageListAxios.jest.test.js

it('should render correct image items when have data',
async () => {
  const mockedData = {
    list: [
      {
        id: '1',
        title: 'Build a Fast Website: Improve User Experience
        and Traffic',
        images: ['https://bit.ly/4228ITO'],
      },
      {
        id: '2',
        title: 'Shimanami Kaido: A Cycling Island-Hopping
        Adventure',
        images: ['https://bit.ly/4b5nLPO'],
      },
    ],
  };
  axios.get.mockResolvedValue(mockedData);

  const { getAllByTestId } = await act(async () =>
render(<ImageList />));

  expect(getAllByTestId('image-item-title')).toHaveLength(2);
});
```

However, the test throws an error:

```
x should render correct image items when have data (18 ms)

TestingLibraryElementError: Unable to find an element by:
[data-test-id="image-item-title"]
```

CHAPTER 7   FREQUENTLY ASKED QUESTIONS

What should you do when the error message doesn't provide enough details, or when the error message is unclear?

What If the Element Can't Be Found?

Since we're expecting to find a specific element that isn't appearing, we can inspect the current screen to see what's rendered. To do this, you can print out the current view to check what's actually being displayed. In Testing Library, you can use screen.debug, screen.logTestingPlaygroundURL, or generate a snapshot for this purpose.

```
// src/ImageList/ImageListAxios.jest.test.js

it('should render correct image items when have data',
async () => {
  // ...skip...
  const { getAllByTestId } = await act(async () =>
render(<ImageList />));

  screen.debug(); // Add this line to print the rendered output

  expect(getAllByTestId('image-item-title')).toHaveLength(2);
});
```

screen.debug will print the HTML structure of the current screen, and inspecting this reveals that it's showing the "No data" prompt.

```
<body>
  <div>
    <div data-test-id="no-data-prompt">No data to
    display.</div>
  </div>
</body>
```

CHAPTER 7   FREQUENTLY ASKED QUESTIONS

Alternatively, you can use Jest's `toMatchSnapshot` method to generate a snapshot of the rendered HTML.

```
// src/ImageList/ImageListAxios.snapshot.jest.test.js
it('should render correct image items when have data',
async () => {
  // ...skip...
  const { getAllByTestId } = await act(async () =>
  render(<ImageList />));

  // Generate a snapshot after rendering the component
  const wrapper = renderer.create(<ImageList />).toJSON();
  expect(wrapper).toMatchSnapshot();

  expect(getAllByTestId('image-item-title')).toHaveLength(2);
});
```

The snapshot output also shows that the "No data" section was rendered.

```
// src/ImageList/__snapshots__/ImageListAxios.snapshot.jest.
test.js.snap

exports[`ImageList should render correct image items when have data 1`] = `
<div
  data-test-id="no-data-prompt"
>
  No data to display.
</div>
`;
```

There are two possible reasons for this: (1) no data was fetched, or (2) the data fields don't match correctly. Let's investigate further.

CHAPTER 7   FREQUENTLY ASKED QUESTIONS

How Do You Trace the Data Flow?

First, let's check whether any data was actually fetched. Add a `console.log` to the component to print out the retrieved data.

```
// src/ImageList/ImageListAxios.js
```

```
const response = await axios.get('https://dummyjson.com/products');
console.log(response); // Add this line to inspect the fetched data
```

Upon inspection, we see that data was indeed fetched.

```
{
  list: [
    {
      id: '1',
      title: 'Build a Fast Website: Improve User Experience and Traffic',
      images: [Array],
    },
    {
      id: '2',
      title: 'Shimanami Kaido: A Cycling Island-Hopping Adventure',
      images: [Array],
    },
  ];
}
```

CHAPTER 7   FREQUENTLY ASKED QUESTIONS

Next, let's check whether the data fields are mapped correctly.

```
// src/ImageList/ImageListAxios.js

// Add these lines to inspect the response data
console.log(response); // Result: { list: [...] }
console.log(response?.data); // Result: undefined
console.log(response?.data?.products); // Result: undefined
```

Comparing the code with `response?.data?.products`, we see that response doesn't have a data field, let alone a `products` field. This results in an empty array and triggers the "No data" section.

So, we need to modify the test data to use `products` instead of `list`.

```
// src/ImageList/ImageListAxios.jest.test.js
const mockedData = {
  // Change mockedData's list to products
  products: [
    {
      id: '1',
      title: 'Build a Fast Website: Improve User Experience and
      Traffic',
      images: ['https://bit.ly/4228ITO'],
    },
    {
      id: '2',
      title: 'Shimanami Kaido: A Cycling Island-Hopping
      Adventure',
      images: ['https://bit.ly/4b5nLPO'],
    },
  ],
};
```

CHAPTER 7 FREQUENTLY ASKED QUESTIONS

Also, make sure the returned value includes the data field.

```
// src/ImageList/ImageListAxios.jest.test.js

axios.get.mockResolvedValue({ data: mockedData });
```
After making these changes, the test should pass successfully.

```
✓ should render correct image items when have data (21 ms)
```

In this example, we used simple methods to debug the issue. In real projects, you may need additional tools, and you can choose whichever methods and tools suit your needs and preferences.

Notes

- Note 1: For the screen structure and layout of the image list feature, refer to Chapter 3 for more details.

How to Test Localization?

When testing localized interfaces, a common issue is that while everything may look well arranged when testing in Chinese (Note 1), using other languages—such as English, Japanese, or Arabic—can result in layout breakage. So how can we tackle this?

For example, the ordering system of the dessert shop "Summer's dessert shop" is available in both Chinese and English. As shown in Figure 7-1, the Chinese version looks perfectly fine.

CHAPTER 7   FREQUENTLY ASKED QUESTIONS

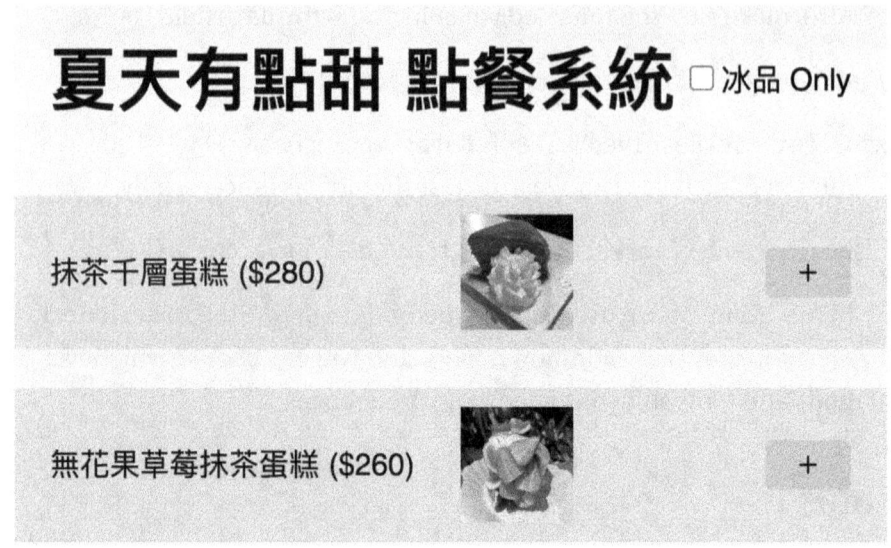

Figure 7-1. The Chinese version of the ordering system for "Summer's dessert shop"

Now, let's look at the English version (Figure 7-2). It also seems okay at first glance.

CHAPTER 7   FREQUENTLY ASKED QUESTIONS

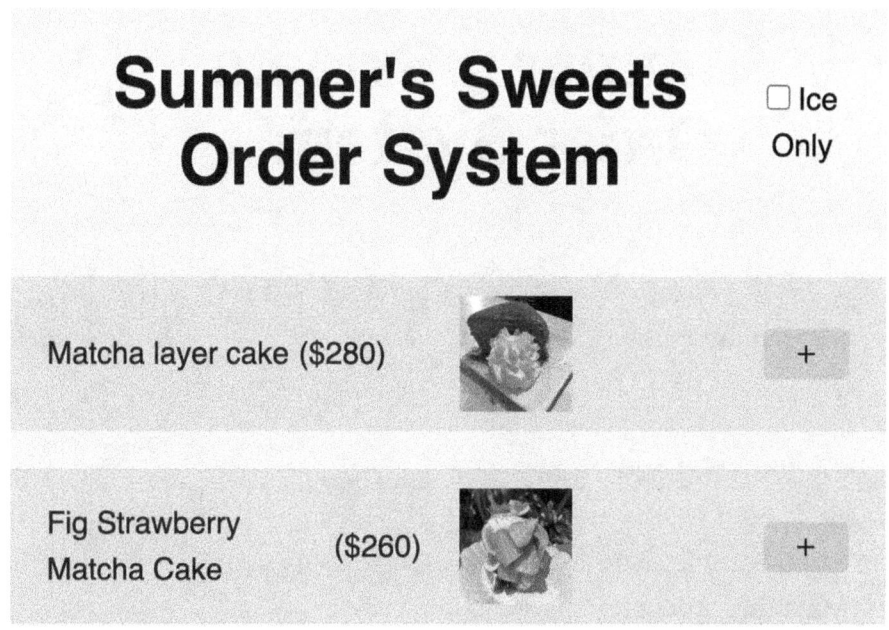

Figure 7-2. The English version of the ordering system for "Summer's dessert shop"

One day, an English translator updated the dessert names, giving them trendy new titles. After renaming, the English version of "Fig Strawberry Matcha Cake" had a longer name, causing the display to look crowded (Figure 7-3). How can we quickly identify such issues and notify developers that the layout needs fixing?

CHAPTER 7　FREQUENTLY ASKED QUESTIONS

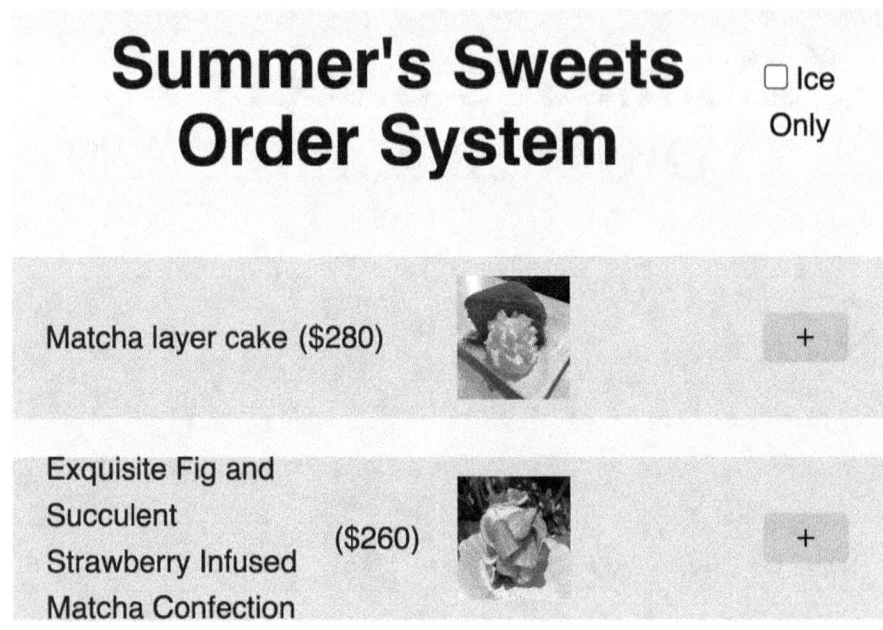

Figure 7-3. The updated English version of the ordering system for "Summer's dessert shop"

Visual testing can help with this. In this example, due to the renaming of "Fig Strawberry Matcha Cake," we can use Percy for visual testing to highlight the updated parts. This allows developers to review the changes and determine if they meet expectations (Figure 7-4). If the changes are as expected, the new view can be set as the new baseline for future comparisons. If not, adjustments need to be made. Visual testing can be set as part of the PR review criteria, ensuring that if an unexpected visual change occurs, it will be flagged and the PR will not be merged into the main branch. This helps maintain product quality.

CHAPTER 7   FREQUENTLY ASKED QUESTIONS

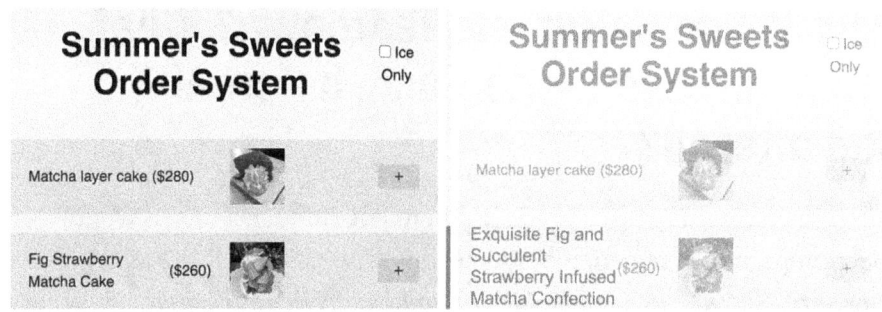

Figure 7-4. *Visual testing using Percy for "Summer's dessert shop" ordering system*

How is this implemented? For components, you can import strings in different languages into Storybook to generate accurate snapshots. Similarly, for pages, you can switch between languages and capture snapshots of the view. Each time a component or page is modified, it can be compared against this baseline. If the update is expected, it can be accepted as the new baseline. If not—such as when layout issues arise—adjustments must be made before updating.

Since English or other languages may not be as familiar to us as Chinese, visual testing's ability to detect subtle layout differences makes it highly effective. It makes it easier to identify issues, especially in non-native languages, and helps solve readability and user experience problems when switching between languages on websites.

Notes

- Note 1: In this section, as the author originally wrote the book in Chinese, it is dedicated to translating non-English terms into English.

CHAPTER 7   FREQUENTLY ASKED QUESTIONS

How to Use Setup and Teardown? What Are beforeEach, afterEach, beforeAll, and afterAll?

When implementing tests, it's common to encounter scenarios where some preparation is needed before testing, and cleanup is required afterward. But why do we need this, and how do we implement it?

Repeated Setup

To maintain the independence of each test case and avoid unintended interference that can lead to unstable test results (Note 1), we can use the beforeEach and afterEach hooks to encapsulate repetitive setup and teardown tasks. This ensures that each test case runs in a clean environment. For example, if one test case modifies the value of a variable and the next test case doesn't reset it, subsequent tests might fail.

For instance, here is a Counter class that allows incrementing or decrementing a number via the increment and decrement methods, with the current count retrievable through the getCount method.

```
// src/Counter/Counter.js

class Counter {
  constructor() {
    this.count = 0;
  }
  increment() {
    this.count++;
  }
```

```
  decrement() {
    this.count--;
  }

  getCount() {
    return this.count;
  }
}
```

The test is written as follows. The first test case checks the `increment` method, and the second test case checks the `decrement` method. These two test cases share the same counter instance. Initially, the counter starts at 0. Logically, if the test cases run in order, the first should return 1 (0 + 1 = 1), and the second should return 0 (1 − 1 = 0).

```
describe('Counter class', () => {
  let counter = new Counter();

  // 0 + 1 = 1
  test('should get 1 when increment from 0', () => {
    counter.increment();
    expect(counter.getCount()).toBe(1);
  });

  // 1 - 1 = 0
  test('should get 0 when decrease', () => {
    counter.decrement();
    expect(counter.getCount()).toBe(0);
  });
});
```

CHAPTER 7　FREQUENTLY ASKED QUESTIONS

What happens if the test cases don't run in order? If the second test case runs first, it will fail. This is because the expected results depend on the order of execution. In such cases, test cases can interfere with each other due to dependencies, leading to failures. The solution is to ensure each test case remains independent and unaffected by the others.

Here's how we can modify the test:

- Use beforeEach to initialize a new counter instance before each test case.
- Adjust the expected result of the second test case to make it independent.

```
// src/Counter/Counter.flaky.test.js
describe('Counter class', () => {
  let counter = new Counter();

  beforeEach(() => {
    counter = new Counter();
  });

  test('should get 1 when increment from 0', () => {
    counter.increment();
    expect(counter.getCount()).toBe(1);
  });

  test('should get -1 when decrease from 0', () => {
    counter.decrement();
    expect(counter.getCount()).toBe(-1);
  });
});
```

CHAPTER 7   FREQUENTLY ASKED QUESTIONS

After these changes, we ensure that every test case starts from the same state, reducing the likelihood of unstable results. You could also use afterEach in a similar way to ensure that each test case ends in a consistent state.

The beforeEach and afterEach hooks can be applied in various scenarios:

- When testing components, you can initialize and render the component before each test and clean up afterward.

- In cookie-related tests, you could clear cookies before or after each test.

- When using mocks, you could mock certain objects before the tests and clean up afterward (Note 2).

One-Time Setup

One-time setup avoids repetitive setup tasks, improving test efficiency. It ensures a consistent and safe testing environment. For instance, before testing, you can use the beforeAll hook to set up the environment for all test cases. After testing is complete, the afterAll hook cleans up the environment, preventing any lingering effects.

Here's an example. Before testing, beforeAll calls Jest's useFakeTimers method to replace real timers with test-controlled ones. After testing, afterAll calls useRealTimers to restore the original timer settings, ensuring other tests are not affected (Note 3).

```
// src/Timer/Timer.js
describe('Timer component', () => {
  beforeAll(() => {
    jest.useFakeTimers();
  });
```

275

CHAPTER 7   FREQUENTLY ASKED QUESTIONS

```
  afterAll(() => {
    jest.useRealTimers();
  });

  // ...test cases...
});
```

beforeAll and afterAll are useful in scenarios such as

- Logging in before running all test cases and logging out afterward when testing checkout functionality
- Loading test data before testing a menu feature and cleaning it up afterward

Summary

When implementing tests, we often need to set up before tests and clean up afterward. Depending on whether the tasks are repeated or one-time setups, you can use the appropriate before* and after* hooks. In summary, beforeEach and afterEach are best for repeated setups, while beforeAll and afterAll are for one-time setups. These hooks ensure a consistent and safe testing environment, improving the efficiency and reliability of your tests.

Notes

- Note 1: For details and examples of "flaky tests," see the section "Why Do Some Test Cases Succeed Sometimes and Fail Other Times?" in this chapter.
- Note 2: For more on mockClear testing and examples, see Chapter 3, section "Mocking Components, API Responses, and Third-Party Libraries."
- Note 3: For more on time-related testing and examples, see the section "How to Test the Timer?" in this chapter.

CHAPTER 7   FREQUENTLY ASKED QUESTIONS

Should Tests Include Type Checking?

Should we perform type checking during testing? Consider the following example where the addNumbers function is used to sum two numbers (Note 1):

```
// src/utils/addNumbers/addNumbers.js

const addNumbers = (a, b) => Number((a + b).toFixed(1));
```

If we want to ensure that the inputs to addNumbers are always numbers, how should we handle it?

Option 1: Implement Type Checking Inside the addNumbers Function

One approach is to add type-checking logic within the addNumbers function itself. If the input is not a number, an error message is returned.

```
// src/utils/addNumbers/addNumbers.js

const addNumbers = (a, b) => {
  if (typeof a !== 'number' || typeof b !== 'number') {
    return 'Inputs must be numbers.';
  }
  return Number((a + b).toFixed(1));
};
```

CHAPTER 7   FREQUENTLY ASKED QUESTIONS

When writing tests, add corresponding type-checking test cases. In the test case below, we verify that when the inputs are strings `'1'` and `'2'`, the `addNumbers` function returns the expected error message `'Inputs must be numbers.'`:

```
// src/utils/addNumbers/addNumbers.test.js
```

```
test('should get error when inputs are not number', () => {
  expect(addNumbers('1', '2')).toBe('Inputs must be numbers.');
});
```

This approach shows that adding too much defensive code can make the `addNumbers` function overly complex. Whether to include such defensive logic in the implementation is a subject of debate. Some developers believe it adds unnecessary complexity, while others feel it strengthens the code and enhances test reliability. From the above example, adding type checking within the `addNumbers` function increases complexity and makes testing more difficult, which may not be ideal (Note 2).

Option 2: Use Tools for Type Checking

Instead of checking types directly within functions or tests, developers can use tools such as `prop-types` (for React components) or TypeScript's type system to handle type checking (Note 3). This keeps the `addNumbers` function simple and avoids unnecessary complexity.

For example, using TypeScript, you can define the inputs a and b of `addNumbers` as numbers.

```
// src/utils/addNumbers/addNumbers.ts
```

```
const addNumbers = (a: number, b: number) => Number((a + b).toFixed(1));
```

278

CHAPTER 7 FREQUENTLY ASKED QUESTIONS

If addNumbers is used somewhere with valid number inputs, no issues arise.

// src/utils/addNumbers/helloNumbers.ts

const a = addNumbers(1, 2);

However, if strings are passed in, TypeScript will warn that this is incorrect and requires fixing.

// src/utils/addNumbers/helloNumbers.ts

const b = addNumbers('1', '2');

The error message would be

Argument of type 'string' is not assignable to parameter of type 'number'.

By using type-checking tools instead of implementing type checks within functions or tests, you can keep the addNumbers function and its test cases clean and readable while ensuring the robustness of your codebase.

Notes

- Note 1: Before running all tests, consider performing "static analysis" depending on the project's requirements. Static analysis is a technique that examines the structure, syntax, and quality of the code without actually executing it. Tools such as TypeScript and ESLint are highly recommended for static analysis.
- Note 2: Defensive programming is a coding style designed to prevent and handle potential errors or issues, improving the robustness and reliability of programs. However, repeatedly checking types in this way can lead to unnecessary complexity.

A more effective solution is to use contracts, like TypeScript's type checking, which ensures correctness during development while improving code readability and maintainability.

- Note 3: TypeScript is not only a programming language but also a static analysis tool. It provides type checking during development, helping developers catch potential issues early on. By checking variable types, function parameters, return types, and more, TypeScript helps maintain high-quality code throughout the development process.

Why Do Some Test Cases Succeed Sometimes and Fail Other Times?

Flaky tests refer to test cases that produce inconsistent results under different executions. These inconsistencies can be caused by various factors such as network latency, database state, execution environment differences, or poor test design. Flaky tests are a common problem in automated testing. While developers may not be able to control external factors, they can reduce the occurrence of flaky tests by improving the test code itself. Let's explore the causes of flaky tests and how to address them.

Resource Dependencies

Dependencies on internal and external resources such as time, network, data sources, or execution environments can cause tests to be unreliable. For example, consider the `checkValentinesDay` function, which checks if today is Valentine's Day. If the current date is February 14, it returns `Happy Valentine's Day`; otherwise, it returns `Today is not Valentine's Day` (Note 1).

```
// src/utils/checkValentinesDay/checkValentinesDay.js

const checkValentinesDay = () => {
  const today = getToday();
  return today === '2/14' ? 'Happy Valentine's Day' : 'Today is not Valentine's Day';
};
```

If today is February 10 (not Valentine's Day), the function will return `Today is not Valentine's Day`, causing the test to fail. However, on February 14, the function will return `Happy Valentine's Day`, making the test pass.

```
// src/utils/checkValentinesDay/checkValentinesDay.test.js

describe('checkValentinesDay', () => {
  it('today should be Valentines Day', () => {
    expect(checkValentinesDay()).toBe('Happy Valentine's Day');
  });
});
```

This test case does not consistently produce the same result, making it a flaky test. This happens because the `checkValentinesDay` function relies on the `getToday` function, which introduces variability. To address this, we can use mocking to isolate dependencies. Unreliable tests make it difficult to evaluate if the functionality is working correctly.

For tests with dependencies, you can use mock data or fixed test data to isolate the dependencies. For example, you can mock the `getToday` function (Note 2) to ensure that `checkValentinesDay` behaves consistently

CHAPTER 7 FREQUENTLY ASKED QUESTIONS

regardless of the actual date. By isolating getToday, you can prevent test instability. In the test cases below, the mockReturnValue function is used to return specific dates (Note 3):

```
// src/utils/checkValentinesDay/checkValentinesDay.test.js
jest.mock('./getToday', () => ({
  getToday: jest.fn(),
}));
```

The following test cases check two scenarios:

- When today is February 12, the function should return Today is not Valentine's Day.
- When today is February 14, the function should return Happy Valentine's Day.

```
// src/utils/checkValentinesDay/checkValentinesDay.test.js
describe('checkValentinesDay', () => {
  // When today is February 12, expect the function to return
  `Today is not Valentine's Day`
  it('2/12 should not be Valentines Day', () => {
    getToday.mockReturnValue('2/12');

    expect(checkValentinesDay()).toBe('Today is not
    Valentine\'s Day');
  });

  // When today is February 14, expect the function to return
  `Happy Valentine's Day`
  it('2/14 should be Valentines Day', () => {
    getToday.mockReturnValue('2/14');

    expect(checkValentinesDay()).toBe('Happy Valentine\'s Day');
  });
});
```

CHAPTER 7   FREQUENTLY ASKED QUESTIONS

Test Dependencies

When test cases depend on each other or rely on execution order, they can become flaky tests. This often occurs when test cases share a state that may differ between tests, leading to inconsistent results.

For example, the following `Counter` class has methods `increment` and `decrement` to increase or decrease a counter and `getCount` to retrieve the current count:

```
// src/Counter/Counter.js
class Counter {
  constructor() {
    this.count = 0;
  }

  increment() {
    this.count++;
  }

  decrement() {
    this.count--;
  }

  getCount() {
    return this.count;
  }
}
```

CHAPTER 7   FREQUENTLY ASKED QUESTIONS

The test cases below share a single `counter` instance. The first test case tests `increment`, and the second tests `decrement`. Initially, the counter starts at 0, and when run in sequence, the first test case should result in 1 (0 + 1 = 1), and the second in 0 (1 − 1 = 0).

```
describe('Counter class', () => {
  let counter = new Counter();

  // 0 + 1 = 1
  test('[dev1] should get 1 when increment from 0', () => {
    counter.increment();

    expect(counter.getCount()).toBe(1);
  });

  // 1 - 1 = 0
  test('[dev2] should get 0 when decrease', () => {
    counter.decrement();

    expect(counter.getCount()).toBe(0);
  });
});
```

Running these tests in order will pass.

```
yarn test Counter.flaky.test.js
PASS  src/Counter/Counter.flaky.test.js
  Counter class
    ✓ [dev1] should get 1 when increment from 0 (3 ms)
    ✓ [dev2] should get -1 when decrease from 0 (2 ms)
```

But if the test order is changed, the tests may fail. If the second test runs first, the counter starts at 0, and the result is −1 (0 − 1 = −1), causing the test to fail.

```
FAIL  src/Counter/Counter.flaky-skip-and-only.test.js
  Counter class
    ✗ [dev2] should get 0 when decrease (5 ms)
    ✗ [dev1] should get 1 when increment from 0 (1 ms)
```

To avoid this dependency, initialize a new counter instance before each test using beforeEach, and adjust the test expectations to ensure each test runs independently.

```
// src/Counter/Counter.flaky.test.js
describe('Counter class', () => {
  let counter = new Counter();

  beforeEach(() => {
    counter = new Counter();
  });

  test('[dev1] should get 1 when increment from 0', () => {
    counter.increment();
    expect(counter.getCount()).toBe(1);
  });

  test('[dev2] should get -1 when decrease from 0', () => {
    counter.decrement();
    expect(counter.getCount()).toBe(0);
  });
});
```

Now, the tests will pass regardless of the execution order.

```
PASS  src/Counter/Counter.flaky.test.js
  Counter class
    ✓ [dev1] should get 1 when increment from 0 (3 ms)
    ✓ [dev2] should get -1 when decrease from 0 (2 ms)
```

CHAPTER 7   FREQUENTLY ASKED QUESTIONS

Conclusion

The causes and solutions for flaky tests are summarized in Table 7-1.

Table 7-1. The Causes and Solutions for Flaky Tests

Cause	Solution
Resource dependencies	Isolate dependencies with mocks or fixed data
Test dependencies	Ensure no dependencies and reset state before each test

If a flaky test cannot be resolved immediately, it can be temporarily skipped (using `skip` or `only`) until fixed (Note 4). Flaky tests can undermine the reliability of test results, confuse developers, and reduce confidence in code quality, so skipping them temporarily is often better than allowing unreliable results.

Notes

- Note 1: For more details on the `checkValentinesDay` example, refer to Chapter 2, section "Minimal Scope Validation Logic."

- Note 2: For more information on mocking, see Chapter 3, section "Mocking Components, API Responses, and Third-Party Libraries."

CHAPTER 7   FREQUENTLY ASKED QUESTIONS

- Note 3: For details on `mockImplementation` and `mockReturnValue`, see Chapter 3, section "Mocking Components, API Responses, and Third-Party Libraries."
- Note 4: For more on using `skip` and `only`, see the section "How to Run Specific Tests? An Example Using Jest" in this chapter.

How to Run Specific Tests? An Example Using Jest

When running tests, developers may want to skip specific test cases for debugging or isolating flaky tests. Below is an explanation using Jest as an example.

Skipping Specific Test Blocks

"Skipping specific test blocks" means ignoring an entire block of test cases in the execution. In Jest, adding `skip` to `describe` will skip all test cases in that block. In the example below, `describe` separates "shallow rendering" and "full rendering" test blocks:

```
// src/Counter/Counter.snapshot.rtl.test.js
describe('Counter component', () => {
  describe.skip('shallow rendering', () => {
    // ... omitted ...
  });
  describe('full rendering', () => {
    // ... omitted ...
  });
});
```

Since `skip` is added to the first block, only the "full rendering" test cases will run, and the "shallow rendering" block will be skipped:

```
PASS  src/Counter/Counter.snapshot.rtl.test.js
  Counter component
    shallow rendering
      ○ skipped should get snapshot correctly
    full rendering
      ✓ should get snapshot correctly (33 ms)
      ✓ should get 1 when click the increment button (26 ms)
```

Skipping Specific Test Cases

To skip individual test cases, you can add `skip` to `it` or `test`. Below are three test cases, but the third one will be skipped:

```
// src/utils/addNumbers/addNumbers.test.js

test('should return 0.3 when 0.1 + 0.2', () => {
  expect(addNumbers(0.1, 0.2)).toBe(0.3);
});

test('should return 2 when 5 - 3', () => {
  expect(addNumbers(5, -3)).toBe(2);
});

test.skip('should get error when inputs are not number', () => {
  expect(addNumbers('1', '2')).toBe('Inputs must be numbers.');
});
```

Since `skip` is added to the third case, only the first two test cases will run:

CHAPTER 7   FREQUENTLY ASKED QUESTIONS

```
PASS  src/utils/addNumbers/addNumbers.test.js
  ✓ should return 0.3 when 0.1 + 0.2 (4 ms)
  ✓ should return 2 when 5 - 3 (1 ms)
  ○ skipped should get error when inputs are not number
```

This is very useful when debugging, especially if you need to check if test cases have dependencies or if you want to temporarily skip unstable tests (Note 1). For example, here is a Counter class where you can increment or decrement a number and retrieve the result using getCount:

```
// src/Counter/Counter.js

class Counter {
  constructor() {
    this.count = 0;
  }

  increment() {
    this.count++;
  }

  decrement() {
    this.count--;
  }

  getCount() {
    return this.count;
  }
}
```

The following two test cases share a single counter instance. Initially, the counter starts at 0. As the tests are run sequentially, the first test case is expected to return 1 (i.e., 0 + 1 = 1), and the second test case should return 0 (i.e., 1 - 1 = 0).

289

CHAPTER 7   FREQUENTLY ASKED QUESTIONS

When the test cases run in order, both tests pass:

```
PASS  src/Counter/Counter.flaky.test.js
  Counter class
    ✓ [dev1] should get 1 when increment from 0 (3 ms)
    ✓ [dev2] should get -1 when decrease from 0 (2 ms)
```

However, when test cases are not run in order, the results may change. If they don't follow the expected sequence, all tests may fail:

```
FAIL  src/Counter/Counter.flaky-skip-and-only.test.js
  Counter class
    ✗ [dev2] should get 0 when decrease (5 ms)
    ✗ [dev1] should get 1 when increment from 0 (1 ms)
```

When all tests fail like this, it becomes difficult to determine which specific test case is causing the issue. In such a scenario, you can use only or skip to narrow down the issue. Let's start by only running the first test case:

```
describe('Counter class', () => {
  let counter = new Counter();

  // 0 + 1 = 1
  test.only('[dev1] should get 1 when increment from 0', () => {
    // ... omitted ...
  });

  // 1 - 1 = 0
  test('[dev2] should get 0 when decrease', () => {
    // ... omitted ...
  });
});
```

If only the first test case runs, it will pass:

```
PASS  src/Counter/Counter.flaky-skip-and-only.test.js
  Counter class
    ✓ [dev1] should get 1 when increment from 0 (2 ms)
    ○ skipped [dev2] should get 0 when decrease
```

Next, run only the second test case:

```
describe('Counter class', () => {
  let counter = new Counter();

  // 0 + 1 = 1
  test('[dev1] should get 1 when increment from 0', () => {
    // ... omitted ...
  });

  // 1 - 1 = 0
  test.only('[dev2] should get 0 when decrease', () => {
    // ... omitted ...
  });
});
```

The second test case fails because its result depends on the first test case. The second test case expects the result after the first test's increment operation, which means the initial value (0) was already incremented by 1 before decrementing. To fix this, reduce the dependencies between the two tests by initializing a new `counter` instance before each test case and adjusting the expected result for the second test case to run independently:

```
FAIL  src/Counter/Counter.flaky-skip-and-only.test.js
  Counter class
    ✗ [dzev2] should get 0 when decrease (8 ms)
    ○ skipped [dev1] should get 1 when increment from 0

    ● Counter class › [dev2] should get 0 when decrease
```

```
expect(received).toBe(expected) // Object.is equality

Expected: 0
Received: -1
```

You should ensure that each test case starts from the same initial state to avoid this kind of dependency issue. Ideally, tests should not rely on one another. When refactoring test code, changing the order or skipping test cases should not cause failures.

Conclusion

In summary, comparing when to use `.only` vs. `.skip` depends on how many test cases you want to run or skip:

- If you want to skip many test cases, use `.only`.
- If you only need to skip a few, use `.skip`.

Notes

- Note 1: For more information on "flaky tests," see the section "Why Do Some Test Cases Succeed Sometimes and Fail Other Times?" in this chapter.

CHAPTER 8

Leveraging AI for Writing Tests

You will learn the following in this chapter:

- GitHub Copilot can help developers write efficient test cases by generating code from clear, goal-oriented comments, but requires review and adjustments.

- Use Mermaid flowcharts and ChatGPT to efficiently write tests in development for improved product quality.

How to Effectively Use GitHub Copilot for Writing Tests

GitHub Copilot (or Copilot) is an AI-powered code assistant tool provided by GitHub, which can be used with the Visual Studio Code editor (https://code.visualstudio.com/). By providing clear prompts, developers can leverage Copilot to generate code and efficiently write test cases. Although Copilot can generate suggested code based on comments, improving development efficiency and reducing syntax overhead, developers must still carefully review the generated code and adjust it as needed to meet specific testing requirements (Note 1).

CHAPTER 8   LEVERAGING AI FOR WRITING TESTS

How can you use Copilot to help write tests? Let's look at a few examples.

Simple Example

First, since Copilot needs enough information to generate code, it is up to the developer to name files or functions appropriately and write clear, goal-oriented comments to generate test cases (Note 2). For instance, suppose we want to implement a function called addDays, which adds a specified number of days to the current date to calculate a target date. Following the principles of TDD (Note 3), we can first create a test file named hello.test.js and ask GitHub Copilot to help write the test case.

```
// src/utils/timeUtils/hello.test.js

// test this function
```

After pressing Enter, Copilot begins to generate the test case. However, with an unclear file name and vague comment, Copilot cannot produce the desired content. Since the file name contains the word "hello" and does not mention addDays or anything related to dates, Copilot generates a test case for the string Hello World instead.

```
// src/utils/timeUtils/hello.test.js

// test this function
describe('hello', () => {
  test('should return "Hello, World!"', () => {
    const result = hello();

    expect(result).toBe('Hello, World!');
  });
});
```

CHAPTER 8 LEVERAGING AI FOR WRITING TESTS

We can adjust our approach by renaming the test file to addDays.test.js and adding a comment like `// should get the date after adding days` to guide Copilot in generating the correct test case. Then, we ask Copilot to generate the test case based on the comment.

```
// src/utils/timeUtils/addDays.test.js

// should get the date of 5 days from now
```

This time, the generated test case is much more accurate and complete, clearly specifying the date, adding the target number of days, and checking if it matches the expected result. You can follow this process to generate more context-appropriate test cases. While Copilot can generate code based on the given information, it's essential to review and adjust the code to meet your testing needs.

```
// src/utils/timeUtils/addDays.test.js

// should get the date of 5 days from now
test('should get the date of 5 days from now', () => {
  const date = new Date('2020-01-01');
  const result = addDays(date, 5);
  expect(result).toEqual(new Date('2020-01-06'));
});
```

Next, implement the addDays function to verify whether the implementation and the test are working correctly.

```
// src/utils/timeUtils/addDays.js

const addDays = (currentDate, daysToAdd) => {
  // should get the date of daysToAdd days from currentDate
  const result = new Date(currentDate);
  result.setDate(result.getDate() + daysToAdd);
  return result;
};
```

This was a simple example. Now, let's move on to a more complex example.

Implementing Unit Tests

How do we write unit tests for components? For instance, we have a <Counter> component with a simple counting functionality that allows users to increment or decrement a number by clicking buttons (Note 4). In most development scenarios, the functionality is implemented first, followed by writing the tests. In this case, we will first implement the <Counter> component and then call GitHub Copilot to help write the test cases.

```
// src/Counter/Counter.js

const Counter = () => {
  const [count, setCount] = useState(0);
  const increment = () => setCount(count + 1);
  const decrement = () => setCount(count - 1);

  return (
    <>
      <div data-test-id="counter-value">{count}</div>
      <button data-test-id="decrement-button" onClick={decrement}>
        -
      </button>
      <button data-test-id="increment-button" onClick={increment}>
        +
      </button>
    </>
  );
};
```

CHAPTER 8 LEVERAGING AI FOR WRITING TESTS

To write the unit test for the <Counter> component, we can call Copilot and type /tests Counter.js in the Copilot Chat to generate the test cases. Once Copilot produces the test cases (as shown in Figure 8-1), you can review them. If they look good, simply insert them into your test file.

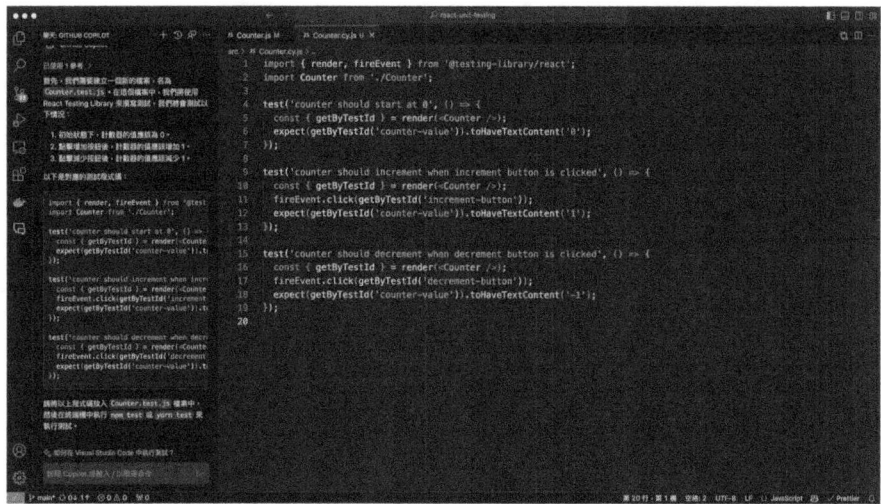

Figure 8-1. *Copilot generates test cases for the Counter component*

As seen here, the more detailed the information you provide, the more accurate the code that Copilot generates. When writing comments, it is advised to clearly specify what needs to be tested, the expected result, and under what conditions the result is valid. This will help generate comprehensive test cases that meet expectations.

Implementing Integration Tests

When implementing integration tests, let's revisit the image list functionality. This feature is split into two components: <ImageList> and <ImageItem> (Note 5). The main purpose of this functionality is to visually display the retrieved image information. The <ImageList> component is responsible for determining how to display the data based on the fetched

CHAPTER 8   LEVERAGING AI FOR WRITING TESTS

image information. If no image data is available, a prompt is shown to notify the user that no images can be displayed. If image data exists, the component uses <ImageItem> to display the images.

```
// src/ImageList/ImageList.js
const ImageList = () => {
  const [images, setImages] = useState([]);

  useEffect(() => {
    async function fetchData() {
      const response = await fetch('https://dummyjson.com/
      products');
      const data = await response.json();
      setImages(data.products);
    }
    fetchData();
  }, []);

  const renderImages = () => {
    return images.map(({ id, title, images }) => (
      <ImageItem key={id} title={title} image={images[0]} />
    ));
  };

  const renderNoDataPrompt = () => {
    return <div data-test-id="no-data-prompt">No data to
    display.</div>;
  };

  return <>{!!images.length ? renderImages() :
renderNoDataPrompt()}</>;
};
```

CHAPTER 8   LEVERAGING AI FOR WRITING TESTS

To write tests for the `<ImageList>` component, integration tests can be a bit more complex since they might require fetching data from APIs and testing across multiple components. To ensure Copilot generates the desired test code, it is recommended to give the test files proper names and write clear comments to reduce the likelihood of generating unintended results.

```
// src/ImageList/ImagesList.cy.js

describe('ImageList', () => {
  it('should render no data prompt when no images', () => {
    // intercept response from https://dummyjson.com/products
    with fixture `empty.json` in fixtures folder
    // mount component `<ImageList />`
    // assert no data prompt "no-data-prompt" exists
  });

  it('should render correct image items when data is
  available', () => {
    // intercept response from https://dummyjson.com/products
    with fixture `products.json` in fixtures folder
    // mount component `<ImageList />`
    // assert image items length is 2
  });
});
```

After writing these comments and selecting the code block, you can enter /tests in Copilot to generate test code. Although the code generated by Copilot might not be entirely correct, you can make some adjustments.

```
// src/ImageList/ImagesList.cy.js

describe('ImageList', () => {
  it('should render no data prompt when no images', () => {
    cy.intercept('https://dummyjson.com/products', {
```

CHAPTER 8   LEVERAGING AI FOR WRITING TESTS

```
      fixture: 'empty.json',
    }).as('getProducts');
    cy.visit('/'); // Not needed, remove this line
    cy.wait('@getProducts'); // Not needed, remove this line
    // Add mount command here
    cy.get('[data-test-id="no-data-prompt"]').should('exist');
  });

  it('should render correct image items when data is
available', () => {
    cy.intercept('https://dummyjson.com/products', {
      fixture: 'products.json',
    }).as('getProducts');
    cy.visit('/'); // Not needed, remove this line
    cy.wait('@getProducts'); // Not needed, remove this line
    // Add mount command here
    cy.get('[data-test-id="image-item-title"]').should('have.
    length', 2);
  });
});
```

After adjusting, the result should look like this. Remove unnecessary code, add the mount command, and format the code into 3A (Arrange, Act, Assert) blocks for better readability (Note 6).

```
// src/ImageList/ImagesList.cy.js

describe('ImageList', () => {
  it('should render no data prompt when no images', () => {
    cy.intercept('GET', 'https://dummyjson.com/products', {
      statusCode: 200,
      body: { products: },
    }).as('apiRequest');

    cy.mount(<ImageList />);
```

CHAPTER 8   LEVERAGING AI FOR WRITING TESTS

```
    cy.get('[data-test-id="no-data-prompt"]').should('exist');
  });

  it('should render correct image items when data is
  available', () => {
    cy.intercept('GET', 'https://dummyjson.com/products', {
      statusCode: 200,
      body: {
        products: [
          {
            id: '1',
            title: 'Build a fast website, starting with
            performance metrics!',
            images: ['https://bit.ly/4228IT0'],
          },
          {
            id: '2',
            title: 'Shimanami Kaido: Cycling Island Hopping
            Adventure',
            images: ['https://bit.ly/4b5nLP0'],
          },
        ],
      },
    }).as('apiRequest');

    cy.mount(<ImageList />);

    cy.get('[data-test-id="image-item-title"]').should('have.
    length', 2);
  });
});
```

CHAPTER 8   LEVERAGING AI FOR WRITING TESTS

Implementing End-to-End Tests

How can you implement an end-to-end test? For example, if you want to write a test for Memori's image upload feature (Note 7), the user flow for testing the image upload feature can be divided into the following steps:

- Step 1: Enter the website URL in the browser.
- Step 2: Input the username and message, and select an image file.
- Step 3: Click the submit button.
- Step 4: Display a success message after the image is uploaded.

Based on the user flow, the following comments can be written to structure the test:

```
// cypress/e2e/memori.upload.cy.js
describe('upload page', () => {
  describe('desktop', () => {
    it('should get success message when uploading an image with png format', () => {
      // go to url "https://memori-ui-upload.web.app/?serviceId=webconf2023"
      // type "summer" into input with data-cy "user-name"
      // type "hello world!" into input with data-cy "message"
      // upload file "cycling.jpeg" into input with data-cy "file-upload"
      // click button with data-cy "submit"
      // expect element with data-cy "success-message" to have text "Success!"
    });
  });
});
```

CHAPTER 8   LEVERAGING AI FOR WRITING TESTS

Once you've written the comments, call Copilot to generate the suggested test code. Select the code block with comments and enter /tests in Copilot to produce the test code (see Figure 8-2).

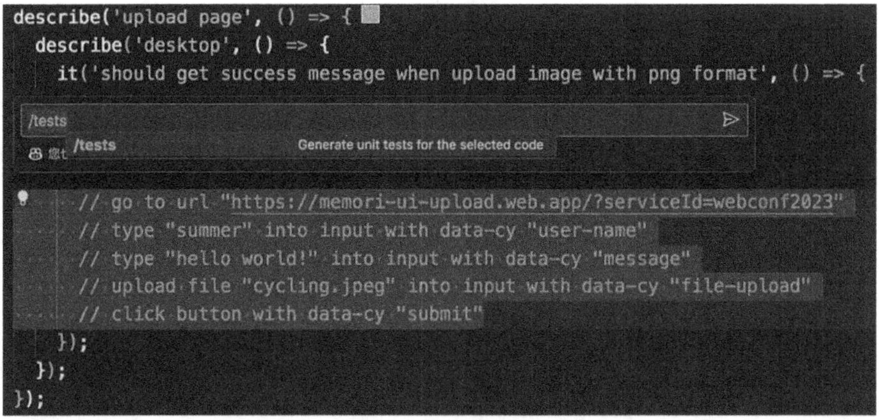

```
describe('upload page', () => {
  describe('desktop', () => {
    it('should get success message when upload image with png format', () => {
      // go to url "https://memori-ui-upload.web.app/?serviceId=webconf2023"
      // type "summer" into input with data-cy "user-name"
      // type "hello world!" into input with data-cy "message"
      // upload file "cycling.jpeg" into input with data-cy "file-upload"
      // click button with data-cy "submit"
    });
  });
});
```

Figure 8-2. *Copilot generating Memori's image upload test code*

Below is the code generated by Copilot. You'll notice that precise naming and clearly defined steps in the comments help generate accurate test code. However, the Copilot-generated code may not be entirely correct, so the developer must adjust it accordingly.

```
// cypress/e2e/memori.upload.cy.js

describe('upload page', () => {
  describe('desktop', () => {
    it('should get success message when uploading an image with jpeg format', () => {
      // go to url "https://memori-ui-upload.web.app/?serviceId=webconf2023"
      cy.visit('https://memori-ui-upload.web.app/?serviceId=webconf2023');
```

```
      // type "summer" into input with data-cy "user-name"
      cy.get('[data-cy="user-name"]').type('summer');

      // type "hello world!" into input with data-cy "message"
      cy.get('[data-cy="message"]').type('hello world!');

      // upload file "cycling.jpeg" into input with data-cy
      "file-upload"
      const fileName = 'cycling.jpeg';
      cy.fixture(fileName).then((fileContent) => {
        cy.get('[data-cy="file-upload"]').attachFile({
          fileContent,
          fileName,
          mimeType: 'image/jpeg',
        });
      });

      // click button with data-cy "submit"
      cy.get('[data-cy="submit"]').click();

      // expect element with data-cy "success-message" to have
      text "Success!"
      cy.get('[data-cy="success-message"]').should('have.text',
      'Success!');
    });
  });
});
```

Conclusion

To effectively use Copilot for writing tests, the first step is to write clear and meaningful comments. Next, it's important to carefully review the code generated by Copilot to ensure it meets the test requirements and works correctly, adjusting or writing code manually as needed. While the

CHAPTER 8   LEVERAGING AI FOR WRITING TESTS

initial results might not always be perfect, once Copilot gains context from similar experiences within your project, it can quickly generate much of the code you need. Integrating Copilot into your workflow can significantly boost productivity.

Summary of steps for using Copilot to help with test writing:

- Step 1: Name the file or function appropriately and write clear, goal-specific comments.
- Step 2: Call Copilot to generate the test code based on the comments.
- Step 3: Review and verify the code generated by Copilot. Copilot's suggestions may not always be entirely correct or suitable, so adjustments are often necessary.
- Step 4: If the generated code doesn't meet your needs, go back to Step 1 or write the code manually.

No time to write tests? With AI, there are no more excuses.

Notes

- Note 1: The purpose of this section is to explain how to use Copilot to efficiently generate test code, so background, operation principles, installation, and experience will not be discussed. For more information, please refer to the official website `https://github.com/features/copilot/`.
- Note 2: Regarding what constitutes a "clear goal," it's recommended to clearly specify what is being tested, define the expected outcome, and outline under what conditions this should occur, for example, get input

element by ID "name" or expect message to be "Success!". For more details, see Chapter 1, section "Naming Conventions."

- Note 3: For more on TDD, refer to Chapter 1, section "Testing Techniques."

- Note 4: For details and examples of the <Counter> component, see Chapter 2, section "Environment Setup, Installation, and Tool Comparison."

- Note 5: For examples and explanations of the image list display structure, refer to Chapter 3, section "Integration Testing."

- Note 6: For information on the 3A principle, see Chapter 1, section "Naming Conventions."

- Note 7: For information about Memori, see Chapter 4, section "Verifying User Flow."

How to Leverage Mermaid and ChatGPT for Writing Tests

In the software development process, implementing functionality is naturally the most important task, but in a fast-paced and constantly evolving development environment, writing tests is essential for improving product quality. Efficiently writing test scripts is one of the goals that developers pursue. In this chapter, we will explore how to effectively use Mermaid and ChatGPT for writing tests.

Mermaid (https://mermaid.js.org/) is a simple and intuitive Markdown-based diagramming tool used to create flowcharts, sequence diagrams, Gantt charts, and more. With simple code, Mermaid can automatically generate complex diagrams.

ChatGPT (https://chatgpt.com/) is a large language model developed by OpenAI. Based on GPT technology, it can understand and generate natural language text. ChatGPT is widely used in areas such as conversations, Q&A, translations, and summaries. By training on vast amounts of data, ChatGPT improves its language understanding and generation abilities, continually updating to adapt to language changes. As a language model, ChatGPT can provide helpful assistance in many fields and can be customized and extended according to users' needs.

So, can we use Mermaid flowcharts to ask ChatGPT to write tests?

Simple Example

First, let's try using a Mermaid flowchart to implement a function. For example, we'll implement an addNumbers function that provides the ability to add two numbers. The flowchart for this function is implemented in Mermaid as shown below:

```
flowchart TD
    Get_Input[get 2 numbers from arguments] --> Add_Numbers[add 2 numbers]
    Add_Numbers --> Round_Result[round the result]
    Round_Result --> Return_Result[return added result]
```

As shown in Figure 8-3, Mermaid generates a preview of the flowchart based on the code.

CHAPTER 8 LEVERAGING AI FOR WRITING TESTS

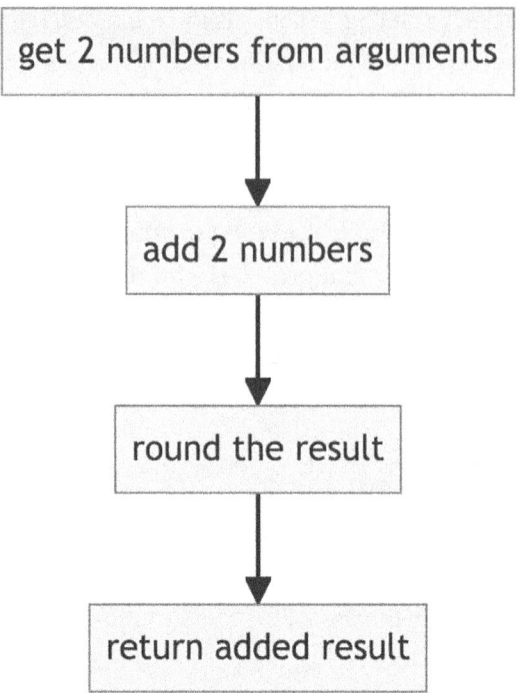

Figure 8-3. Mermaid flowchart for addNumbers

Developer's Request: Implement the Function

Based on the flowchart code, we can ask ChatGPT to help implement this function like this:

Generate a function addNumbers based on this diagram.

```
flowchart TD
    Get_Input[get 2 numbers from arguments] --> Add_Numbers[add
    2 numbers]
    Add_Numbers --> Round_Result[round the result]
    Round_Result --> Return_Result[return added result]
```

CHAPTER 8 LEVERAGING AI FOR WRITING TESTS

ChatGPT's Response

ChatGPT responds within seconds with the following:

Based on the flowchart, here's a possible implementation of the `addNumbers` function:

```
function addNumbers(num1, num2) {
  const sum = num1 + num2;
  const roundedResult = Math.round(sum);
  return roundedResult;
}
```

This function accepts two numbers as parameters, adds them together, rounds the result, and returns it.

The following code is the example implementation of the `addNumbers` function from this book. Compared to ChatGPT's response, the difference lies in the choice between using `Math.round` and `toFixed` for rounding. While both perform rounding, the former returns a number, and the latter returns a string, making the data type different.

```
// src/utils/addNumbers/addNumbers.js

const addNumbers = (a, b) => Number((a + b).toFixed(1));
```

It seems that the return data type was not clearly defined, so we redefine the flowchart as follows:

```
flowchart TD
    Get_Input[get 2 numbers from arguments] --> Add_Numbers[add
    2 numbers]
    Add_Numbers --> Round_Result[round the result]
    Round_Result --> Return_Result[return added result in
    string format]
```

309

CHAPTER 8 LEVERAGING AI FOR WRITING TESTS

As shown in Figure 8-4, Mermaid generates a preview of the updated flowchart based on the new code.

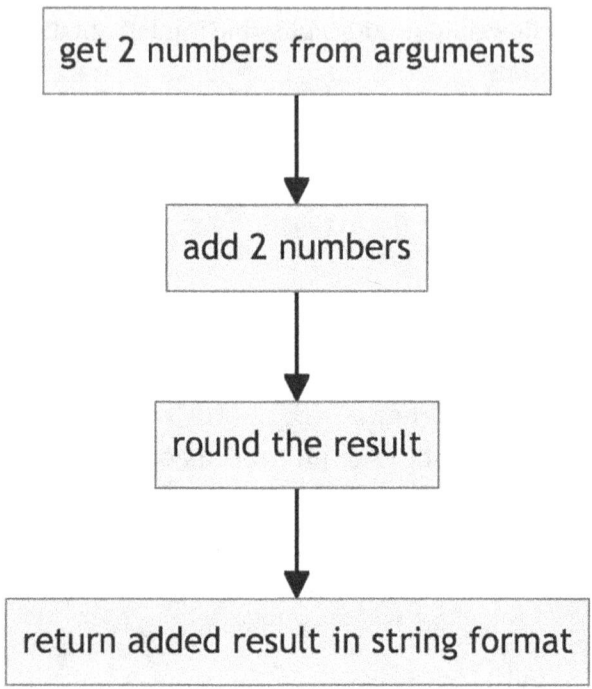

Figure 8-4. *Updated Mermaid flowchart for addNumbers*

Let's ask ChatGPT again if it can generate code that better matches the requirements and specifications.

Generate a function `addNumbers` based on this diagram.

```
flowchart TD
    Get_Input[get 2 numbers from arguments] --> Add_Numbers[add
    2 numbers]
    Add_Numbers --> Round_Result[round the result]
    Round_Result --> Return_Result[return added result in
    string format]
```

CHAPTER 8 LEVERAGING AI FOR WRITING TESTS

ChatGPT responds with the following:

Based on the flowchart, we need to implement a function `addNumbers` that adds two input numbers, rounds the result to an integer, and then returns the result as a string. Here's a possible JavaScript implementation:

```
function addNumbers(num1, num2) {
  const sum = num1 + num2;
  const roundedSum = Math.round(sum);
  return roundedSum.toString();
}
```

This function accepts two parameters, `num1` and `num2`, adds them together, rounds the result using `Math.round()`, and then returns it as a string.

Although the reply does not use `toFixed` as expected for rounding, ChatGPT's response already meets the requirements. The developer can make adjustments based on their preferences or project needs. In this simple example, implementing the `addNumbers` function based on the flowchart works smoothly.

Developer Asks Again: Writing Tests

Not only do we want ChatGPT to help implement the function, but we also want it to write test cases, so we ask again.

Generate test cases based on this diagram in Jest.

```
flowchart TD
    Get_Input[get 2 numbers from arguments] --> Add_Numbers[add
    2 numbers]
    Add_Numbers --> Round_Result[round the result]
    Round_Result --> Return_Result[return added result in
    string format]
```

311

CHAPTER 8   LEVERAGING AI FOR WRITING TESTS

ChatGPT's Response

ChatGPT quickly provides the following response:
   Based on the above diagram, we can write the following test code:

```
import { addNumbers } from './addNumbers';

describe('addNumbers', () => {
  it('should correctly add two numbers and round the result', () => {
    const num1 = 2;
    const num2 = 3;
    const result = addNumbers(num1, num2);
    expect(result).toBe('5');
  });
});
```

This test case tests the addNumbers function to ensure it correctly adds two numbers and rounds the result.

The following is an example test case from this book for the addNumbers function. Compared to ChatGPT's response, the difference lies in considering edge cases. For example, due to binary floating-point arithmetic, adding 0.1 and 0.2 results in 0.30000000000000004 instead of 0.3. If the addNumbers function does not handle this case, users may get unexpected results when inputting such numbers. Therefore, test cases for these special cases are important to ensure the function works as expected, or they can serve as validation after refactoring.

```
// src/utils/addNumbers/addNumbers.test.js

const addNumbers = require('./addNumbers');

test('should return 0.3 when 0.1 + 0.2', () => {
  expect(addNumbers(0.1, 0.2)).toBe(0.3);
});
```

```
test('should return 2 when 5 - 3', () => {
  expect(addNumbers(5, -3)).toBe(2);
});
```

In this simple example, can we rely on Mermaid flowcharts to ask ChatGPT to write tests? It seems that implementing test cases based on the flowchart is not an issue. ChatGPT's response met the requirement of testing the `addNumbers` function for the addition of two numbers. However, it did not consider all edge cases, so developers must make slight adjustments according to their specific needs or preferences when writing the function or tests.

This was a simple example; let's move on to a more complex one.

Writing Unit Tests

How can we write unit tests for components? For example, here we have a `<Counter>` component, where users can click buttons to increase or decrease a number, fulfilling a counting function.

```
// src/Counter/Counter.js

const Counter = () => {
  const [count, setCount] = useState(0);
  const increment = () => setCount(count + 1);
  const decrement = () => setCount(count - 1);

  return (
    <>
      <div data-test-id="counter-value">{count}</div>
      <button data-test-id="decrement-button"
      onClick={decrement}>
        -
      </button>
```

```
      <button data-test-id="increment-button" onClick={increment}>
        +
      </button>
    </>
  );
};
```

Since developers should create a design document before implementing functionality (Note 1), they would write or draw flowcharts according to design specifications to describe the component's behavior. For example, a flowchart depicting the behavior of "clicking the + button should increase the number by 1" might look like this:

```
flowchart TD
    Render_Component[render Counter component] --> Click_Increment_Button[click increment button]
    Click_Increment_Button --> Get_Result[get result]
```

As shown in Figure 8-5, this Mermaid-generated flowchart visualizes the behavior of the Counter component based on the code.

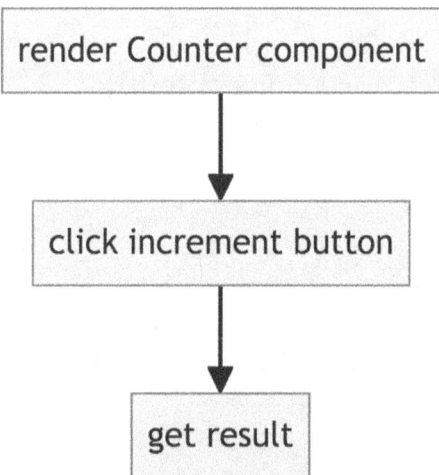

Figure 8-5. *Mermaid flowchart for Counter component*

Developer Inquiry: Implementing Functionality

Based on the flowchart's code, we can ask ChatGPT to assist with implementing the feature as follows:

Generate a component Counter based on this diagram.

```
flowchart TD
    Render_Component[render Counter component] --> Click_Increment_Button[click increment button]
    Click_Increment_Button --> Get_Result[get result]
```

ChatGPT's Response

Within seconds, ChatGPT generates the following response:

Based on the provided flowchart, here is the implementation of the Counter component:

```
import React, { useState } from 'react';

const Counter = () => {
  const [count, setCount] = useState(0);

  const handleIncrement = () => {
    setCount(count + 1);
  };

  return (
    <div>
      <h2>Counter Component</h2>
      <p>Count: {count}</p>
      <button onClick={handleIncrement}>Increment</button>
    </div>
  );
};

export default Counter;
```

CHAPTER 8   LEVERAGING AI FOR WRITING TESTS

This component displays a counter with an initial value of 0. Clicking the "Increment" button increases the count by 1.

For this <Counter> component example, ChatGPT's response meets the requirements. It shows that implementing the <Counter> component based on the flowchart works as expected. However, for a more refined implementation, developers might need to ask further questions or adjust the code according to their preferences or needs. For instance, when developing more complex components, separating the logic, state, and display of the <Counter> component can make the code more maintainable and easier to test (Note 2).

Developer Inquiry: Writing Tests

We not only want ChatGPT to assist in implementing functionality but also to generate test cases. So, we ask again:

Generate test cases based on this diagram by using Jest + React Testing Library.

```
flowchart TD
    Render_Component[render Counter component] --> Click_Increment_Button[click increment button]
    Click_Increment_Button --> Get_Result[get result]
```

ChatGPT's Response

ChatGPT responded in just a few seconds with the following:

Here is the test code using Jest and React Testing Library based on the provided flowchart:

```
import React from 'react';
import { render, fireEvent } from '@testing-library/react';
import Counter from './Counter';

describe('Counter Component', () => {
```

CHAPTER 8 LEVERAGING AI FOR WRITING TESTS

```
  it('should increment count when increment button is
  clicked', () => {
    const { getByText } = render(<Counter />);
    const incrementButton = getByText('Increment');
    fireEvent.click(incrementButton);
    const countElement = getByText('Count: 1');
    expect(countElement).toBeInTheDocument();
  });
});
```

This test checks whether the displayed count increases by 1 when the "Increment" button is clicked.

Below is part of the test code for the <Counter> component implemented in this book. Compared to ChatGPT's response, the main differences lie in how structured and maintainable the code is. For example, using getByText to select elements can be too loose compared to using getByTestId. Additionally, simply checking whether the element exists is not rigorous enough; verifying the element's displayed content would be a more precise approach (Note 3). Finally, using toBeInTheDocument to check if the element is present is not ideal, as the element will always be present but with different content. Using toHaveTextContent would be a better choice (Note 4), and developers should pay attention to these details.

```
// src/Counter/Counter.rtl.test.js

describe('Counter component', () => {
  let counter;
  const renderCounter = () => <Counter />;

  beforeEach(() => {
    counter = render(renderCounter());
  });
```

CHAPTER 8   LEVERAGING AI FOR WRITING TESTS

```
  afterEach(() => {
    counter.unmount();
  });

  it('should get -1 when click the decrement button', () => {
    const { getByTestId } = counter;

    fireEvent.click(getByTestId('decrement-button'));

    expect(getByTestId('counter-value')).
toHaveTextContent('-1');
  });
});
```

So, can we rely on Mermaid's flowcharts to help ChatGPT generate unit tests for components? For this example, implementing the test code based on the flowchart seems to work without major issues. However, a more refined implementation requires developers to adjust the tests according to their needs or preferences. If it doesn't work, it's always fine to adjust the query, the code, or rewrite it manually.

Let's now take a look at a more complex example.

Implementing Integration Test

How should we approach writing integration tests? As an example, let's write test cases for the <Counter> component. In this case, <Counter> is implemented using three child components: <CounterValue>, <DecrementButton>, and <IncrementButton>.

```
// src/Counter/Counter-enhanced.js

const Counter = () => {
  const [count, setCount] = useState(0);
  const increment = () => setCount(count + 1);
```

CHAPTER 8   LEVERAGING AI FOR WRITING TESTS

```
  const decrement = () => setCount(count - 1);
  return (
    <>
      <CounterValue count={count} />
      <DecrementButton onClick={decrement} />
      <IncrementButton onClick={increment} />
    </>
  );
};
```

The flowchart representing the specification "When the + button is clicked, the count should increment by 1" is shown below:

```
flowchart TD
    Render_Component[render Counter component, including
    child component CounterValue, DecrementButton and
    IncrementButton] --> Click_Increment_Button[click
    IncrementButton]
    Click_Increment_Button --> Get_Result[show result in
    CounterValue]
```

As shown in Figure 8-6, Mermaid generates the flowchart based on the code. First, the component and its child components are rendered, then the + button is clicked, and, finally, the result is displayed.

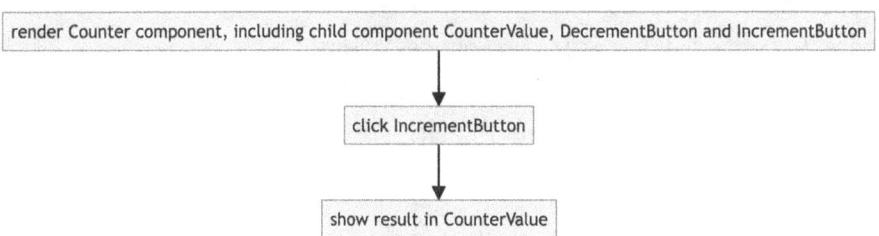

Figure 8-6. *Updated Mermaid flowchart of the Counter component*

CHAPTER 8   LEVERAGING AI FOR WRITING TESTS

In this case, we specifically inform ChatGPT that the <Counter> component includes three child components: <CounterValue>, <DecrementButton>, and <IncrementButton>. The expectation is that ChatGPT will correctly implement the <Counter> component based on this information.

Developer Inquiry: Implementing Functionality

Based on the flowchart, we can ask ChatGPT for assistance in implementing this functionality:

Generate a component Counter based on this diagram.

flowchart TD
    Render_Component[render Counter component, including child component CounterValue, DecrementButton, and IncrementButton] --> Click_Increment_Button[click IncrementButton]
    Click_Increment_Button --> Get_Result[show result in CounterValue]

ChatGPT's Response

ChatGPT responded within seconds with the following:

Based on the provided flowchart, here is the implementation of the Counter component:

```
import React, { useState } from 'react';
import CounterValue from './CounterValue';
import DecrementButton from './DecrementButton';
import IncrementButton from './IncrementButton';

const Counter = () => {
  const [count, setCount] = useState(0);
```

```
  const increment = () => setCount(count + 1);
  return (
    <div>
      <CounterValue count={count} />
      <DecrementButton />
      <IncrementButton onClick={increment} />
    </div>
  );
};

export default Counter;
```

This component includes child components CounterValue, DecrementButton, and IncrementButton. When the IncrementButton is clicked, it increases the count, which is then displayed in the CounterValue component.

As seen from this example, implementing the <Counter> component based on the flowchart posed no significant issues. With clear instructions, ChatGPT generally provides responses that meet the requirements. However, a better implementation approach may involve further questions or adjustments based on specific preferences or project needs.

Developer Inquiry: Writing Tests

We want ChatGPT to help not only with implementing the functionality but also with writing the test cases. So we ask again:

Generate test cases based on this diagram by using Jest + React Testing Library.

CHAPTER 8   LEVERAGING AI FOR WRITING TESTS

```
flowchart TD
    Render_Component[render Counter component, including
    child component CounterValue, DecrementButton, and
    IncrementButton] --> Click_Increment_Button[click
    IncrementButton]
    Click_Increment_Button --> Get_Result[show result in
    CounterValue]
```

ChatGPT's Response

ChatGPT responded in a few seconds with the following:

Here are the test cases using Jest and React Testing Library based on the provided flowchart:

```
import React from 'react';
import { render, fireEvent } from '@testing-library/react';
import Counter from './Counter';

describe('Counter component', () => {
  test('increments count when IncrementButton is clicked', () => {
    const { getByText, getByTestId } = render(<Counter />);
    const incrementButton = getByText('Increment');
    fireEvent.click(incrementButton);
    const counterValue = getByTestId('counter-value');
    expect(counterValue.textContent).toBe('1');
  });
});
```

This test checks whether the count increases when the IncrementButton is clicked and if the result is correctly displayed in the CounterValue component.

When compared with the test implementation from the book for the <Counter> component, the primary difference lies in the structure and maintainability of the test. Similar to the previous example, using getByText to select elements is too loose, and using textContent can be improved by using toHaveTextContent to make the test easier to read and provide better error messages when the test fails. This would be a more recommended approach (Note 6).

```js
// src/Counter/Counter.snapshot.rtl.test.js
describe('Counter component', () => {
  let counter;
  const renderCounter = () => <Counter />;

  beforeEach(() => {
    counter = render(renderCounter());
  });

  afterEach(() => {
    counter.unmount();
  });

  it('should get 1 when click the increment button', () => {
    const { getByTestId } = counter;

    fireEvent.click(getByTestId('increment-button'));

    expect(getByTestId('counter-value')).
    toHaveTextContent('1');
  });
});
```

For slightly more complex examples, we can still rely on Mermaid flowcharts to help ChatGPT write integration tests. However, developers need to provide more precise information to help ChatGPT generate more

Chapter 8 Leveraging AI for Writing Tests

accurate code, or they can adjust it according to their needs. If ChatGPT's solution doesn't work, it's always fine to tweak the question, the code, or simply write it manually.

Let's move on to the most complex example.

Implementing End-to-End Test

Using the photo browsing feature of Memori (Note 5) as an example, we can rely on a Mermaid flowchart and ask ChatGPT to help write the test. The following Mermaid flowchart represents the steps to implement this functionality:

```
flowchart TD
    Init[page loaded] --> Get_Photos[get photos] --> Get_Photos_Status{status?}
    Get_Photos_Status --> |success|Has_Photos{has photos?}
    Get_Photos_Status --> |fail|Show_Error_Message[show error message] --> |wait for some time|Polling
    Has_Photos -->|yes| Render_Photos[render photos with max count] --> |wait for some time|Polling
    Has_Photos -->|no| Show_Empty_Message[show empty message] --> |wait for some time|Polling
    Polling[polling] --> Get_Photos
```

As shown in Figure 8-7, Mermaid generates the flowchart based on the code, representing a sequence where the page loads, photos are fetched, and the API response determines whether to display a photo list or an error message.

CHAPTER 8 LEVERAGING AI FOR WRITING TESTS

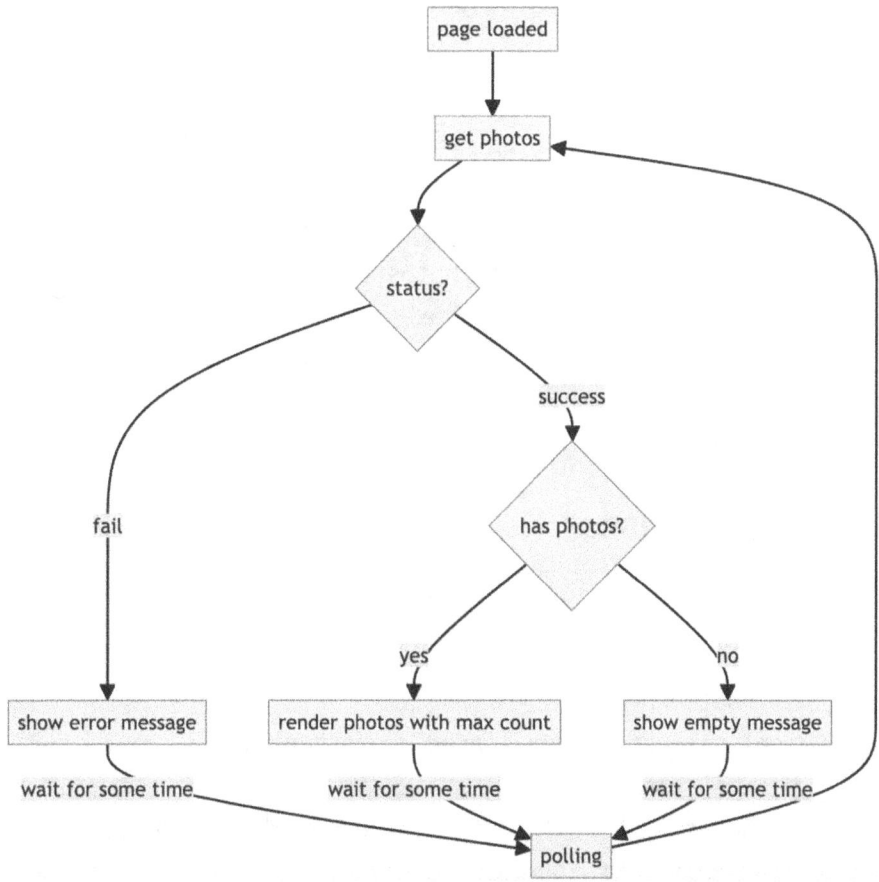

Figure 8-7. Flowchart of Memori's photo browsing functionality

Developer Inquiry

We want to ask ChatGPT to generate test code based on the Mermaid flowchart:

Generate end-to-end test codes based on this diagram by using Cypress.

CHAPTER 8 LEVERAGING AI FOR WRITING TESTS

```
flowchart TD
    Init[page loaded] --> Get_Photos[get photos] -->
    Get_Photos_Status{status?}
    Get_Photos_Status --> |success|Has_Photos{has photos?}
    Get_Photos_Status --> |fail|Show_Error_Message[show error
    message] --> |wait for some time|Polling
    Has_Photos -->|yes| Render_Photos[render photos with max
    count] --> |wait for some time|Polling
    Has_Photos -->|no| Show_Empty_Message[show empty message]
    --> |wait for some time|Polling
    Polling[polling] --> Get_Photos
```

ChatGPT's Response

ChatGPT responded with the following:

Based on the flowchart, the generated Cypress test code is as follows:

```
describe('Photo Page', () => {
  it('displays photos when loaded successfully', () => {
    cy.visit('/photos');
    // Assuming '/photos' is the route for the photo page
    cy.intercept('GET', '/api/photos', { fixture: 'photos.json'
    }); // Mocking API response

    cy.wait('@getPhotos'); // Wait for the photos to be fetched

    cy.get('.photo').should('have.length.above', 0);
    // Check if photos are rendered
  });

  it('displays error message when photos fail to load', () => {
    cy.visit('/photos'); // Assuming '/photos' is the route for
    the photo page
    cy.intercept('GET', '/api/photos', { statusCode: 500 });
    // Mocking failed API response
```

```
    cy.wait('@getPhotos'); // Wait for the failed request

    cy.get('.error-message').should('be.visible');
    // Check if error message is displayed
  });

  it('displays empty message when no photos are
  available', () => {
    cy.visit('/photos');
    // Assuming '/photos' is the route for the photo page
    cy.intercept('GET', '/api/photos', { fixture: 'empty.json'
    }); // Mocking empty API response

    cy.wait('@getPhotos'); // Wait for the photos to be fetched

    cy.get('.empty-message').should('be.visible');
    // Check if empty message is displayed
  });
});
```

This test suite includes three cases that verify the page's behavior when photos load successfully, fail to load, or no photos are available.

Upon reviewing the test code generated by ChatGPT, it shows that indeed, we can use a Mermaid flowchart to guide ChatGPT in writing end-to-end test code. However, developers need to provide more precise details, and ChatGPT's suggestions may not always be fully correct or meet all needs. Therefore, developers must review and adjust the output according to project requirements or preferences. If ChatGPT's suggestions don't work, rephrasing the question and writing the code manually are valid alternatives.

CHAPTER 8   LEVERAGING AI FOR WRITING TESTS

Conclusion

If you want to use Mermaid-generated flowcharts to assist ChatGPT in writing related test code, it's essential to provide clear, step-by-step flowcharts and review the generated code carefully to ensure it meets testing needs and is correct. You may need to adjust or write parts of the code manually. Although results may not be perfect initially, once you gain experience within a project, ChatGPT can quickly generate most of the code, making it an effective way to boost productivity by integrating Mermaid and ChatGPT into your workflow.

Here's a summary of how to leverage Mermaid and ChatGPT for writing tests:

- Step 1: Create a flowchart with clear steps.

- Step 2: Ask ChatGPT to generate suggested test code based on the flowchart.

- Step 3: Review and verify the generated code. ChatGPT's suggestions may not be completely accurate, so developers must adjust the code as necessary.

- Step 4: If the generated code doesn't meet your needs, return to Step 1 or write the code manually.

By generating test code during the design phase using flowcharts, this approach significantly supports the practice of TDD (test-driven development) (Note 7) and boosts development productivity. Finally, the excuse of "no time to write tests" no longer applies—just create the flowchart, and you'll produce a high-quality product. As AI continues to advance, we can't avoid writing tests anymore.

Notes

- Note 1: For advice on writing effective design documents, refer to Sean Chou's "How to Write a Front-End Development Design Document" (`https://bit.ly/48Rp5U5`).

- Note 2: For discussions on refactoring components for better testing, see Chapter 2, section "How to Write Tests for Components? A React Example."

- Note 3: For issues related to "element selection being too loose, too strict, or not clear enough" and "tests containing too many implementation details," see Chapter 7, section "What to Do When UI Updates Cause Test Failures?"

- Note 4: For inspecting whether elements exist in the DOM, their count, or visibility, see Chapter 3, section "Snapshots."

- Note 5: For more information on Memori, see Chapter 4, section "Verifying User Flow."

- Note 6: For suggestions on the `textContent` approach, see Chapter 7, section "What to Do When UI Updates Cause Test Failures?"

- Note 7: For information on TDD, see Chapter 1, section "Testing Techniques."

CHAPTER 9

Summary

Types and Methods of Testing

Testing is a crucial method for ensuring software quality. During development, the proportion and structure of different types of testing should be dynamically adjusted based on the product stage and characteristics.

Product Stage and Testing Ratio

For larger-scale products that require integration with various components, services, or systems, integration testing plays a more significant role. Conversely, in smaller products with simpler functionality, where the focus is on self-contained features, unit testing becomes more prominent.

Common Types of Testing

Here are some common testing types and their objectives:

- Unit testing: Tests whether a single module or function meets the expected outcome
- Integration testing: Tests the interfaces between multiple modules or features to ensure they work together properly

CHAPTER 9   SUMMARY

- End-to-end testing: Ensures the entire flow from the user end to the system back end operates smoothly
- Visual testing: Verifies that the user interface displays correctly and functions seamlessly

Testing Methods and Tools

At different stages of product development, different approaches can be used to continuously ensure product quality. During development, manual scripts or test runners can be employed to provide immediate feedback. Before merging code, testing can be conducted at the `pre-commit`, `pre-push`, and pull request (PR) stages to catch any errors. After merging, projects often run automated tests or scheduled tests to ensure the long-term reliability of the product.

Testing Strategies at Different Stages of Product Development

Different types of tests can be conducted at various stages of product development. During the development phase, unit testing, integration testing, and end-to-end testing ensure core functionality. Before product release, end-to-end and visual testing can optimize the user experience.

Leveraging AI to Improve Testing Efficiency

With the advancement of AI technology, many AI tools are available to assist developers in implementing tests. By effectively using AI tools, testing efficiency can be improved, reducing development costs.

Conclusion

Testing is an indispensable part of software development. Effective testing improves product quality and reduces development costs. In today's fast-paced, ever-evolving development environment, testing helps us achieve the dual goals of high productivity and high quality.

Index

A

AI, *see* Artificial intelligence (AI)
API, *see* Application programming interface (API)
Application programming interface (API), 116–122
Arrange, Act, and Assert (AAA) pattern, 25, 26
Artificial intelligence (AI), 333
    Copilot (*see* Copilot)
Automated tests
    configuration file, 206
    continuous integration (CI), 215
    merging code (*see* Merging code)
Automating tests
    manual test, 207–209
    package.json file, 206
    pre-commands, 206

B

BDD, *see* Behavior-driven development (BDD)
Behavioral testing, 80, 81
Behavior-driven development (BDD), 16, 112
Behavior testing, 97
Black-box testing, 81

C

CD, *see* Continuous delivery/deployment (CD)
ChatGPT
    addNumbers function, 308, 309, 312
    E2E testing, 324–327
    integration tests, 318–324
    JavaScript implementation, 311
    language model, 307
    refactoring, 312
    response, 309–312
    unit testing, 316–318
    unit tests, 313–318
    write test cases, 311
    writing tests, 328
CI, *see* Continuous integration (CI)
Code coverage
    <Count> component, 218–220
    Count.js, 220, 221
    limitations, 218
    modification, 222
    product quality, 218
    recommendations, 218
    testing efforts, 223

INDEX

Component-level testing
    different viewports, 179–183
    interactions
        CI tools, 187–189
        CSS trigger, 185–187
        hover state, 186
        JavaScript, 183–185
        props and flags, 186
        snapshots, 183
    Mixtini home page, 181
    page (*see* Page-level testing)
    shared components, 178
    snapshot testing, 178
    Storybook, 178
    tool comparison, 198
Continuous delivery/deployment (CD), 193
Continuous integration (CI), 178, 193
    code interactions, 215
    code merge process, 216
    cost/limitations, 216
    development/automated testing, 215
    integration, 187
    merging code, 217
    potential risks, 216
    strategies, 217
    test instability, 215
Copilot
    addDays function, 295
    context-appropriate test, 295
    counter component, 297
    end-to-end test, 302–304
    hello.test.js, 294–296
    integration tests, 297–302
    test writing, 305
    unit tests, 296, 297
    write tests, 294
Cypress
    components, 50, 97
    Counter.cy.js, 52
    E2E testing, 152–154
    explanations, 51, 54
    features, 48
    integration, 104–106
    long-term support, 53
    Memori, 162–164
    mount command, 50
    output process, 52
    package.json file, 48
    package manager, 48
    pretest commands, 54
    setup interface, 50
    testing framework, 194
    testing process, 52
    test process, 53

D

Debugging process
    components, 260
    data flow, 265–267
    elements, 263, 264
    error message, 263

INDEX

<ImageList> and
    <ImageItem>, 260–262
toMatchSnapshot method, 264
writing tests, 260
DevOps, 17
Double, 30, 31, 33

E

End-to-end (E2E) testing
    advantages, 153
    Copilot, 302–304
    Cypress, 152–154
    describe/it function, 152
    environment/installation
        configuration, 155
        Cypress, 154
        file structure, 156
        network request, 157
        package manager, 154
        Puppeteer, 156–158
        testing frameworks, 154
        web page, 155
    frameworks, 10
    learning process, 151
    scenarios, 10
    types, 332
    user flow verification
        comprehensive, 159
        Memori, 160–169
        principles, 159
        user environment, 159
    web interfaces, 151
    writing test
        ChatGPT response, 326
        developer inquiry, 325
        flowchart, 325
        implementation, 324–327
        photo list/error message, 324
Enzyme, 42–46

F

Flaky tests
    causes/solutions, 286
    inconsistent results, 280
    internal/external
        resources, 280–283
    scenarios, 282
    test dependencies, 283–286
Front-end web testing
    advantage/disadvantages,
        13, 14
    concepts, 1
    E2E testing, 10
    error handling/edge cases, 13
    factors, 2
    features, 2, 3
    goals, 32
    integration, 8, 9
    meaning, 2
    scenarios, 15
    testing pyramid model, 4, 5
    types/methods, 4, 12, 13
    unit testing, 5–8
    variations, 15
    visual testing, 11, 12
    writing test, 3, 4

INDEX

Full rendering
    comparison, 95
    components, 90, 97
    enzyme, 89–92
    features, 96
    HTML structure, 93
    increment method, 91, 92, 94
    libraries, 89
    meaning, 89
    React testing library, 92–94
    snapshot, 90, 91
Functional testing, *see* Integration testing

G

GitHub Copilot, *see* Copilot

H

Handle duplicate tests, 249–253

I

Integration testing
    components, 101
    Copilot, 297–302
    cy.mount method, 106
    Cypress, 104–106
    definition, 8, 9, 99
    description, 109–111
    error message, 107
    explanation, 103, 104
    features, 108
    <ImageItem> code, 104
    <ImageItem> component, 106–108
    <ImageList>, 102
    image list structure, 100
    learning process, 99
    mock (*see* Mocking techniques)
    principles, 108
    React Testing Library, 102
    realism, 110–112
    real-world scenarios, 149
    snapshot, 130–141
    state management
        implementation, 144, 145, 148
        initial quantity, 145
        modification, 142
        Redux, 141
        scenarios, 143
        shop ordering system, 141, 142
        test implementation, 142
        toEqual method, 145
        toHaveTextContent, 143
        user's perspective, 146–148
    types, 331
    user's perspective, 108–110
    writing tests
        ChatGPT response, 320–324
        child components, 318–324
        Counter components, 320
        flowchart representation, 319

INDEX

Mermaid flowchart, 319
react testing library, 321

J, K

JavaScript
  applications (*see* Jest)
  component-level testing, 183
Jest, 39–48
  addNumbers function, 40
  describe function, 41
  Enzyme, 42–46
  getCount, 289
  implementation, 40
  installation, 39
  only *vs.* skip, 292
  package.json file, 40
  React applications, 42
  running test, 287
  scenarios, 41
  shallow/full rendering, 287, 288
  test case fails, 291
  test cases, 288–292
  testing library, 46–48

L

Localization testing
  Chinese version, 268
  components, 271
  English version, 268–270
  ordering system, 267, 268
  visual testing, 270, 271

M

Manual testing
  commands, 207
  configuration file, 208
  monitoring file, 207, 208
  testing process, 209
  triggers, 209
Memori
  advantages, 170
  considerations, 168
  cross-browser/cross-platform, 165–167
  failure message, 163–165
  image upload function, 161–163
  image uploading, 303
  implementation, 170
  interface, 160
  iterations, 169
  learning process, 169
  photo browsing function, 325
  photo sharing and browsing, 160
  product flow, 170
  testing strategies, 168
  user interaction flows, 167
Merging code
  benefits, 212
  codebase functions, 210
  code hosting services, 213
  GitHub actions, 213
  Git version control, 214
  Husky, 215
  Lint-Staged, 215

INDEX

Merging code (*cont.*)
 pre-commit workflow, 211, 212
 pre-push workflow, 212–214
 PR submission, 213, 214
Mermaid
 ChatGPT (*see* ChatGPT)
 counter component, 314, 315
 flowcharts, 307, 308, 310
 writing test, 306
Mixtini, 172–174
Mock, 27, 28, 33
Mocking techniques
 API responses, 116–122
 axios, 130
 beforeEach function, 121
 benefits, 113
 components, 114–116
 data structure, 125, 126
 debugging techniques, 129
 dependencies, 113
 external factors, 129
 features, 113
 filterList function, 119, 121
 getStatusById function, 119
 image list structure, 129
 interactions, 126, 127
 mockImplementation/
  mockReturnValue, 119
 real-world implementation,
  127–129
 third-party libraries, 122–125
Mocking testing
 modules, 258–260
 user interface (UI), 234–236

N, O

Naming conventions
 advantage, 26
 3A pattern, 25, 26
 descriptions, 22
 error message, 22
 Given-When-Then (GWT),
  23, 24
 identification, 26
 it should, 24

P, Q

Page-level testing
 CI tools, 190
 components, 189
 features, 190
 integration, 190–192
 Percy's platform, 189
 tool comparison, 198

R

Repetitive setup/teardown tasks
 beforeAll/afterAll, 275
 beforeEach, 274
 beforeEach/afterEach,
  272, 275
 increment/decrement
  method, 273
 getCount method, 272
 one-time setup, 275, 276
 repeated setup, 272–275

INDEX

S

Shallow rendering
    components, 83, 97
    <Counter> component, 85
    createRenderer function, 88
    Enzyme, 83–87
    increment method, 86
    libraries, 83
    React testing library, 87–89
Snapshot testing
    comparisons, 135
    components, 130, 136
    convenient method, 134
    elements, 139
    HTML structure, 135
    image blocks, 137
    <ImageList>/<ImageItem>, 130, 131
    implementation details, 132
    no-data scenario, 137
    scenarios, 133, 134
    shallow rendering, 138
    timestamp and renders, 134
    toBeInTheDocument, 140
    toBeVisible, 140
    toHaveLength, 140
    toMatchSnapshot method, 132
Snapshot, visual testing
    advantages, 176
    benefits, 176
    branch creation, 174
    differences, 174–176
    prototypes/diagrams, 176
    pull request, 175
    rejecting process, 175
    third-party tools/services, 176
Spy, 28–30, 33

T

TDD, *see* Test-driven development (TDD)
Test-driven development (TDD), 16, 328
Testing techniques, 16
    Agile/Scrum, 16
    AI technology, 333
    behavior-driven development, 16
    data flows, 21
    development processes, 17, 18
    DevOps, 17
    feature toggle, 20
    Mermaid and ChatGPT, 22
    objectives, 331
    product development, 332
    product stage/ratio, 331
    pull request (PR) stages, 332
    quality assurance, 21
    test-driven development, 16
    types/method, 331
    UI development, 18–20, 33
Timer testing, 254–258
Type checking
    addNumbers function, 277, 278
    defensive programming, 279

Type checking (*cont.*)
　static analysis, 279
　tools, 278–280
　TypeScript, 280

U

UI, *see* User interface (UI)
Unit testing
　addNumbers function, 36, 37
　advantages, 7
　benefits, 35, 37
　code modifications/user
　　actions, 36
　code quality, 37
　components/user behavior, 38
　conversion limitations, 37
　cost efficiency, 38
　Cypress, 48–53
　divideNumbers function, 6
　full rendering, 89–96
　implementation/behavior
　　beforeEach function, 63
　　behavior, 65–69
　　components, 61
　　differences, 68
　　getByTestId method, 66
　　implementation, 63–65
　　increment/decrement
　　　methods, 61
　　internal structure, 69
　　setState method, 61
　　snapshots, 69
　　stages, 69
　integration (*see* Integration
　　testing)
　Jest, 39–48
　logic/presentation
　　calculate button, 69–72
　　code explanation, 72
　　collaboration, 79
　　differences, 79
　　guidelines, 82
　　implementation, 69
　　maintainability, 79
　　pull requests (PRs), 79
　　refactoring, 73, 75, 76, 82
　　reusability, 79
　　testability, 79
　　useCalculatorHook, 77–79
　minimal scope validation
　　logic, 54–60
　　checkValentinesDay
　　　function, 54–58
　　components, 60
　　efficiency and accuracy, 60
　　functional units, 54
　　getToday function, 57
　　isolate dependencies, 58–60
　　key principles, 54
　　mocking, 60
　potential errors, 38
　primary goals, 38
　refactoring code, 38
　setup/installation process, 39
　shallow rendering, 82–89

smallest unit, 5–8, 36
types, 331
writing test
    ChatGPT response, 315–318
    components, 313
    counting function, 313
    design specifications, 314
    implementation, 315
    Mermaid flowchart, 314
    react testing library, 316
User interface (UI), 177
    element selection method
        clear enough, 231–233
        data-* attributes, 233, 234
        HTML structure, 230
        loose, 226–230
        strict, 230, 231
    implementation details
        comparison, 237–239
        logic/state/UI rendering, 239–248
        mocking, 234–236
        snapshots, 236, 237
    principles, 248
    test failures, 225
    testing development, 18–20
    visual testing, 171
    XPath (XML Path Language), 249

V, W, X, Y, Z

Visual testing
    accuracy verification
        component-level, 178–189
        components/web pages, 177
        page-level, 189–194
        workflow, 192
    advantages, 11, 203
    benefits, 202
    component-level testing, 203
    learning process, 171
    localization testing, 270
    Mixtini, 11, 12, 172–174
    page-level testing, 202
    Percy snapshot comparison, 174
    snapshot comparison work, 174–176
    tool comparison, 194
        approaches, 200
        browser support, 199
        Chromatic marks, 195
        comparison, 199–201
        component-level testing, 198
        merge checks, 197
        page-level testing, 198
        pull requests (PRs), 197
        snapshot file types/structure, 195, 196
    types, 332
    UI changes, 171